SwiftUI
by Tutorials

By Antonio Bello, Phil Laszkowicz, Bill Morefield & Audrey Tam

SwiftUI by Tutorials

By Antonio Bello, Phil Łaszkowicz, Bill Morefield & Audrey Tam

Copyright ©2019 Razeware LLC.

Notice of Rights

All rights reserved. No part of this book or corresponding materials (such as text, images, or source code) may be reproduced or distributed by any means without prior written permission of the copyright owner.

Notice of Liability

This book and all corresponding materials (such as source code) are provided on an "as is" basis, without warranty of any kind, express of implied, including but not limited to the warranties of merchantability, fitness for a particular purpose, and noninfringement. In no event shall the authors or copyright holders be liable for any claim, damages or other liability, whether in action of contract, tort or otherwise, arising from, out of or in connection with the software or the use of other dealing in the software.

Trademarks

All trademarks and registered trademarks appearing in this book are the property of their own respective owners.

ISBN: 978-1-942878-83-4

About the Authors

Antonio Bello is an author of this book. Antonio has spent most of his life writing code, and he's gained a lot of experience in several languages and technologies. A few years ago he fell in love with iOS development, and that's what he mostly works on since then, although he's always open for challenges and for playing with new toys. He believes that reputation is the most important skill in his job, and that "it cannot be done" actually means "it can be done, but it's not economically convenient." When he's not working, he's probably playing drums or making songs in his small, but well fitted, home recording studio.

Phil Łaszkowicz is an author of this book. Phil's been delivering large-scale software solutions for many years, as well as working with startups as a board member, mentor, and coach. He's worked with neural networks for over a decade, and enjoys combining deep learning with intuitive and elegant user experiences across mobile and web. In his spare time he writes music, drinks coffee at a professional level, and can be found scaling cliff walls, composing music, sea kayaking, or taking part in competitive archery.

Bill Morefield is an author of this book. Bill has spent most of his professional life writing code. At some point he has worked in almost every language other than COBOL. He bought his first Apple computer to learn to program for the iPhone and got hooked on the platform. He manages the web and mobile development team for a college in Tennessee, where he still gets to write code. When not attached to a keyboard he enjoys hiking and photography.

Audrey Tam is an author of this book. As a retired computer science academic, she's a technology generalist with expertise in translating new knowledge into learning materials. Audrey now teaches short courses in iOS app development to non-programmers, and attends nearly all Melbourne Cocoaheads monthly meetings. She also enjoys long train journeys, knitting, and trekking in the Aussie wilderness.

About the Editors

Pablo Mateo is the final pass editor for this book. He is Technical Lead at Banco Santander, and was also founder and CTO of a Technology Development company in Madrid. His expertise is focused on web and mobile app development, although he first started as a Creative Art Director. He has been for many years the Main Professor of the iOS and Android Mobile Development Masters Degree at a well-known technology school in Madrid (CICE). He is currently specializing in Artificial Intelligence & Machine-Learning.

Morten Faarkrog is a tech editor for this book. Morten is Technical Director at a full-service digital agency in Copenhagen, Denmark. He has a background as an iOS developer and loves tinkering with new innovative technologies—one of which you'll shortly be diving into. He an advocate of trying new things and taking calculated risks, and thinks you should be, too!

Kelvin Lau is a tech editor for this book. Kelvin is a senior mobile engineer at Instacart. He loves space related stuff, and wishes to head up there someday. Outside of programming work, he's an aspiring entrepreneur and musician. You can find him on Twitter: @kelvinlauKL

About the Artist

Vicki Wenderlich is the designer and artist of the cover of this book. She is Ray's wife and business partner. She is a digital artist who creates illustrations, game art and a lot of other art or design work for the tutorials and books on raywenderlich.com. When she's not making art, she loves hiking, a good glass of wine and attempting to create the perfect cheese plate.

Dedications

"To Magdalena, Andrea and Alex, for their support and patience, watching me tapping on the keyboard all day long."

— *Antonio Bello*

"To Isabella for being the best inspiration when distractions are too easy to find, and the best distraction for when work is too easy to lose myself in."

— *Phil Laszkowicz*

"To my parents for buying me that first computer when it was a lot weirder idea than it is now. To them and rest of my family for putting up with all those questions as a child."

— *Bill Morefield*

"To my parents and teachers, who set me on the path thatled me to the here and now."

— *Audrey Tam*

Table of Contents

Book License 12

Book Source Code & Forums 13

What You Need 15

About the Cover 17

Section I: Beginning SwiftUI 19

Chapter 1: Introduction 21
About this book 22

Chapter 2: Getting Started 23
Getting started 24
Creating your UI 29
Updating the UI 35
Making Reusable Views 37
Presenting an Alert 41
Challenge 43
Key points 44

Chapter 3: Understanding SwiftUI 45
Why SwiftUI? 45
Getting started 47
Declaring views 47
Declaring data dependencies 63
Challenge 66
Key points 68

Chapter 4: Integrating SwiftUI 69
Getting started 70
Hosting a SwiftUI view in a UIKit project 71
Hosting a view controller in a SwiftUI project 74

    Hosting a UIKit view with data dependencies 79
    Key points. 85
    Where to go from here?. 85
    Challenge 86

Chapter 5: The Apple Ecosystem 87
    Getting started 88
    Creating a Swift package 90
    Designing for the strengths of each platform. 97
    Improving the watchOS app 98
    Extending the Mac Catalyst app. 100
    Creating a MacOS BullsEye app. 106
    Creating a tvOS BullsEye app 108
    Key points 114

Chapter 6: Intro to Controls: Text & Image. 117
    Getting started 118
    Text 120
    Image 129
    Brief overview of stack views 133
    More on Image 135
    Splitting Text 139
    Key points 142
    Where to go from here? 142

Chapter 7: State & Data Flow 145
    What is state? 147
    Starting with @State 147
    Environmental state. 152
    The happy middle-ground: @ObservedObject 159
    Combine and other beasts 164
    Key points 164
    Where to go from here? 165

Chapter 8: Controls & User Input 167
A simple registration form... 167
Creating the registration view 170
Power to the user: the TextField 173
Taps and buttons 185
Toggle Control.. 193
Other controls.. 195
Key points 198
Where to go from here?... 199

Chapter 9: Introducing Stacks and Containers.............. 201
Layout and priorities 202
Stack views 208
Back to Kuchi... 219
Key points 230
Where to go from here?... 231

Chapter 10: Lists & Navigation.......................... 233
Getting started 233
Navigating through a SwiftUI app 234
Creating navigation views... 235
Using navigation views 237
Displaying a list of data... 239
Making your data more compatible with iteration 241
Showing scrolling data 243
Creating lists 245
Adding navigation links... 249
Adding items to the navigation bar.............................. 252
Displaying a modal sheet 253
Programmatically dismissing a modal 255
Using alerts, action sheets and popovers.................... 257
Key points 264
Where to go from here?... 265

Section II: Intermediate SwiftUI 267

Chapter 11: Testing and Debugging........................ 269
Different types of tests... 270
Debugging SwiftUI apps.. 270
Adding UI tests 274
Creating a UI Test 275
Accessing UI elements 277
Reading the user interface 279
Fixing the bug 280
Adding more complex tests 281
Simulating user interaction... 282
Testing multiple platforms.. 285
Key points 286
Challenge... 287
Where to go from here?.. 288

Chapter 12: Handling User Input........................... 291
Adding the learn feature 292
Your first gesture.. 304
Custom gestures 305
Combining gestures for more complex interactions 308
Key points 310
Where to go from here?.. 310

Chapter 13: Drawing & Custom Graphics.................. 311
Creating shapes 312
Using gradients 315
Rotating shapes 317
Adding images... 318
Scaling drawings in views... 320
Other shapes 322
Drawing lines with paths 322

    Drawing dashed lines... 325
    Drawing arcs and curves 327
    Drawing quadratic curves 327
    Key points 331
    Where to go from here?... 331

Chapter 14: Animations 333
    Animating state changes 334
    Adding animation... 335
    Animation types 337
    Eased animations 338
    Spring animations 341
    Removing and combining animations 344
    Animating from state changes................................. 345
    Adjusting animations 346
    Animating view transitions....................................... 348
    Challenge 352
    Key points 352
    Where to go from here?... 352

Section III: Advanced SwiftUI....................... 353

Chapter 15: Complex Interfaces 355
    Integrating with other frameworks 356
    Building reusable views 360
    Key points 372
    Challenge... 373

Conclusion... 375

Book License

By purchasing *SwiftUI by Tutorials*, you have the following license:

- You are allowed to use and/or modify the source code in *SwiftUI by Tutorials* in as many apps as you want, with no attribution required.

- You are allowed to use and/or modify all art, images and designs that are included in *SwiftUI by Tutorials* in as many apps as you want, but must include this attribution line somewhere inside your app: "Artwork/images/designs: from *SwiftUI by Tutorials*, available at www.raywenderlich.com".

- The source code included in *SwiftUI by Tutorials* is for your personal use only. You are NOT allowed to distribute or sell the source code in *SwiftUI by Tutorials* without prior authorization.

- This book is for your personal use only. You are NOT allowed to sell this book without prior authorization, or distribute it to friends, coworkers or students; they would need to purchase their own copies.

All materials provided with this book are provided on an "as is" basis, without warranty of any kind, express or implied, including but not limited to the warranties of merchantability, fitness for a particular purpose and noninfringement. In no event shall the authors or copyright holders be liable for any claim, damages or other liability, whether in an action or contract, tort or otherwise, arising from, out of or in connection with the software or the use or other dealings in the software.

All trademarks and registered trademarks appearing in this guide are the properties of their respective owners.

Book Source Code & Forums

If you bought the digital edition

The digital edition of this book comes with the source code for the starter and completed projects for each chapter. These resources are included with the digital edition you downloaded from store.raywenderlich.com.

The digital edition of this book also comes with free access to any future updates we may make to the book!

The best way to get update notifications is to sign up for our monthly newsletter. This includes a list of the tutorials that came out on raywenderlich.com that month, any important news like book updates or new books, and a list of our favorite iOS development links for that month. You can sign up here:

- www.raywenderlich.com/newsletter

If you bought the print version

You can get the source code for the print edition of the book here:

https://store.raywenderlich.com/products/swift-ui-by-tutorials-source-code

Forums

We've also set up an official forum for the book at forums.raywenderlich.com. This is a great place to ask questions about the book or to submit any errors you may find.

Digital book editions

We have a digital edition of this book available in both ePUB and PDF, which can be handy if you want a soft copy to take with you, or you want to quickly search for a specific term within the book.

Buying the digital edition version of the book also has a few extra benefits: free updates each time we update the book, access to older versions of the book, and you can download the digital editions from anywhere, at anytime.

Visit our *SwiftUI by Tutorials* store page here:

- https://store.raywenderlich.com/products/swift-ui-by-tutorials.

And if you purchased the print version of this book, you're eligible to upgrade to the digital editions at a significant discount! Simply email support@razeware.com with your receipt for the physical copy and we'll get you set up with the discounted digital edition version of the book.

What You Need

To follow along with this book, you'll need the following:

- A Mac running **macOS Mojave** (10.14.4) or later. Optionally, you can use **macOS Catalina** (10.15), which is still in Beta. You'll need an Apple Developers account in order to install it.

- **Xcode 11 or later.** Xcode is the main development tool for iOS. You'll need Xcode 11 or later to make use of SwiftUI. You can download the latest version of Xcode from Apple's developer site here: apple.co/2asi58y.

> **Note**: You can use the same link to install the beta version of macOS Catalina. Bear in mind that because it is still in beta, you might find some bugs and unexpected errors while following along the tutorials if you are using the beta version or macOS Mojave. SwiftUI is a new technology that still needs some polish, so don't expect perfect behavior in every situation. Use the book's forum to ask any questions you might have.

If you haven't installed the latest version of Xcode, be sure to do that before continuing with the book. The code covered in this book depends on Swift 5.1, macOS Catalina and Xcode 11 — you may get lost if you try to work with an older version.

About the Cover

The pearl oyster is found in numerous locations around the world, throughout the tropical and sub-tropical regions of the ocean. Although most of us hold a romantic notion of ocean divers finding lone oysters with a beautiful, rare pearl inside, the majority of jewelry-quality pearls come from commercially farmed pearl oysters.

Natural pearls form when an irritant, such as a tiny parasite, invades the shell of the oyster. In commercial applications, the "irritant" is actually an implanted bead or piece of mother-of-pearl. In either case, the oyster coats the irritant with layer after layer of a coating called "nacre", sometimes for years, until a lustrous pearl is formed.

SwiftUI is the pearl in your own development oyster; although initially it feels out of place, as you create layers upon layers of views in your SwiftUI app, you'll come to learn that declarative UI development can really bring some luster to your apps. And just like the strings of pearls in a necklace, the collection of SwiftUI views in your app will come together to form something beautiful and quite valuable — no skin-diving necessary!

Section I: Beginning SwiftUI

Start your SwiftUI journey with the foundations you need. Specifically, you will learn:

Chapter 1: Introduction

Chapter 2: Getting Started: Get started with SwiftUI! Learn about the basic terminology, and discover the power of building your interface directly in the preview canvas. Check how SwiftUI makes declarative development easy and straightforward, and how you can drag and drop as you used to do with storyboards.

Chapter 3: Understanding SwiftUI: SwiftUI changes the way we must think about views, data, and control. Get a better understanding of the differences with UIKit; Learn how ViewControllers are being replaced or powerful concepts like @ObjectBinding and @EnvironmentObject.

Chapter 4: Integrating SwiftUI: Check how SwiftUI and UIKit/AppKit can be good friends and work together, side-by-side by integrating them in a single app. Learn how to navigate between both implementations and how to create and manage SwiftUI packages and frameworks.

Chapter 5: The Apple Ecosystem: Check the differences between Apple´s platforms when dealing with SwiftUI. Learn how to focus on getting the best use of the device, its unique features and its way to handle input. Customize an app and update it for AppKit, UIKit, WatchKit, tvOS, iPadOS and Catalyst.

Chapter 6: Intro to Controls: Text & Image: Learn how to add and configure different SwiftUI controls within your apps. Discover modifiers in a practical way and how they can be shared across controls or used individually. Get an introduction to container views and how to use them with SwiftUI.

Chapter 7: State & Data Flow: Learn how to bind data to the UI, about reactive updates to the UI through state management, and in-depth usage of the attributes related to SwiftUI.

Chapter 8: Controls & User Inputs: Learn about some of the main and most used controls in user interfaces such as TextFields, Buttons, Toggles, Sliders, Steppers and Pickers and how to use them with SwiftUI.

Chapter 9: Introducing Stacks & Containers: Learn the powerful capabilities of vertical and horizontal stacks. See how easy it is to apply them to your app layout and to nest them to generate almost any possible combination. Stacks are back stronger than before and will for sure become a game-changer in SwiftUI.

Chapter 10: Lists & Navigation: Increase your knowledge with more advanced SwiftUI controls. Lists are a must in almost any app. Here you will learn how to deal with any sort of list to get the best out of them. You will learn about navigation and start working with the most powerful user feedback an app can provide, Alerts, Modals, and Popovers. Need to provide users with extra functionality? Sheets and ActionSheets have also been prepared for SwiftUI.

Chapter 1: Introduction

> *"SwiftUI is an innovative, exceptionally simple way to build user interfaces across all Apple platforms with the power of Swift."*
>
> — Apple

SwiftUI is a new paradigm in Apple-related development. In 2014, after years of programming apps with Objective-C, Apple surprised the world with a new open-source language: **Swift**. Since its release, Swift has updated and evolved, eventually becoming one of the most beloved and powerful programming languages today.

SwiftUI's introduction in 2019 creates another opportunity for a paradigm shift in the industry. After years using UIKit and AppKit to create user interfaces, SwiftUI presents a fresh, new way to create UI for your apps. IN many ways, SwiftUI is much simpler and powerful than its predecessors, and even more importantly, it's cross-platform over the Apple ecosystem.

One of the most important things, though, is SwiftUI's declarative nature. For years, developers have worked with imperative programming models, dealing with state-management problems and complex code. But now, you have in our hands a declarative, straight-forward way to build amazing user interfaces. And don´t worry; if you loved working with UIKit or AppKit, rest assured that you can integrate those frameworks with your SwiftUI code.

SwiftUI still has room for improvement; just as Swift has had to evolve since v1.0, so will SwiftUI. But just as Swift has become one of the industry standards for progressive, modern programming languages, SwiftUI will surely follow the same path.

Come embark upon the exciting voyage waiting for you inside this book; you'll learn all the tips and tricks we have to share of this new way of creating user interfaces. You´ll discover what SwiftUI has to offer, how powerful it is, and how quickly and easy it is to start working with it.

About this book

We wrote this book with beginner-to-advanced developers in mind. The only requirements for reading this book are a basic understanding of Swift and iOS development. SwiftUI is new for all of us, so developers of all backgrounds are welcome to discover this great technology with us. As you work through this book, you'll progress from beginner topics to more advanced concepts in a paced, familiar fashion.

If you've worked through our classic beginner books — the *Swift Apprentice* https://store.raywenderlich.com/products/swift-apprentice and the *iOS Apprentice* https://store.raywenderlich.com/products/ios-apprentice — or have similar development experience, you're ready to read this book. You'll also benefit from a working knowledge of design patterns — such as working through *Design Patterns by Tutorials* https://store.raywenderlich.com/products/design-patterns-by-tutorials — but this isn't strictly required.

Chapter 2: Getting Started

By Audrey Tam

SwiftUI is some of the most exciting news since Apple first announced Swift in 2014. It's an enormous step towards Apple's goal of getting everyone coding; it simplifies the basics so that you can spend more time on custom features that delight your users.

If you're reading this book, you're just as excited as I am about developing apps with this new framework. This chapter will get you comfortable with the basics of creating a SwiftUI app and (live-) previewing it in Xcode. You'll create a small color-matching game, inspired by our famous *BullsEye* app from our book *iOS Apprentice*. The goal of the app is to try and match a randomly generated color by selecting colors from the RGB color space:

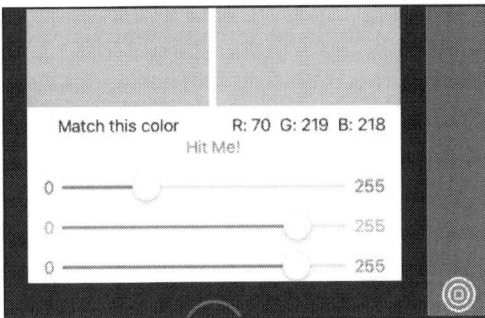

Playing the game

In this chapter, you will:

- Learn how to use the Xcode canvas to create your UI side-by-side with its code, and see how they stay in sync—a change to one side always updates the other side.
- Create a reusable view for the sliders seen in the image.
- Learn about @State variables and use them to update your UI whenever a state value changes.
- Present an alert to show the user's score.

Time to get started!

Getting started

Open the **RGBullsEye** starter project from the chapter materials, and build and run:

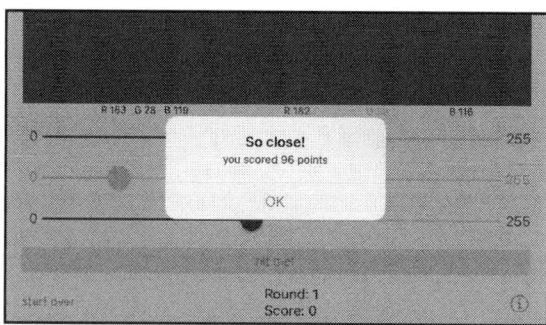

UIKit RGBullsEye starter app

This app displays a target color with randomly generated red, green and blue values. The user moves the sliders to make the left color block match the right side. You're about to create a SwiftUI app that does the exact same thing, but more swiftly!

Creating a new SwiftUI project

To start, create a new Xcode project (**Shift-Command-N**), select **iOS ▸ Single View App**, name the project **RGBullsEye**, then select **SwiftUI** in the **User Interface** menu:

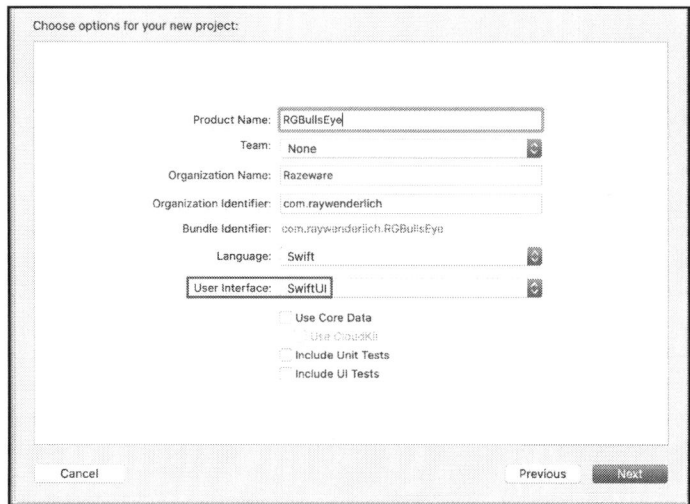

Use SwiftUI checkbox

Save your project somewhere *outside* the **RGBullsEye-Starter** folder.

In the project navigator, open the **RGBullsEye** group to see what you got: the **AppDelegate.swift**, which you may be used to seeing, is now split into **AppDelegate.swift** *and* **SceneDelegate.swift**. The latter has the `window`:

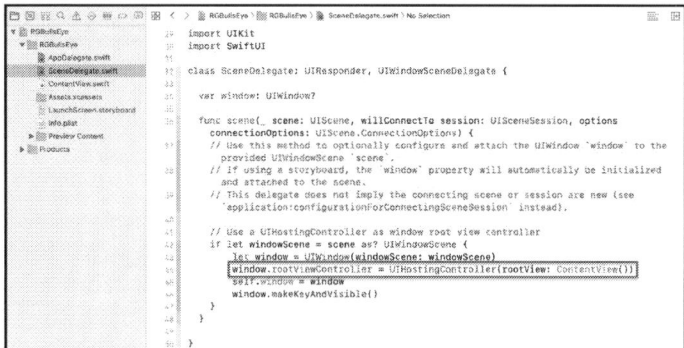

SceneDelegate.swift

`SceneDelegate` itself isn't specific to SwiftUI, but this line is:

```
window.rootViewController = UIHostingController(rootView:
  ContentView())
```

`UIHostingController` creates a view controller for the SwiftUI view `ContentView`.

> **Note**: `UIHostingController` enables you to *integrate* SwiftUI views into an existing app. You'll learn how in Chapter 4, "Integrating SwiftUI."

When the app starts, `window` displays an instance of `ContentView`, which is defined in **ContentView.swift**. It's a `struct` that conforms to the `View` protocol:

```
struct ContentView: View {
  var body: some View {
    Text("Hello World")
  }
}
```

This is SwiftUI declaring that the body of `ContentView` contains a `Text` view that displays **Hello World**.

Previewing your ContentView

Down in the `DEBUG` block, `ContentView_Previews` contains a view that contains an instance of `ContentView`:

```
struct ContentView_Previews : PreviewProvider {
  static var previews: some View {
    ContentView()
  }
}
```

This is where you can specify sample data for the preview, and you can compare different font sizes and color schemes. But where *is* the preview?

There's a big blank space next to the code, with this at the top:

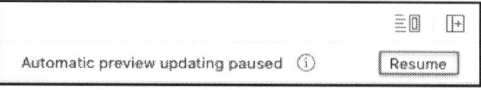

Preview Resume button

Click **Resume**, and wait a while, to see the preview:

Hello World preview

Note: If you don't see the **Resume** button, click the **Editor Options** button, and select **Canvas**:

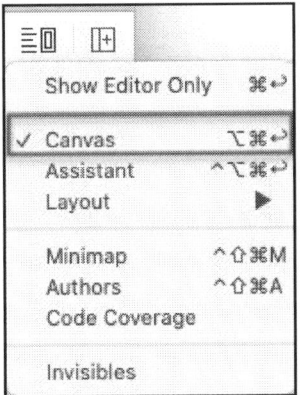

Editor options

If you still don't see the **Resume** button, make sure you're running macOS Catalina (10.15).

> **Note**: Instead of clicking the **Resume** button, you can use the very useful keyboard shortcut **Option-Command-P**. It works even when the **Resume** button isn't displayed immediately after you change something in the view.

Previewing in landscape

RGBullsEye looks best in landscape orientation. However, at the time of writing, Xcode 11 doesn't provide an easy way to preview in landscape orientation. For now, you have to specify fixed width and height values—inside the static `previews` property, add a `previewLayout` modifier to `ContentView()`:

```
ContentView().previewLayout(.fixed(width: 568, height: 320))
```

These values display an iPhone SE-sized window in landscape orientation.

To see a list of dimensions for other iPhone models, go to, see this article, *"The Ultimate Guide To iPhone Resolutions,"* which you can access here: bit.ly/29Ce3Ip.

> **Note**: To save some display space here, I set the editor layout to **Canvas on Bottom**.

Preview iPhone SE in landscape

Creating your UI

Your SwiftUI app doesn't have a storyboard or a view controller—**ContentView.swift** takes over their jobs. You can use any combination of code and drag-from-object-library to create your UI, and you can perform storyboard-like actions directly in your code! Best of all, everything stays in sync all the time!

SwiftUI is **declarative**: you declare how you want the UI to look, and SwiftUI converts your declarations into efficient code that gets the job done. Apple encourages you to create as many views as you need to keep your code easy to read. Reusable parameterized views are especially recommended—it's just like extracting code into a function, and you'll create one later in this chapter.

For this chapter, you'll mostly use the canvas, similar to how you'd layout your UI in Interface Builder (IB).

Some SwiftUI vocabulary

Before you dive into creating your views, there's a little vocabulary you must learn.

- **Canvas and Minimap**: To get the full SwiftUI experience, you need **Xcode 11** and **macOS 10.15**—then you'll be able to preview your app's views in the **canvas**, alongside the code editor. Also available is a **minimap** of your code: It doesn't appear in my screenshots because I hid it: **Editor ▸ Hide Minimap**.

- **Container views**: If you've previously used stack views, you'll find it pretty easy to create this app's UI in SwiftUI, using HStack and VStack **container views**. There are other container views, including ZStack and Group—you'll learn about them in _Chapter 9, "Containers"_.

In addition to container views, there are SwiftUI views for many of the UIKit objects you know and love, like Text, Button and Slider. The + button in the toolbar displays the **Library** of SwiftUI views.

Modifiers: Instead of setting attributes or properties of UIKit objects, you can attach **modifiers**—for foreground color, font, padding and a lot more.

Creating the target color block

In RGBullsEye, the target color block, which is the color your user is trying to match, is a Color view above a Text view. But in SwiftUI you can't have more than one view at the top-level of body, so you'll need to put them into a container view—a VStack (vertical stack) in this scenario.

The workflow is as follows:

1. **Embed** the `Text` view in a `VStack` and edit the text.
2. Add a `Color` view to the stack.

Step 1: **Command-click** the **Hello World** `Text` view in the canvas—notice Xcode highlights the code line—and select **Embed in VStack**:

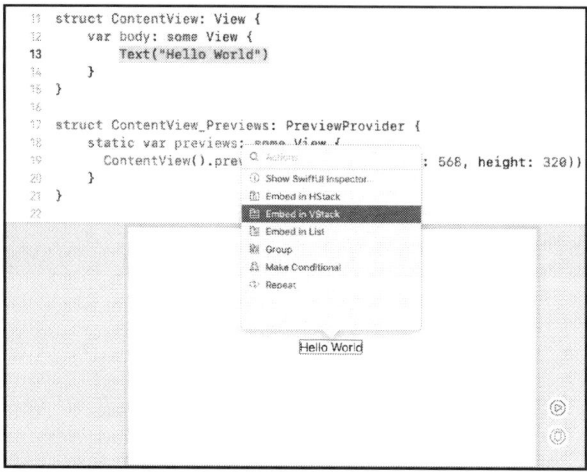

Embed Text view in VStack

> **Note**: If **Command-click** jumps to the definition of `Text`, use **Control-Command-click** instead.

The canvas looks the same, but there's now a `VStack` in your code.

Change "`Hello World`" to "`Match this color`": You could do this directly in the code, but, just so you know you can do this, **Command-click** the `Text` view in the canvas, and select **Inspect...**:

Inspect Text view

Then edit the text in the inspector:

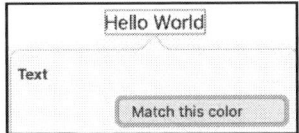

Edit text in inspector

Your code updates to match! Just for fun, change the text in your code, and watch it change in the canvas. Then change it back. Efficient, right?

Step 2: Click the + button in the toolbar to open the **Library**. Search for **Color**. Then drag this object onto the Text view in the canvas; while dragging, move the cursor down until you see the hint **Insert Color Into Vertical Stack**—*not* **Add Color to a new Vertical Stack along with existing Vertical Stack**—but keep the cursor near the top of the Text view. Then release the Color object.

Insert Color into VStack

And there's your Color view inside the VStack, in both the canvas and your code!

```
        VStack {
            Color(red: 0.5, green: 0.5, blue: 0.5)
            Text("Match this color")
        }
    }
}

struct ContentView_Previews: PreviewProvider {
    static var previews: some View {
        ContentView().previewLayout(.fixed(width: 568, height: 320))
```

Color view in VStack

> **Note**: In IB, you could drag several objects onto the view, then select them all, and embed them in a stack view. But the SwiftUI **Embed** command only works on a *single* object.

Creating the guess color block

The guess color block looks a lot like the target color block, but with different text. It needs to be on the *right-side* of the target color block; that means using an `HStack` (horizontal stack) as the top-most view.

In SwiftUI, it's easier to select nested objects in the code than in the canvas.

In your code, **Command-click** the `VStack`, and select **Embed in HStack**.

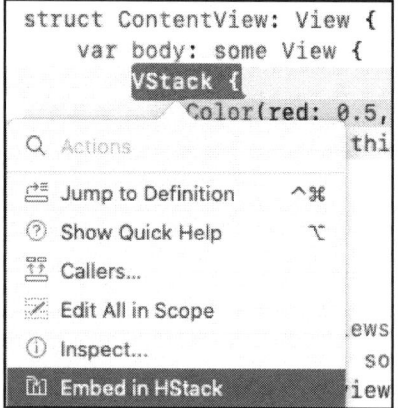

Embed color block VStack in HStack

Then copy the `VStack` closure, paste it inside the `HStack`, and change the `Text` in the *second* `VStack` to "R: 127 G: 127 B: 127". Your `HStack` now looks like this:

```
HStack {
  VStack {
    Color(red: 0.5, green: 0.5, blue: 0.5)
    Text("Match this color")
  }
  VStack {
    Color(red: 0.5, green: 0.5, blue: 0.5)
    Text("R: 127   G: 127   B: 127")
  }
}
```

Creating the button and slider

In the original app, the **Hit me!** button and color sliders went *below* the color blocks; again a container view is needed. To achieve the desired result, you need to put your `HStack` with color blocks inside a `VStack`.

> **Note**: To keep the **Library** open, **Option-click** the + button.

First, in your code, embed the `HStack` in a `VStack`, then drag a `Button` from the **Library** into your *code*: Hover *slightly below* the `HStack` view's closing brace until a new line opens for you to drop the object.

Press **Option-Command-P** or click **Resume** to see your button:

```
VStack {
    HStack {
        VStack {
            Color(red: 0.5, green: 0.5, blue: 0.5)
            Text("Match this color")
        }
        VStack {
            Color(red: 0.5, green: 0.5, blue: 0.5)
            Text("R: 127   G: 127   B: 127")
        }
    }
    Button(action: {}) {
        Text("Button")
    }
}
```

Add Button to code

Now that the button makes it clear where the VStack bottom edge is, you can drag a **Slider** from the **Library** onto your canvas, just below the Button:

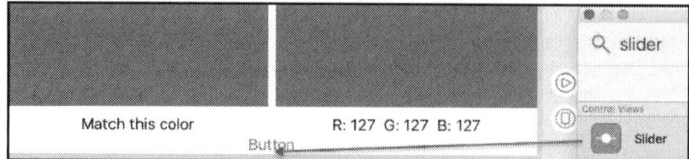

Insert Slider into VStack

Change the Button Text to "Hit Me!", and set the Slider value to **.constant(0.5)**.

Here's what it looks like:

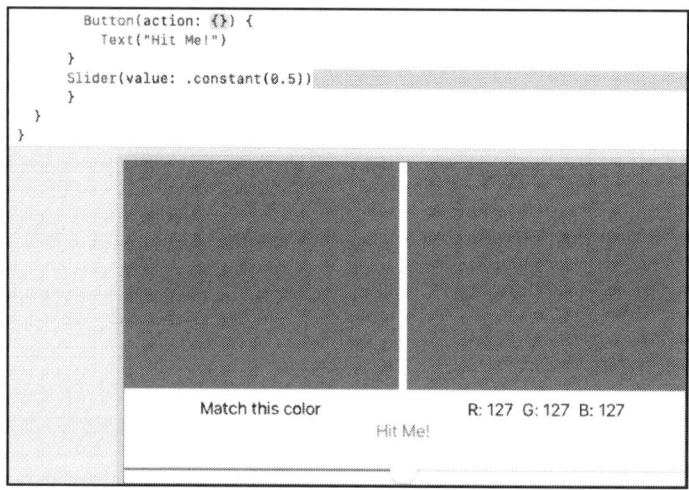

Button & Slider in VStack

> **Note**: If your slider thumb isn't centered, press **Option-Command-P** until it is.

Well, yes, you do need *three* sliders, but the slider values will update the UI, so you'll first set up the red slider, then replicate it for the other two sliders.

Updating the UI

You can use "normal" constants and variables in SwiftUI, but if the UI should update when its value changes, you designate a variable as a `@State` variable. In SwiftUI, when a `@State` variable changes, the view invalidates its appearance and recomputes the body. To see this in action, you'll ensure the variables that affect the guess color are `@State` variables.

Using @State variables

Add these properties at the top of `struct ContentView`, above the body property:

```
let rTarget = Double.random(in: 0..<1)
let gTarget = Double.random(in: 0..<1)
let bTarget = Double.random(in: 0..<1)
@State var rGuess: Double
@State var gGuess: Double
@State var bGuess: Double
```

In the RGB color space, R, G and B values are between 0 and 1. The target color doesn't change during the game, so its values are constants, initialized to random values. You could also initialize the *guess* values to 0.5, but I've left them uninitialized to show you what you must do, if you don't initialize some variables.

Scroll down to the `ContentView_Previews` struct, which instantiates a `ContentView` to display in the preview. The initializer now needs parameter values for the guess values. Change `ContentView()` to this:

```
ContentView(rGuess: 0.5, gGuess: 0.5, bGuess: 0.5)
```

This makes sure the sliders' thumbs are centered when previewing the view.

You must also modify the initializer in `SceneDelegate`, in `scene(_:willConnectTo:options:)` — replace `ContentView()` in this line:

```
window.rootViewController = UIHostingController(rootView:
   ContentView(rGuess: 0.5, gGuess: 0.5, bGuess: 0.5))
```

When the app loads its root scene, the slider thumbs will be centered.

Updating the Color views

In the `VStack` containing `Text("Match this color")`, edit the `Color` view to use the target values:

```
Color(red: rTarget, green: gTarget, blue: bTarget)
```

Press **Option-Command-P** to see a random target color.

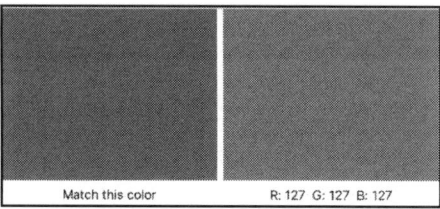
Random target color

> **Note**: The preview refreshes itself periodically, as well as when you click **Resume** or the live preview button (more about this soon), so don't be surprised to see the target color change, all by itself, every so often.

Similarly, modify the **guess** `Color` to use the guess values:

```
Color(red: rGuess, green: gGuess, blue: bGuess)
```

When the R, G and B values are all 0.5, you get gray. To check these guess values are working, change them in the preview—for example:

```
static var previews: some View {
  ContentView(rGuess: 0.7, gGuess: 0.3, bGuess: 0.6)
    .previewLayout(.fixed(width: 568, height: 320))
}
```

And see the preview update to something like this:

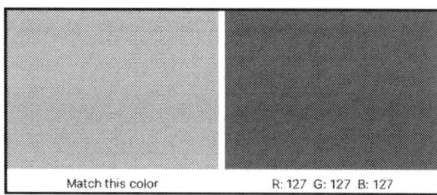
Non-gray color to check guess values

The R, G and B values in the `Text` view are still 127, but you'll fix that soon.

Change the preview values back to **0.5**.

Making Reusable Views

Because the sliders are basically identical, you'll define *one* slider view, then *reuse* it for the other two sliders—exactly as Apple recommends.

Making the red slider

First, pretend you're not thinking about reuse, and just create the red slider. You should tell your users its minimum and maximum values with a `Text` view on either side of the `Slider`. To achieve this layout, you'll need an `HStack`.

Embed the `Slider` in an `HStack`, then insert `Text` views above and below (in code) or to the left and right (in canvas). Change the `Placeholder` text to 0 and 255, then update the preview to see how it looks:

Slider from 0 to 255

> **Note:** You and I know the slider goes from 0 to 1, but the **255** end label and 0-to-255 RGB values are for your users, who might feel more comfortable thinking of RGB values between 0 and 255, as in the hexadecimal representation of colors.

The numbers look cramped, so you'll fix that, and also make this look and behave like a red slider.

Edit the slider `HStack` code to look like this:

```
HStack {
  Text("0").foregroundColor(.red)
  Slider(value: $rGuess)
  Text("255").foregroundColor(.red)
}.padding(.horizontal)
```

You've modified the `Text` views to be red, set the `Slider` value to $rGuess—the position of its thumb—and modified the `HStack` with some horizontal padding. But what's with the $? You'll find out real soon, but first, check that it's working.

Down in the preview code, change `rGuess` to something different from 0.5, then press **Option-Command-P**:

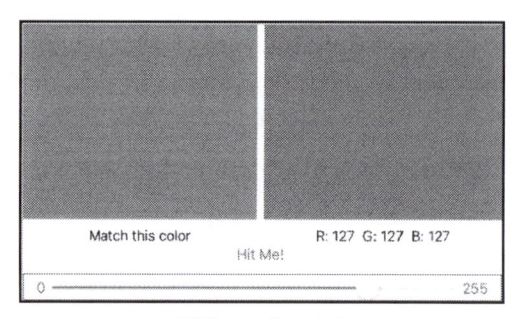

Slider value 0.8

Awesome—I set `rGuess` to **0.8**, and the slider thumb is right where I expect it to be! And the numbers are red, and not squashed up against the edges.

Bindings

So back to that `$`—it's actually pretty cool and ultra powerful for such a little symbol. `rGuess` by itself is just the value—read-only. `$rGuess` is a read-write **binding**; you need it here, to update the guess color while the user is changing the slider's value.

To see the difference, set the values in the Text view below the guess `Color` view: Change `Text("R: 127 G: 127 B: 127")` to the following:

```
Text("R: \(Int(rGuess * 255.0))"
  + "  G: \(Int(gGuess * 255.0))"
  + "  B: \(Int(bGuess * 255.0))")
```

Here, you're only *using* (read-only) the guess values, not changing them, so you don't need the `$` prefix.

Press **Option-Command-P**:

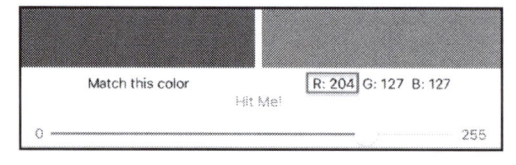

*R value 204 = 255 * 0.8*

And now the R value is **204**—that's 255 * **0.8**, as it should be!

Extracting subviews

Now, the purpose of this section is to create a reusable view from the red slider `HStack`. To be reusable, the view will need some parameters. If you were to **Copy-Paste-Edit** this `HStack` to create the green slider, you'd change `.red` to `.green`, and `$rGuess` to `$gGuess`. So those are your parameters.

Command-click the red slider `HStack`, and select **Extract Subview**:

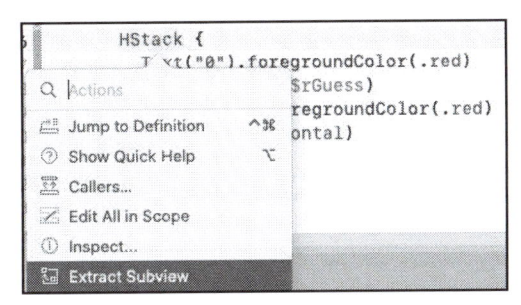

Extract HStack to subview

This works the same as **Refactor ▸ Extract to Function**, but for SwiftUI views.

Don't worry about all the error messages that appear; they'll go away when you've finished editing your new subview.

Name the extracted view **ColorSlider**, then add these properties at the top, before the body property:

```
@Binding var value: Double
var textColor: Color
```

For the `value` variable, you use `@Binding` instead of `@State`, because the `ColorSlider` view doesn't *own* this data—it receives an initial value from its parent view and mutates it.

Now, replace `$rGuess` with `$value`, and `.red` with `textColor`:

```
Text("0").foregroundColor(textColor)
Slider(value: $value)
Text("255").foregroundColor(textColor)
```

Then go back up to the call to `ColorSlider()` in the `VStack`, and add your parameters:

```
ColorSlider(value: $rGuess, textColor: .red)
```

Check that the preview still shows the red slider correctly, then **Copy-Paste-Edit** this line to replace the Text placeholders with the other two sliders:

```
ColorSlider(value: $gGuess, textColor: .green)
ColorSlider(value: $bGuess, textColor: .blue)
```

Change the guess values in the preview code, then update the preview:

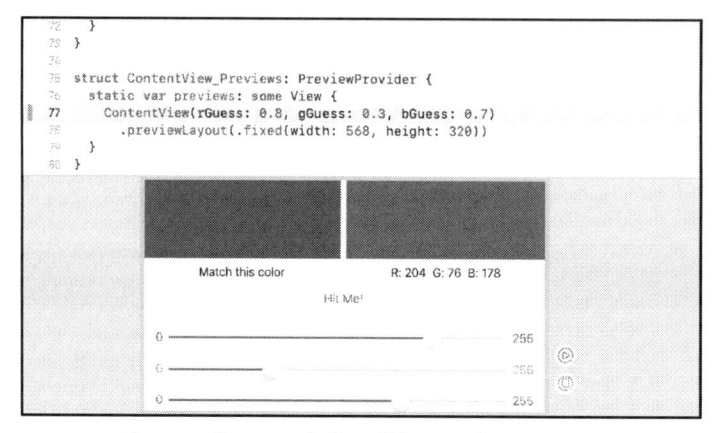

Guess values work for sliders and guess text

Everything's working! You can't wait to play the game? Coming right up!

But first, set the guess values back to **0.5** in the preview code.

Live Preview

You don't have to fire up Simulator to play the game: Down by the lower-right corner of the preview device, click the **live preview** button:

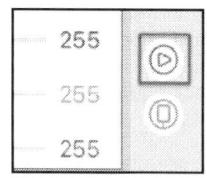

Live preview button

Wait for the **Preview spinner** to stop; if necessary, click **Try Again**.

Now move those sliders to match the color!

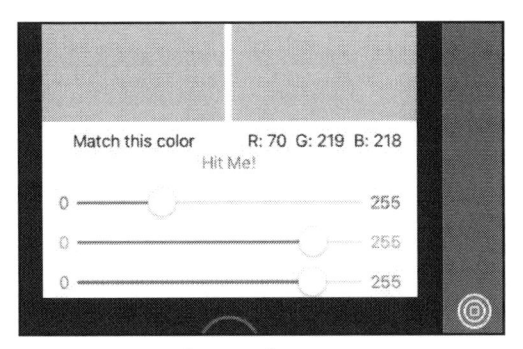

Playing the game

> **Note**: At the time of writing, Xcode's live preview doesn't use the fixed width and height settings. Instead, it uses the Simulator device that's selected in the project's scheme — in this case, iPhone 8.

Stop and think about what's happening here, compared with how the UIKit app works. The SwiftUI views *update themselves* whenever the slider values change! The UIKit app puts all that code into the slider action. Every @State variable is a **source of truth**, and views depend on **state**, not on a sequence of events.

How amazing is that! Go ahead and do a victory lap to the kitchen, get your favorite drink and snacks, then come back for the final step! You want to know your score, don't you?

Presenting an Alert

After using the sliders to get a good color match, your user taps the **Hit Me!** button, just like in the original UIKit game. And just like in the original, an Alert should appear, displaying the score.

First, add a method to ContentView to compute the score. Between the @State variables and the body, add this method:

```
func computeScore() -> Int {
  let rDiff = rGuess - rTarget
  let gDiff = gGuess - gTarget
  let bDiff = bGuess - bTarget
  let diff = sqrt(rDiff * rDiff + gDiff * gDiff + bDiff * bDiff)
  return Int((1.0 - diff) * 100.0 + 0.5)
}
```

The `diff` value is just the distance between two points in three-dimensional space. You subtract it from 1, then scale it to a value out of 100. Smaller `diff` yields a higher score.

Next, you'll work on your `Button` view:

```
Button(action: {}) {
  Text("Hit Me!")
}
```

A `Button` has an action and a label, just like a `UIButton`. The action you want to happen is the presentation of an `Alert` view. But if you just create an `Alert` in the `Button` action, it won't do anything.

Instead, you create the `Alert` as one of the subviews of `ContentView`, and add a `@State` variable of type `Bool`. Then you set the value of this variable to `true` when you want the `Alert` to appear—in the `Button` action, in this case. The value resets to `false` when the user dismisses the `Alert`.

So add this `@State` variable, initialized to `false`:

```
@State var showAlert = false
```

Then add this line as the `Button` action:

```
self.showAlert = true
```

You need the `self` because `showAlert` is inside a closure.

Finally, add an `alert` modifier to the `Button`, so your `Button` view looks like this:

```
Button(action: { self.showAlert = true }) {
  Text("Hit Me!")
}.alert(isPresented: $showAlert) {
  Alert(title: Text("Your Score"),
        message: Text(String(computeScore())))
}.padding()
```

You pass the `$showAlert` **binding** because its value will change when the user dismisses the alert.

SwiftUI has simple initializers for `Alert` views, just like the ones that many developers have created for themselves, in a `UIAlertViewController` extension. This one has a default `OK` button, so you don't even need to include it as a parameter.

Finally, you add some padding, to make the button stand out better.

Turn off **live preview**, click **Resume** to refresh the preview, then turn on **live preview**, and try your hand at matching the target color:

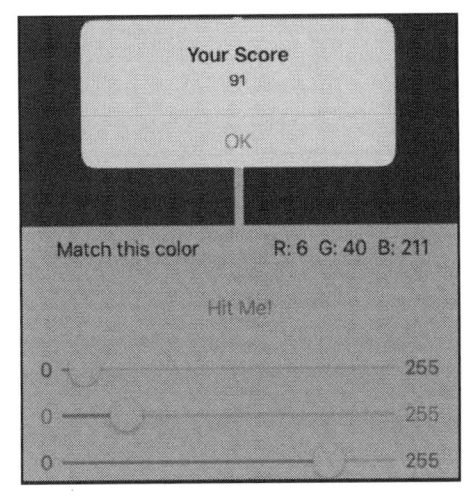

Score!

Hey, when you've got live preview, who needs Simulator?

Challenge

Challenge: Create a SwiftUI app

The **challenge/starter** folder contains a UIKit version of our "famous" BullsEye app from our book *iOS Apprentice*. Your challenge is to create a SwiftUI app with the same UI and behavior.

The UIKit app doesn't use a stack view for the slider, but you'll find it really easy to create your SwiftUI UI using stacks.

The solution is in the **challenge/final** folder for this chapter.

Key points

- The Xcode canvas lets you create your UI side-by-side with its code, and they stay in sync—a change to one side always updates the other side.

- You can create your UI in code or in the canvas or using any combination of the tools.

- You organize your view objects with horizontal and vertical stacks, just like using stack views in storyboards.

- **Preview** lets you see how your app looks and behaves with different environment settings or initial data, and **Live Preview** lets you interact with your app without firing up Simulator.

- You should aim to create reusable views — Xcode's **Extract Subview** tool makes this easy.

- SwiftUI updates your UI whenever a `@State` variable's value changes. You pass a reference to a subview as a `@Binding`, allowing read-write access to the `@State` variable.

- Presenting alerts is easy again.

Chapter 3: Understanding SwiftUI

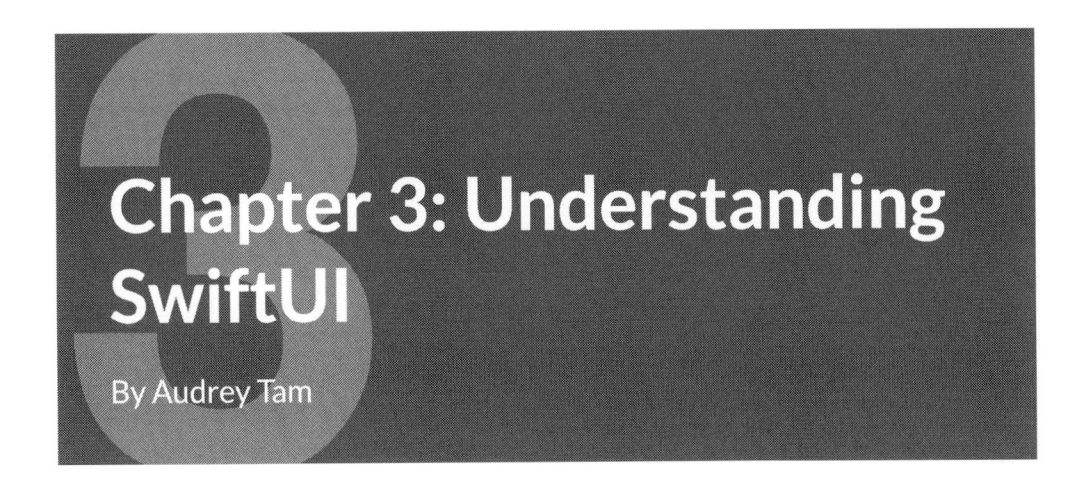

By Audrey Tam

This chapter gives you an overview of how SwiftUI can help you develop great apps faster. You'll learn about declarative app development — declarative UI plus declarative data dependencies — and how to "think different" about your app design.

Why SwiftUI?

Interface Builder (IB) and storyboards helped a lot of us get up to speed developing apps, making it easy to layout adaptive user interfaces and setting up segues for navigation.

But many developers prefer to create their production views in code, partly because it's more efficient to copy or edit UI when it's written out in code, but mostly because IB and storyboards have built-in gotchas—you edit the name of an `IBAction` or `IBOutlet` or delete it from your code, and your app crashes because IB doesn't see changes to code. Or you've fumed about stringly-typed identifiers for segues or table view cells that you have to use in your code, but Xcode can't check for you because they're strings.

SwiftUI lets you ignore Interface Builder (IB) and storyboards without having to write detailed step-by-step instructions for laying out your UI. You can preview a SwiftUI view side-by-side with its code—a change to one side will update the other side, so they're always in sync. There aren't any identifier strings to get wrong. And it's code, but a lot less than you'd write for UIKit, so it's easier to understand, edit and debug. What's not to love?

SwiftUI doesn't replace UIKit—like Swift and Objective-C, you can use both in the same app. In this chapter, you'll use a non-SwiftUI class as a data source in RGBullsEye. In Chapter 4, **Integrating SwiftUI**, you'll see how easy it is to use a SwiftUI view in a UIKit app, and vice versa.

The SwiftUI APIs are consistent across platforms, so it's easy to develop the same-ish app on multiple platforms using the same source code on each. In Chapter 5, **Frameworks**, you'll learn how to take advantage of the features of macOS, watchOS and tvOS.

Is SwiftUI ready for production? Maybe, if you don't have to support older OS versions—SwiftUI apps need the latest operating systems on all the Apple platforms.

Declarative app development

SwiftUI enables you to do **declarative** app development—you'll develop great apps faster… once you learn to "think different." Declarative app development means you declare both how you want the views in your UI to look and also what data they depend on. The SwiftUI framework takes care of creating views when they should appear and updating them whenever there's a change to data they depend on.

You declare how your view's state affects its appearance, and how SwiftUI should *react* to changes in view's data dependencies. Yes, there's a definite *reactive* feeling to SwiftUI! So if you're already using one of the reactive programming frameworks, you'll probably have an easier time picking up SwiftUI.

These features help to speed up your app development:

- **Views**: Declarative UI stays in sync with code, with no stringly-typed identifiers. Use views for layout and navigation, and encapsulate presentation logic for a piece of data. Another benefit of declarative UI: the API is consistent *across platforms*, so you can learn once, then apply everywhere. Controls describe their *role*, not their appearance, so the same control looks appropriate for the platform. You'll learn more about the other platforms in Chapter 5, **Frameworks**.

- **Data**: Declarative data dependencies update views when data changes—the framework recomputes the view and all its children, then renders what has changed. A view's state depends on its data, so you declare how the view uses data —how the view reacts to data changes or how data affect the view. You declare the possible states for your view, and how the view appears for each state.

- **Navigation**: Conditional subviews can replace navigation: see Chapter 10, **Lists & Navigation**.

- **Integration**: It's easy to integrate SwiftUI into a UIKit app and vice versa: see Chapter 4, **Integrating SwiftUI**.

Getting started

Open the starter project, or continue with your project from the previous chapter.

SwiftUI vs. UIKit

Also, open the UIKit version of RGBullsEye, and take a closer look at the differences between UIKit and SwiftUI.

To create the UIKit app, I laid out several labels, a button and three sliders on the storyboard, connected them to outlets and actions in the view controller, then wrote code in the actions and some helper methods to keep the UI in sync with changes to the slider values. When the user moves a slider, its action updates a color value, a label and a label's background color. I had to think about the correct order to do things—it would be easy to forget a step.

To create the SwiftUI app, you listed the `Color`, `Text`, `Button` and `Slider` subviews in the order you wanted them to appear—much easier than setting auto-layout constraints!—and declared *within each subview* how it depends on changes to the app's data. SwiftUI manages data dependencies to keep views consistent with their state, so you don't have to worry about doing things in the right order, or forgetting to update a UI object. The canvas preview means you don't need a storyboard. The subviews keep themselves updated, so you don't need a view controller either. And live preview means you rarely need to launch the simulator.

Time-efficient, right?

Declaring views

A SwiftUI view is a piece of your UI: You combine small views to build larger views. There are lots of primitive views like `Text` and `Color`, which you can use as basic building blocks for your custom views.

Inside a view, click the + button (or **Command-Shift-L**) to open the **Library**:

Views	Modifiers
Layout Views	*Layout Modifiers*
Vertical Stack	Padding
Horizontal Stack	Frame
Z Stack	Background
Spacer	Aspect Ratio
Control Views	Hidden
List	Fixed Size
Text	Relative Size
Button	Relative Width
Toggle	Relative Height
Date Picker	Scale to Fill
Slider	Scale to Fit
Text Field	Offset
Tabbed View	Overlay
Stepper	Content Shape
Navigation View	Edges Ignoring Safe Area
Picker	*Effect Modifiers*
Scroll View	Border
Horizontal Split View	Opacity
Vertical Split View	Corner Radius
Other Views	Blur
Image	Clipped
Color	Grayscale
Rectangle	Clip Shape
Ellipse	Hue Rotation
Circle	Blend Mode
Rounded Rectangle	

Library of primitive views and modifiers.

The first tab lists **primitive views** for layout and control, plus Other Views and Paints. Many of these—especially the control views—are familiar to you as UIKit elements, but some are unique to SwiftUI. You'll learn how to use them in upcoming chapters.

The second tab lists **modifiers** for layout, effects, text, events and other purposes like presentation, environment and accessibility. A modifier is a method that creates a new view from the existing view. You can chain modifiers like a pipeline to customize any view.

SwiftUI encourages you to create small reusable views, then customize them with modifiers for the specific context where you use them. And don't worry, SwiftUI collapses the modified view into an efficient data structure, so you get all this convenience with no visible performance hit.

You can apply many of these modifiers to any type of view. And sometimes the ordering matters, as you'll soon see.

Environment values

Several environment values affect your whole app. Many of these correspond to device user settings like accessibility, locale, calendar and color scheme. You'll usually try out environment values in `previews`, to anticipate and solve problems that might arise from these settings on a user's device. Later in this chapter, you'll see another (easier) way to check for environment issues.

You can find a list of built-in `EnvironmentValues` at apple.co/2yJJk7T.

To start, open up **ContentView.swift** and add the following environment modifier to `ContentView` in `previews`:

```
ContentView(rGuess: 0.5, gGuess: 0.5, bGuess: 0.5)
    .previewLayout(.fixed(width: 568, height: 320))
    .environment(\.colorScheme, .dark)
```

Also, in body, embed your top-level `VStack` in a `NavigationView`:

```
var body: some View {
  NavigationView {
    VStack {
      HStack { ... }
      Button(...)
      ColorSlider(...)
      ColorSlider(...)
      ColorSlider(...)
```

```
    }
    .navigationBarTitle("", displayMode: .inline)
    .navigationBarHidden(true)
  }
}
```

> **Note**: At the time of writing, you need a `NavigationView` as your top-level view for `.environment(\.colorScheme, .dark)` to work. But then the (large) navigation bar covers the color blocks, so the two `navigationBar` modifiers make the bar smaller and hide it ... sort of. This might be a bug in Xcode.

Refresh the preview, and now it's in dark mode!

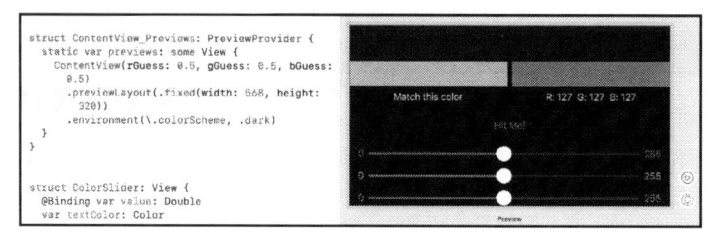

Dark mode applied to preview.

But, build and run the app, and you will see the following:

Modifying the preview doesn't affect your app—if you want your app to default to dark mode *at startup*, you need to set the environment value for the app's top-level view.

To do this, first delete or comment out the preview's `.environment` modifier you just added, and refresh the preview (**Option-Command-P**)—yes, it's back to light mode.

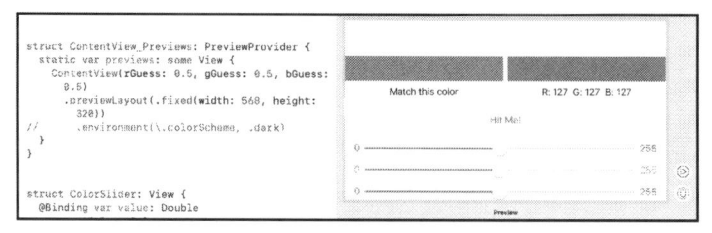

No dark mode applied to preview.

Then add the `.environment` modifier to the *top level* view of body—`NavigationView`—instead:

```
var body: some View {
  NavigationView {
    VStack {
      HStack { ... }
      Button(...)
      ColorSlider(...)
      ColorSlider(...)
      ColorSlider(...)
    }
  }
  .environment(\.colorScheme, .dark)
}
```

Now, refresh the preview:

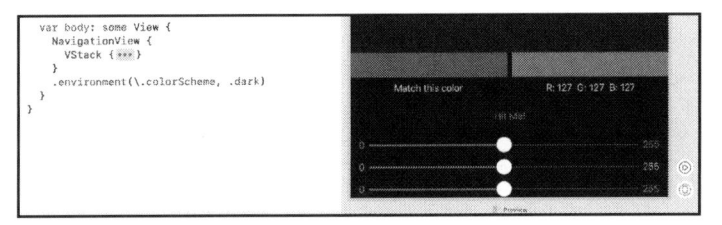

Dark mode applied to top level of body.

Then build and run—your app starts up in dark mode!

Now delete or comment out the `.environment` modifier, to see the full effect of my future magic trick ;].

Modifying reusable views

In the starter project, take a look at the body of the `ColorSlider` view you created in the previous chapter:

```
HStack {
  Text("0").foregroundColor(textColor)
  Slider(value: $value)
  Text("255").foregroundColor(textColor)
}.padding(.horizontal)
```

The `HStack` has a `padding()` modifier that adds some space at either end.

Your UI has three `ColorSlider` views, just bundled into the top-level `VStack`, at the same level as the `HStack` with the `Color` views and the button:

```
VStack {
  HStack { ... }
  Button(...)
  ColorSlider(value: $rGuess, textColor: .red)
  ColorSlider(value: $gGuess, textColor: .green)
  ColorSlider(value: $bGuess, textColor: .blue)
}
```

Here's how it currently looks:

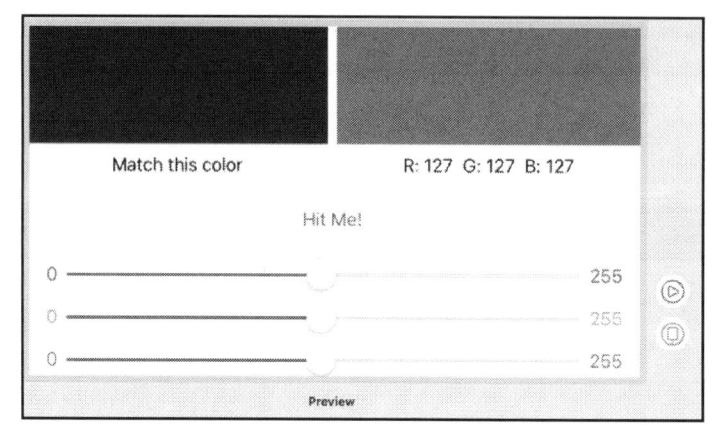

Padding happens in ColorSlider.

But these three `ColorSlider` views are a logical unit, and it makes sense to manage the padding for the *unit*, not for each individual `ColorSlider`. If you embed them in a VStack, then you can add padding to the VStack so it fits just right in your UI— padding() is one of those modifiers that can be applied to any type of view.

So embed the three `ColorSlider` views in a VStack and add horizontal padding to the VStack:

```
VStack {
  ColorSlider(value: $rGuess, textColor: .red)
  ColorSlider(value: $gGuess, textColor: .green)
  ColorSlider(value: $bGuess, textColor: .blue)
}.padding(.horizontal)
```

> **Note**: **Command-click** the first `ColorSlider` to embed it in a VStack, then move the closing brace after the third `ColorSlider`. The canvas must be open, or you won't see **Embed in VStack** in the menu. If **Command-click** jumps to the definition of `ColorSlider`, use **Control-Command-click** instead.

Then remove the padding from the `HStack` in the `ColorSlider` view, so it looks like this:

```
struct ColorSlider: View {
  @Binding var value: Double
  var textColor: Color
  var body: some View {
    HStack {
      Text("0").foregroundColor(textColor)
      Slider(value: $value)
      Text("255").foregroundColor(textColor)
    }
  }
}
```

Now refresh the preview (**Option-Command-P**) to see that it looks the same:

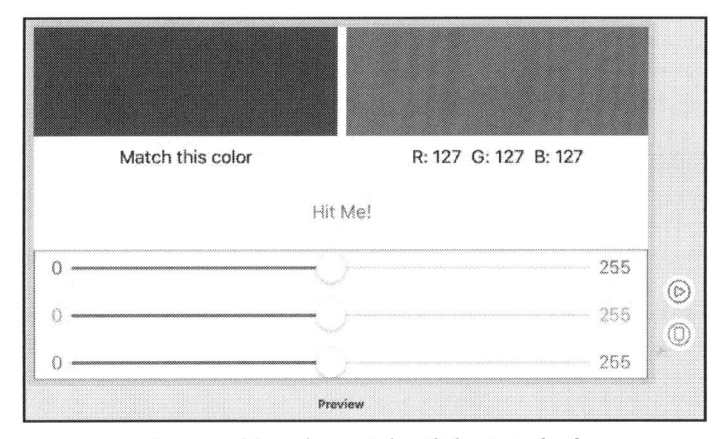

Move padding from ColorSlider into body.

The difference is that now you can tweak the padding of the 3-`ColorSlider` `VStack` as you fine-tune your UI—you might decide to add padding all around, or some top and side padding, but no bottom padding. And `ColorSlider` is just that little bit more reusable, now that it doesn't bring along its own horizontal padding.

Adding modifiers in the right order

SwiftUI applies modifiers in the order that you add them—adding a background color then padding produces a different visual effect than adding padding then background color.

To start, add modifiers to `Slider` in `ColorSlider`, so it looks like this:

```
Slider(value: $value)
  .background(textColor)
  .cornerRadius(10)
```

You're adding a background color to match the 0 and 255 labels, then rounding the corners a little.

Then refresh the preview (**Option-Command-P**) to see the effect:

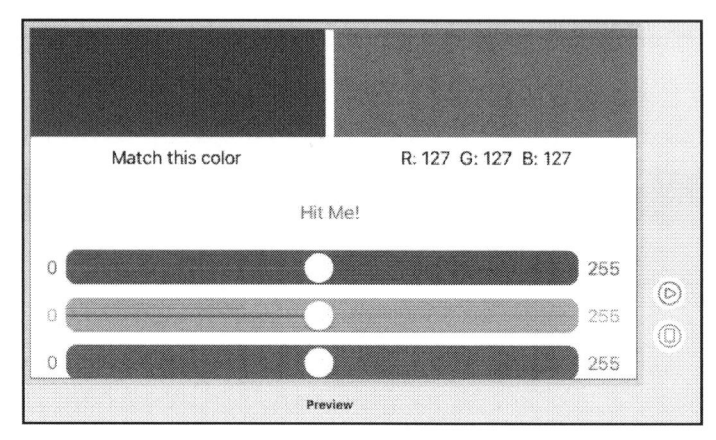

Adding background color and rounded corners to sliders.

Now swap the order:

```
Slider(value: $value)
  .cornerRadius(10)
  .background(textColor)
```

And refresh the preview:

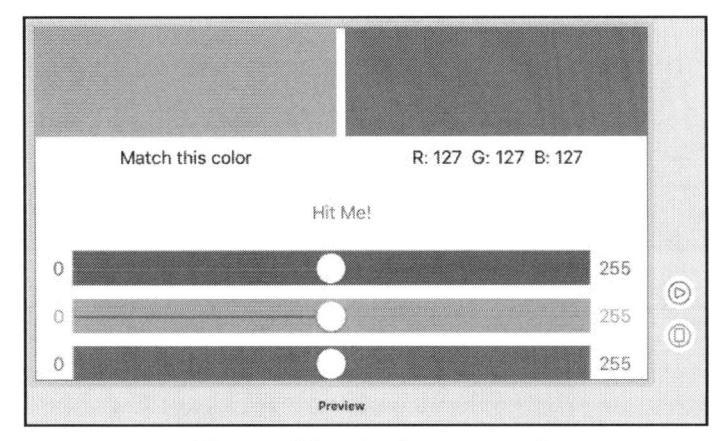

Adding modifiers in the wrong order.

What, no rounded corners!? Well, they're there, but there isn't anything "underneath" for the corner-rounding to clip. So the background color affects the whole rectangle.

Now switch the modifiers back to the first ordering, so the background modifier returns a `Slider` with background color, then the `cornerRadius` modifier returns a `Slider` with background color with rounded corners.

Showing conditional views

RGBullsEye already has a view that appears only when a certain condition is true: `Alert` appears when `showAlert` is true. The condition is in the `.alert` modifier:

```
.alert(isPresented: $showAlert)
```

You can also write explicit conditions.

In the target color `VStack`, replace `Text("Match this color")` with the following:

```
self.showAlert ? Text("R: \(Int(rTarget * 255.0))"
  + "  G: \(Int(gTarget * 255.0))"
  + "  B: \(Int(bTarget * 255.0))")
  : Text("Match this color")
```

When you show the user their score, you also display the target color values to provide additional feedback to the user.

Now refresh the preview (**Option-Command-P**), then start the **Live Preview**, and tap **Hit Me!**:

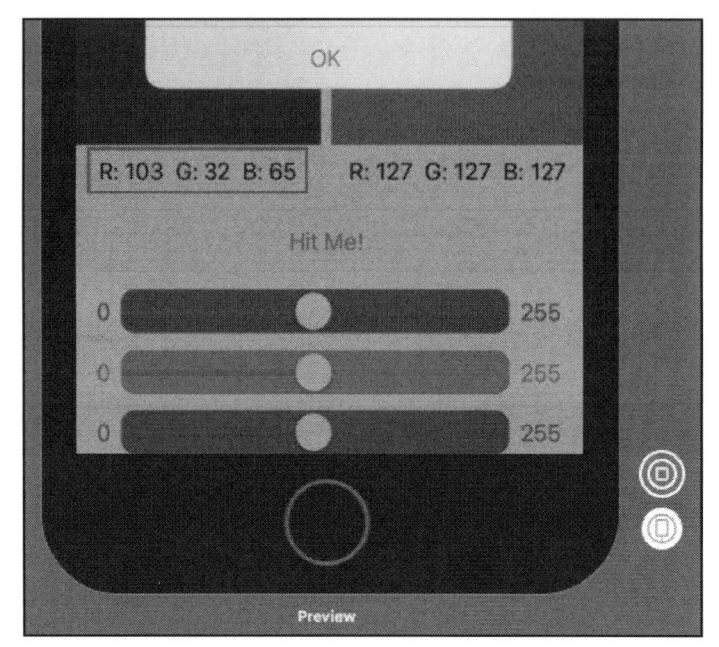

Displaying the target values with the score.

And there are the target values!

Turn off **Live Preview** for now.

Using ZStack

When you play RGBullsEye, there's no incentive to match the target color *quickly*—you can keep moving the sliders back and forth for as long as it takes, or until you give up.

So, to make it more difficult, you'll add a time counter to the game! But where? How about in the center of the guess `Color` view? But how to do that with just `HStack` and `VStack`? This is a job for `ZStack`!

First, embed the guess `Color` view in a `ZStack`:

```
ZStack { Color(red: rGuess, green: gGuess, blue: bGuess) }
```

> **Note**: The **Command-click** menu doesn't include **Embed in ZStack**, so just embed it in an `HStack`, then change "H" to "Z."

Z Stack!? The Z-direction is *perpendicular* to the screen surface — items *lower* in a `ZStack` appear *higher* in the stack. It's similar to how the *positive* Y-direction in the window is *down*.

To see this, add a `Text` view to the `ZStack`, **below** the `Color` view:

```
ZStack {
  Color(red: rGuess, green: gGuess, blue: bGuess)
  Text("60")
}
```

Refresh the preview:

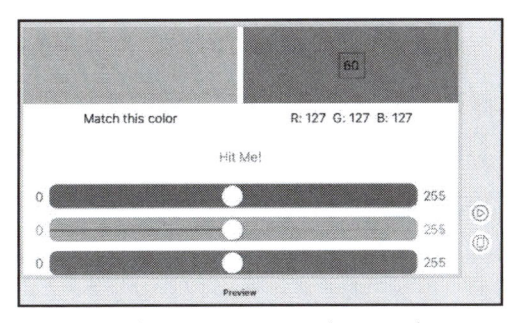

ZStack: Text appears above Color.

And there's the `Text` view!

Now move the `Text` **above** `Color`:

```
ZStack {
  Text("60")
  Color(red: rGuess, green: gGuess, blue: bGuess)
}
```

And refresh the preview:

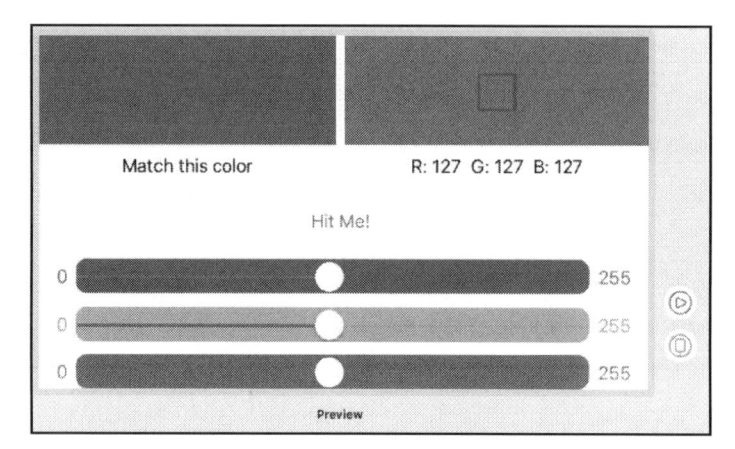

ZStack: Text appears below Color.

You can see the `Text` view's outline, but it's now hidden by the `Color` view. If you don't see anything, tap the `Text` view in the code, to highlight it in the canvas.

Next, move `Text` back below `Color`, then modify it:

```
Text("60")
  .padding(.all, 5)
  .background(Color.white)
  .mask(Circle())
}
```

You've added padding around the text, set the background color to white, so it shows up against the guess color, and added a circle mask, to make it look nice.

Next, add a center-alignment to your `ZStack` so the text is centered:

```
ZStack(alignment: .center) {
  ...
}
```

Refresh the preview to admire your work:

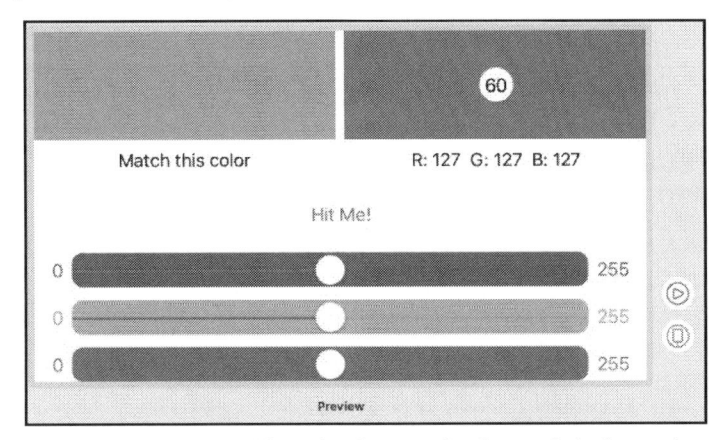

Timer text with padding, background color and circle mask.

You'll soon replace the constant string "60" with a data dependency on a real `Timer` object. But now is a good time to explore runtime debugging.

Debugging

> **Note**: To see the effect of the following instructions, make sure you've deleted or commented out any `.environment(\.colorScheme, .dark)` modifiers applied to your body and preview.

Here's how you do runtime debugging in Xcode's Live Preview: **Control-click** or **Right-click** the **Live Preview** button, then select **Debug Preview** from the menu:

Attach a debug session to Live Preview.

This will take a while, but eventually, you get all the normal debugging tools, plus environment overrides, runtime issue scanning and runtime issue breakpoints:

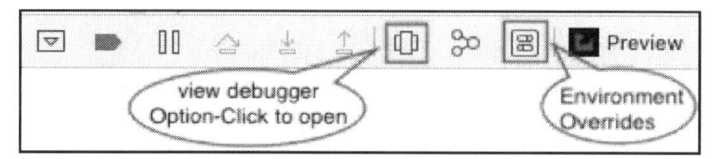

Debug preview session.

> **Note**: The debug session is tied to the lifetime of the preview, so be sure to keep the preview open while you open the view debugger—use the new editor split feature: **Option-click** the view debugger icon.

For now, just look at the environment overrides options: Click the **Environment Overrides** button—the one with two toggles—and switch on **Interface Style**. The Live Preview changes to dark mode:

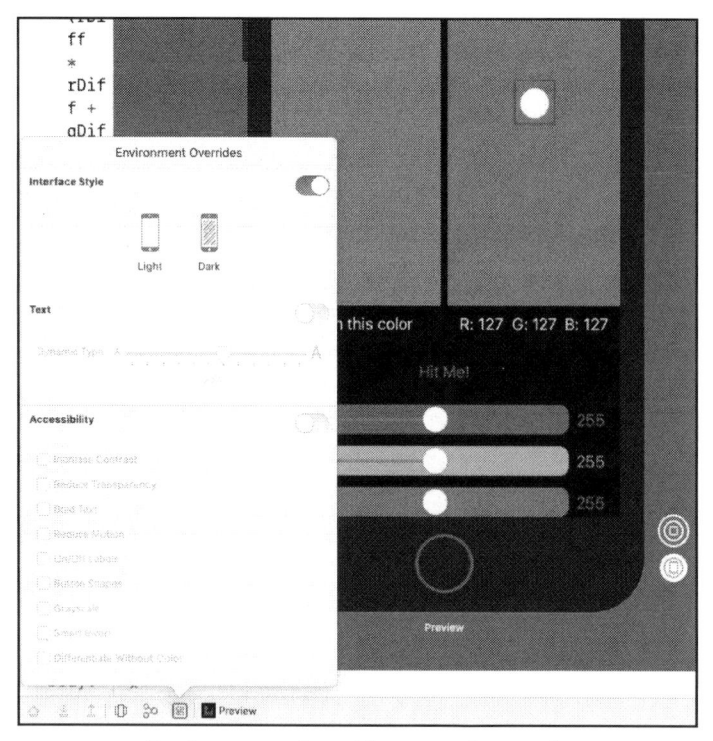

Environment Overrides: Interface Style

It looks very cool, but the timer text is invisible because its color defaults to the color scheme's primary color, which is white for dark mode. So add the `.foregroundColor` modifier:

```
Text("60")
    .padding(.all, 5)
    .background(Color.white)
    .mask(Circle())
    .foregroundColor(.black)
```

Refresh the live debug preview (**Option-Command-P** as usual), and turn on **Environment Overrides ▸ Interface Style**:

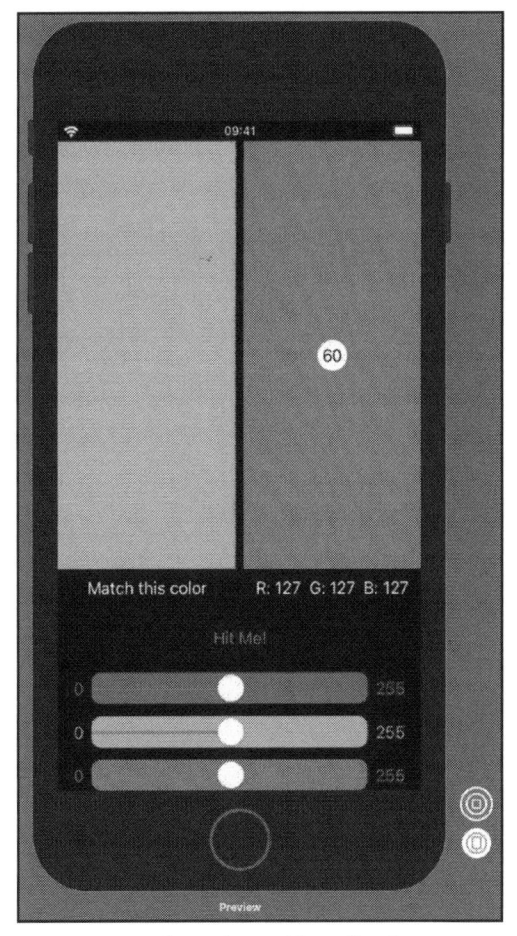

Dark mode problem fixed.

And now the problem is fixed!

Earlier in this chapter, you added a dark mode modifier to `previews` in `ContentView_Previews`, but environment overrides don't need any code... or forethought!

Notice you can also try out different text sizes and accessibility modifiers, all on the fly!

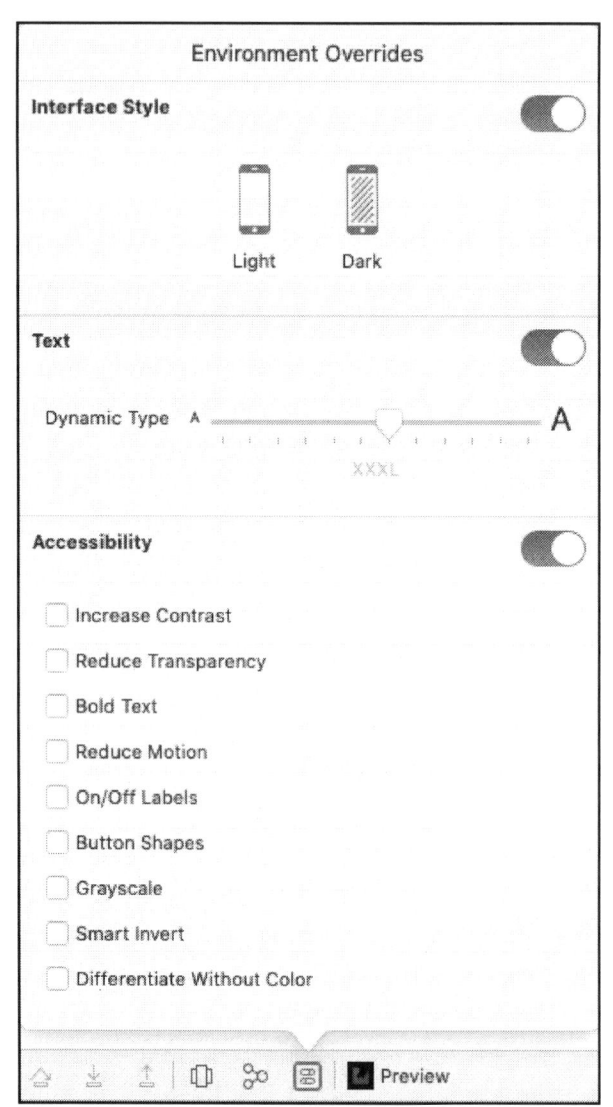

Debug mode

Environment overrides.

Awesome, right? But for now, turn back off the debug preview.

> **Note**: It's well worth your time to watch Apple's WWDC 2019 Session 412 "Debugging in Xcode 11"—it's all about debugging SwiftUI, from the nine-minute mark, which you can access, here: apple.co/2Kfcm5F.

Declaring data dependencies

Guiding principles

SwiftUI has two guiding principles for managing how data flows through your app:

- **Data access = dependency**: Reading a piece of data in your view creates a dependency for that data in that view. Every view is a function of its data dependencies—its inputs or state.

- **Single source of truth**: Every piece of data that a view reads has a source of truth, which is either owned by the view or external to the view. Regardless of where the source of truth lies, you should always have a *single* source of truth. This is why you didn't declare `@State value` in `ColorSlider`—it would have created a *duplicate* source of truth, which you'd have to keep in sync with `rValue`. Instead, you declared `@Binding value`, which means the view depends on a `@State` variable from another view.

In UIKit, the view controller keeps the model and view in sync. In SwiftUI, the declarative view hierarchy plus this single source of truth means you no longer need the view controller.

Tools for data flow

SwiftUI provides several tools to help you manage the flow of data in your app.

Property wrappers augment the behavior of variables. SwiftUI-specific wrappers—`@State`, `@Binding`, `@ObservedObject` and `@EnvironmentObject`—declare a view's dependency on the data represented by the variable.

Each wrapper indicates a different *source of data*:

- `@State` variables are owned by the view. `@State var` allocates persistent storage, so you must initialize its value. Apple advises you to mark these `private` to emphasize that a `@State` variable is owned and managed by that view specifically.

> **Note**: You can initialize the `@State` variables in `ContentView` to remove the need to pass parameters from `SceneDelegate`. Otherwise, if you make them `private`, you won't be able to initialize `ContentView` as the root view.

- `@Binding` declares dependency on a `@State` var owned by another view, which uses the `$` prefix to pass a binding to this state variable to another view. In the receiving view, `@Binding` var is a *reference* to the data, so it doesn't need an initial value. This reference enables the view to edit the state of any view that depends on this data.

- `@ObservedObject` declares dependency on a *reference type* that conforms to the `ObservableObject` protocol: It implements an `objectWillChange` property to publish changes to its data. You'll soon implement a timer as an `ObservableObject`.

- `@EnvironmentObject` declares dependency on some shared data—data that's visible to all views in the app. It's a convenient way to pass data indirectly, instead of passing data from parent view to child to grandchild, especially if the child view doesn't need it.

You normally don't use `@State` variables in a reusable view—use `@Binding` or `@ObservedObject` instead. You should create a `private` `@State` var only if *the view should own the data*, like the `highlighted` property of `Button`. Think about whether the data should be owned by a parent view or by an external source.

Observing a reference type object

OK, it's time to add a real timer to RGBullsEye! Create a new (plain old) Swift file, and name it **TimeCounter.swift**. Add this import below `import Foundation`:

```
import Combine
```

That's right, you'll be using the new **Combine** framework! You'll set up `TimeCounter` to be a **publisher**, and your `ContentView` will **subscribe** to it. Learn more about it in our book *Combine: Asynchronous Programming with Swift*.

Now, start creating your `TimeCounter` class:

```
class TimeCounter: ObservableObject {
  var timer: Timer?
  @Published var counter = 0
```

```
    @objc func updateCounter() {
       counter += 1
    }
  }
```

The magic is in the `ObservableObject` protocol and the `Published` property wrapper. Whenever `counter` changes, it publishes itself to any subscribers.

> **Note**: `ObservableObject` and `Published` provide a general-purpose Combine publisher that you use when there isn't a more specific Combine publisher for your needs. The `Timer` class has a Combine publisher `TimerPublisher`, but it's better to learn about that in our Combine book.

Next, initialize `timer` to call `updateCounter()` every second:

```
init() {
   timer = Timer.scheduledTimer(timeInterval:1, target: self,
     selector:#selector(updateCounter), userInfo: nil, repeats:
true)
}
```

And finally, add this method to get rid of `timer` when it's no longer needed:

```
func killTimer() {
   timer?.invalidate()
   timer = nil
}
```

That's your `TimeCounter` done. Now head back to `ContentView` to subscribe to it.

First, add this new property:

```
@ObservedObject var timer = TimeCounter()
```

You're declaring a data dependency on the `TimeCounter` class, which conforms to the `ObservableObject` protocol. In Combine terminology, you're subscribing to the `TimeCounter` publisher.

Next, down in your `ZStack`, edit `Text("60")` so it looks like this:

```
Text(String(timer.counter))
```

This will update your UI whenever `timer` updates its `counter`—after each second.

Lastly, add this line to the button's `action`:

```
self.timer.killTimer()
```

You want the timer to stop when the user taps **Hit Me!**.

And that's all there is to it!

Build and run. Watch the timer count the seconds, then tap **Hit Me!** to see the timer stop:

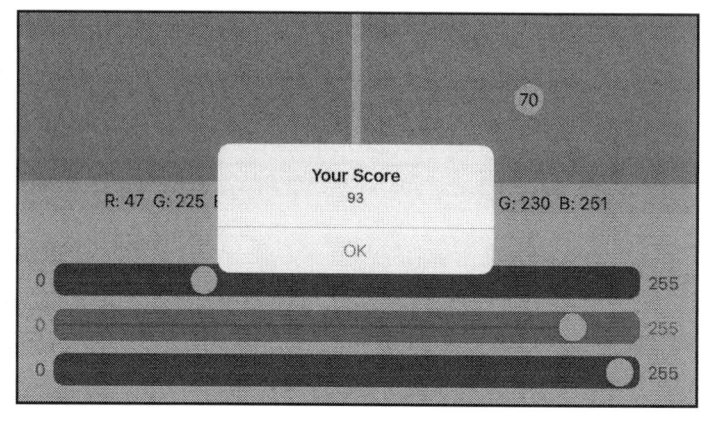

Counting the seconds.

Congratulations, you've just integrated something non-SwiftUI into your SwiftUI app! There are other ways to integrate SwiftUI with UIKit, and you'll learn about these in Chapter 4, **Integrating SwiftUI**.

Challenge

Challenge: Opacity feedback for BullsEye

When you play RGBullsEye, you get continuous feedback on how close you are to the target color. But you don't get any help when playing BullsEye. Your challenge is to add some feedback, by changing the slider background color's opacity as the user moves closer to or further away from the target.

Open the **BullsEye** app in the **challenge/starter** folder:

- Add a background color to the slider, and set the color to blue.

- Add an opacity modifier whose value *decreases* as the score *increases*.

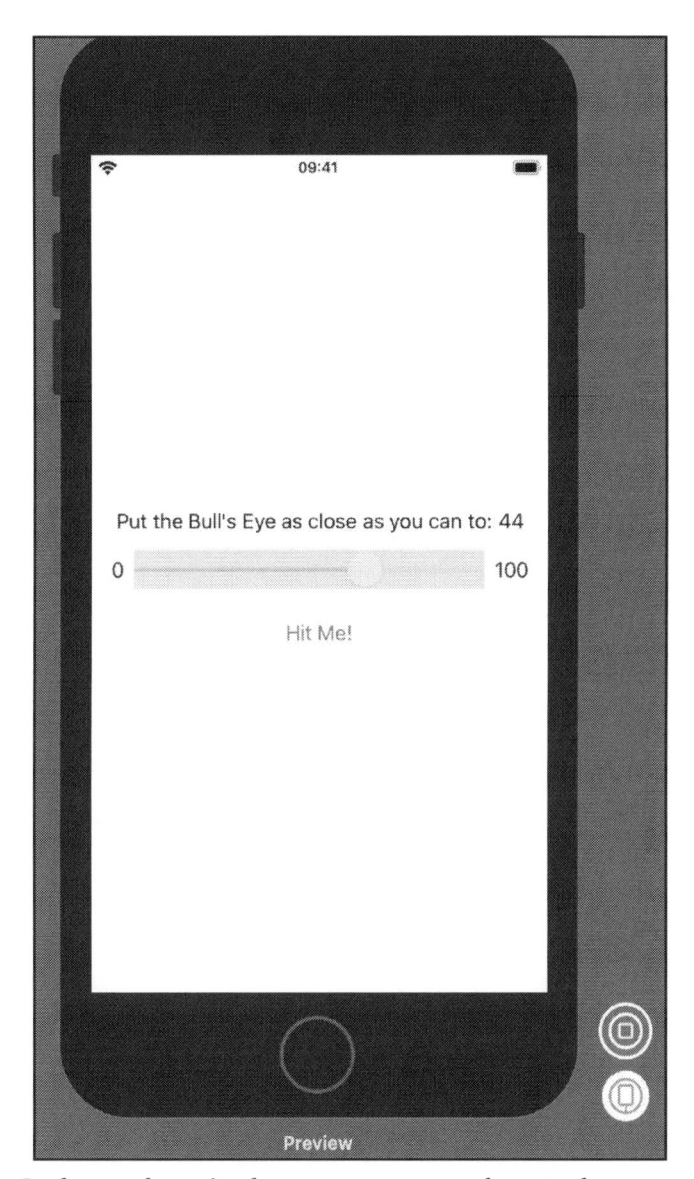

Background opacity decreases as you get closer to the target.

As you get closer to the target value, the slider effectively vanishes. If you go past the target, the increase in opacity indicates you've gone too far.

The solution is in the **challenge/final** folder for this chapter.

Key points

- Declarative app development means you declare both how you want the views in your UI to look and also what data they depend on. The SwiftUI framework takes care of creating views when they should appear and updating them whenever there's a change to data they depend on.
- The **Library** contains a list of primitive views and a list of modifier methods.
- Some modifiers can be applied to all view types, while others can be applied only to specific view types, like `Text`. Changing the ordering of modifiers can change the visual effect.
- Data access = dependency: Reading a piece of data in your view creates a dependency for that data in that view.
- Single source of truth: Every piece of data has a source of truth, internal or external. Regardless of where the source of truth lies, you should always have a *single* source of truth.
- Property wrappers augment the behavior of variables: `@State`, `@Binding`, `@ObservedObject` and `@EnvironmentObject` declare a view's dependency on the data represented by the variable.
- `@Binding` declares dependency on a `@State var` owned by another view. `@ObservedObject` declares dependency on a reference type that conforms to `ObservableObject`. `@EnvironmentObject` declares dependency on some shared data.
- For runtime debugging, **Control-click** or **Right-click** the **Live Preview** button, then select **Debug Preview** from the menu. You get all the normal debugging tools, plus runtime issues scanning and runtime breakpoints. **Option-click** the view debugger icon to open a view debugger.

Chapter 4: Integrating SwiftUI

Audrey Tam

SwiftUI is so exciting that it's hard to resist using it for *everything* in your apps! But you probably have a lot of apps already that are written in plain old Swift using UIKit — there's no way you have time to rewrite them all in SwiftUI. What to do?

No need to fear — Apple has your back. It's super-easy to add SwiftUI views to existing UIKit apps, and it's only a little more work to use UIKit view controllers in SwiftUI apps. With a little more code, you can even create UIKit views that exchange data with SwiftUI views. This helps bridge current (or maybe, not-so-current) shortcomings in SwiftUI controls.

> **Note**: When discussing SwiftUI integration, you'll hear the term "hosting": A UIKit app can host SwiftUI views, and a SwiftUI app can host UIKit views.

In this chapter, you'll learn how to do the following:

- Host a SwiftUI view in a UIKit project.
- Host a view controller in a SwiftUI project.
- Host a UIKit view with data dependencies in a SwiftUI project.

Time to get started!

Getting started

First, duplicate (using **Command-D**) the **BullsEye** starter project in the chapter materials. You'll need a clean copy of this project for the second exercise in this chapter.

Now open the **BullsEye** starter project, and build and run:

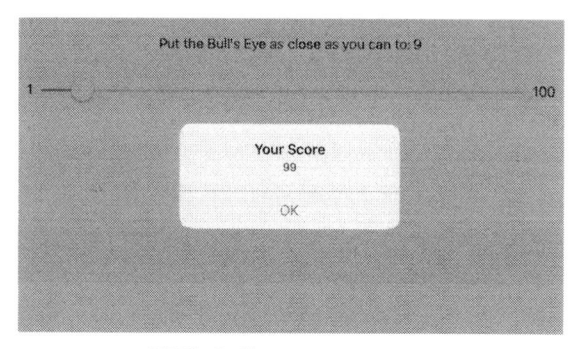

UIKit BullsEye starter app

This UIKit app displays a random target value between 1 and 100. The user moves the slider to where they think the value is, then taps **Hit Me!** to see their score.

Also in the starter folder is the final RGBullsEye project from Chapter 2, "Getting Started", with a few of the improvements from Chapter 3, "Understanding SwiftUI".

You're about to integrate this SwiftUI view into the UIKit BullsEye app!

Targeting iOS 13

SwiftUI requires iOS 13, so check that your UIKit app's deployment target is iOS 13:

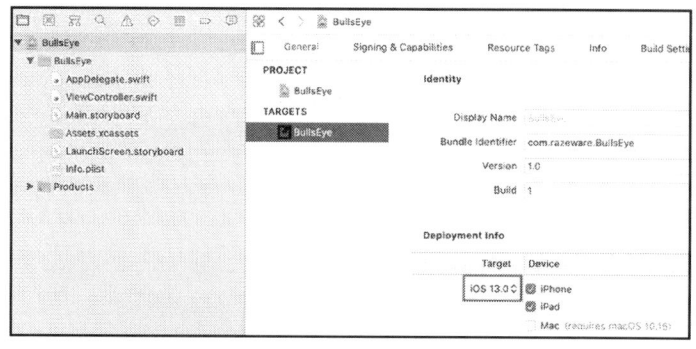

UIKit BullsEye deployment target is iOS 13.

Hosting a SwiftUI view in a UIKit project

The absolute easiest integration to perform is to host a SwiftUI view in an existing UIKit app. All you have to do is:

1. Add the SwiftUI view file to your project.

2. Add a button to play RGBullsEye.

3. Drag a **Hosting Controller** onto your storyboard and create a segue to it.

4. Connect the segue to an `@IBSegueAction` in your view controller code and set the hosting controller's `rootView` to an instance of your SwiftUI view.

So to start, open the **project navigator** and drag **ContentView.swift** from **Finder** into the BullsEye project. Check the **Destination** box **Copy items if needed**.

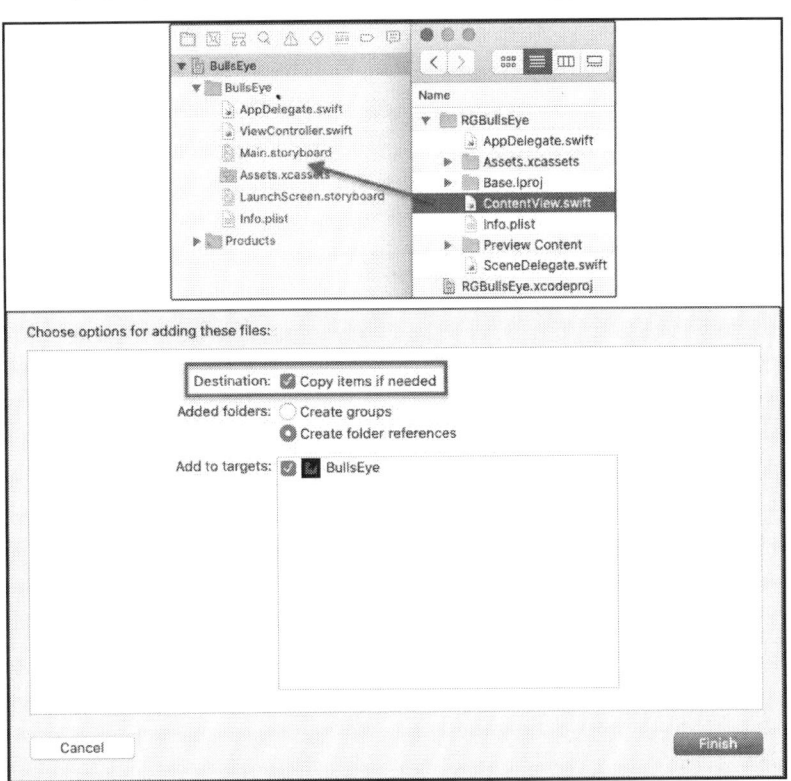

Add ContentView.swift to BullsEye project.

Next, in the storyboard, open the **Library**, add a **button**, and change its title to **Play RGBullsEye**. Also set constraints to pin the button's bottom edge to the view's bottom margin, and center it horizontally in the view:

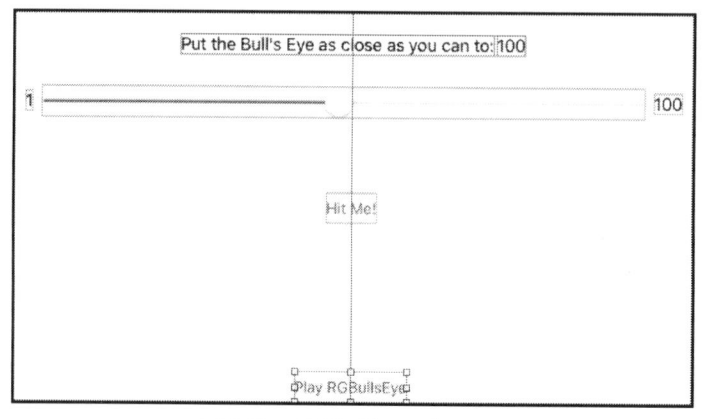

Add Play RGBullsEye button.

That was step 2. Now for the good part: From the **Library**, drag a **Hosting Controller** onto the storyboard, then **Control-drag** to it from the **Play RGBullsEye** button, and select **Show**:

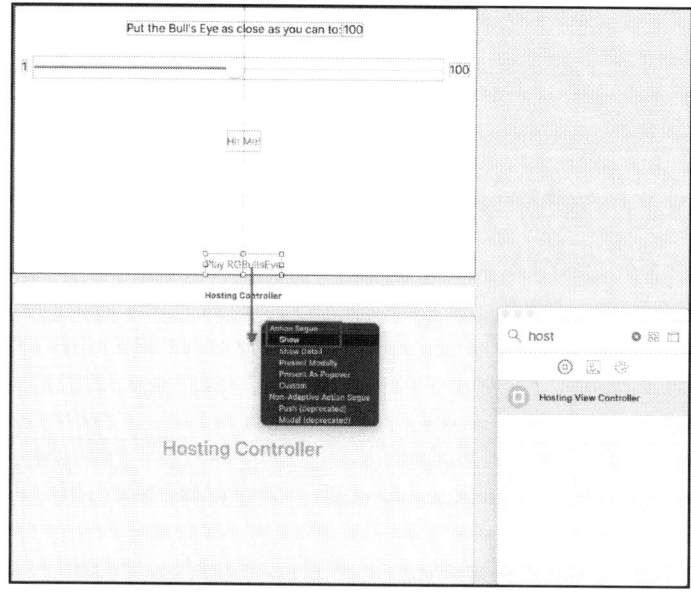

Create segue from button to Hosting Controller.

A `UIHostingController` is a `UIViewController` whose `Content` is a SwiftUI `View`. You've already seen it in `SceneDelegate` when you load `ContentView` into the window:

```
window.rootViewController = UIHostingController(rootView:
  ContentView(...))
```

And that was step 3!

Now, for step 4.

In the **storyboard**, select **View Controller**, and open the **assistant editor** (**Control-Option-Command-Return**). Add `import SwiftUI` to **ViewController.swift**.

Control-drag from the **segue** in the storyboard into `ViewController` to create an `@IBSegueAction`. Name it **openRGBullsEye**:

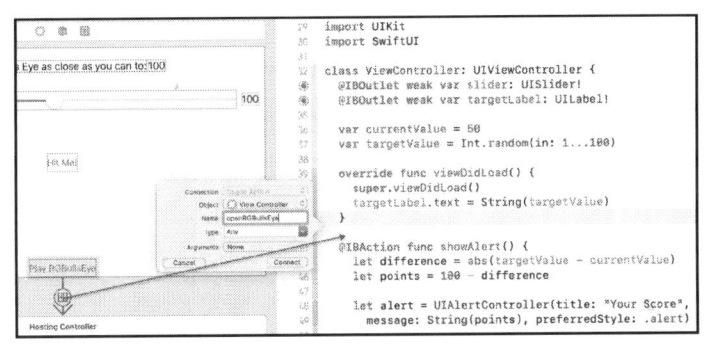

Create @IBSegueAction in ViewController.

`@IBSegueAction` is new in Xcode 11. You can use it in UIKit apps instead of `prepare(for:sender:)`. It's especially useful if you want to set properties in the destination view controller *when you create it*. And because it's connected directly to a segue, you don't even need a segue identifier!

Finally, add this code to `openRGBullsEye(_:)`:

```
UIHostingController(coder: coder, rootView:
  ContentView(rGuess: 0.5, gGuess: 0.5, bGuess: 0.5))
```

> **Note**: In Swift 5.1, you don't need the `return` keyword if there's only one line of code.

Build and run, then tap **Play RGBullsEye** — hey presto! To prove it works, move the sliders, then tap **Hit Me!**:

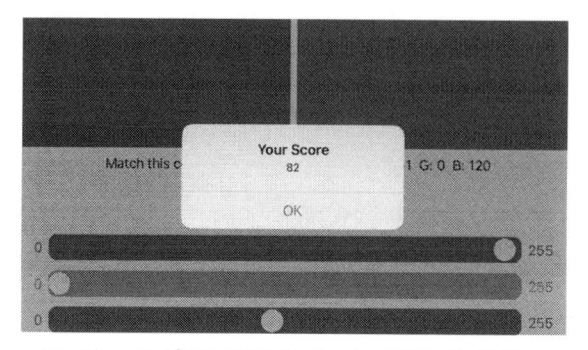

Hosting SwiftUI RGBullsEye in UIKit BullsEye.

How easy was that!? Now you can go wild adding SwiftUI views to your existing apps!

Hosting a view controller in a SwiftUI project

Now, to do the opposite — host the BullsEye view controller in RGBullsEye — here's what you'll do:

1. Add **ViewController.swift** and **Main.storyboard** to **RGBullsEye**.

2. In the storyboard's **identity inspector**, set the **Storyboard ID** for `ViewController`.

3. Create a representation `struct` for `ViewController`.

4. Add a `NavigationLink` to `ContentView`.

Seems straightforward enough – let's get started.

Open the **RGBullsEye** starter project, then open the **project navigator**.

From **the clean copy** of the starter BullsEye project in **Finder**, drag **ViewController.swift** and **Main.storyboard** into the **RGBullsEye** project.

Check the **Destination** box **Copy items if needed**.

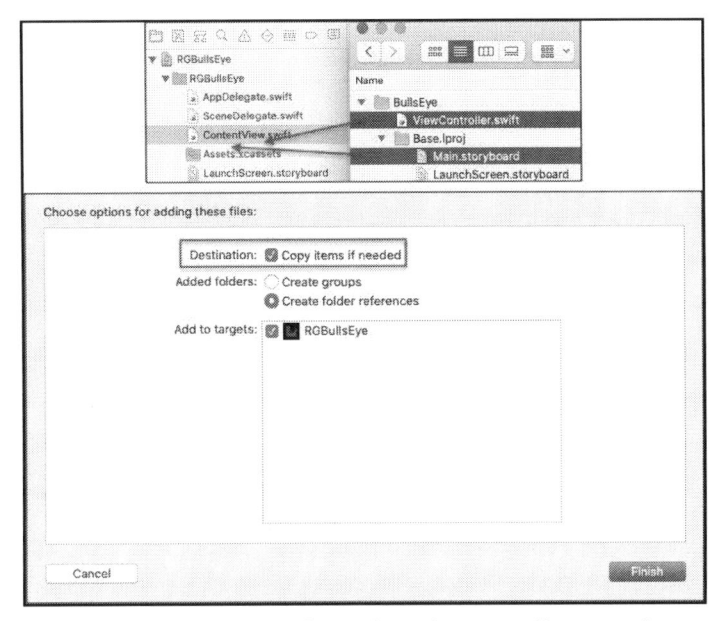

Add ViewController and storyboard to RGBullsEye project.

Next, in the **storyboard**, select **View Controller** and, in the **identity inspector**, set its **Storyboard ID** to **ViewController**:

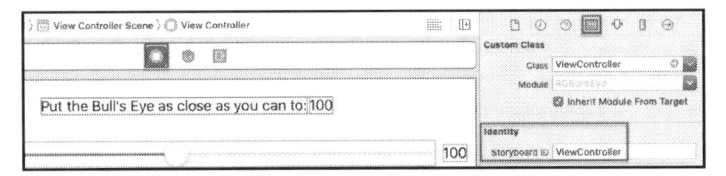

Set View Controller's Storyboard ID.

You'll use this stringly-typed ID in the next step.

Conforming to UIViewControllerRepresentable

This is where the magic happens.

At the top of **ViewController.swift**, add the following statement:

```
import SwiftUI
```

Below the `ViewController` class, create `ViewControllerRepresentation`:

```swift
struct ViewControllerRepresentation:
UIViewControllerRepresentable {

  func makeUIViewController(
    context: UIViewControllerRepresentableContext
    <ViewControllerRepresentation>) -> ViewController {
    UIStoryboard(name: "Main", bundle: nil)
      .instantiateViewController(withIdentifier:
"ViewController")
      as! ViewController
  }

  func updateUIViewController(_ uiViewController:
ViewController,
    context: UIViewControllerRepresentableContext
    <ViewControllerRepresentation>) {

  }
}
```

The `UIViewControllerRepresentable` protocol requires a make method and an update method. The `makeUIViewController(context:)` method instantiates a `ViewController` from **Main.storyboard** — that's why you had to give it a Storyboard ID.

> **Note**: If your view controller doesn't use the storyboard, or you just want an empty view controller, creating it is even easier simply use its default constructor.

You'll leave the other required method `updateUIViewController(_:context:)` empty, as `ViewController` doesn't depend on your SwiftUI view for any data. If Xcode tries to get you to implement a `Coordinator`, ignore it: `ViewControllerRepresentation` doesn't need one, because your SwiftUI view doesn't depend on `ViewController` for any data. But there's no fear of missing out — the next section needs both of these!

Navigating to the view controller

Almost finally, add this code to the bottom of the top-level `VStack` in `ContentView`, below the `VStack` of `ColorSliders`:

```
NavigationLink(destination: ViewControllerRepresentation()) {
  Text("Play BullsEye")
}.padding(.bottom)
```

Note: You'll learn all about navigation in Chapter 9, "Lists and Navigation".

And *finally* finally, embed the top-level `VStack` in a `NavigationView`:

```
var body: some View {
  NavigationView {
    VStack { ... }
  }
}
```

Refresh the preview (**Option-Command-P**), start **Live Preview**, then tap **Play BullsEye**. Move the slider, then tap **Hit Me!**:

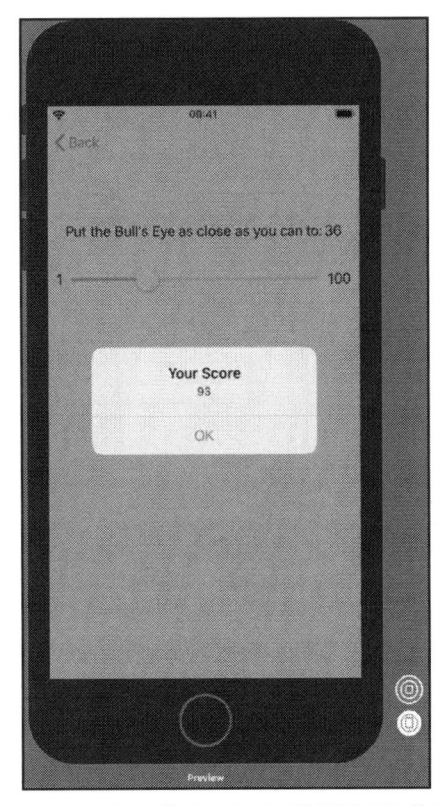

Hosting UIKit BullsEye in SwiftUI RGBullsEye.

Notice you get a **Back** button, just like you'd expect from a navigation controller!

Previewing UIKit views

So that didn't take long to do. But wait, there's more! Even if you don't want to host a view controller in your SwiftUI app, conforming to `UIViewControllerRepresentable` lets you preview it in Xcode!

Head back to **ViewController.swift** and scroll down to `ViewControllerRepresentation`. Add this code *below* the `struct`:

```
struct ViewControllerPreviews: PreviewProvider {
  static var previews: some View {
    ViewControllerRepresentation()
  }
}
```

This is just like the usual preview code that you see below every SwiftUI view.

Refresh the preview, start Live Preview, and play the game:

Live previewing ViewControllerRepresentation.

Your representation is as live-previewable as a SwiftUI view!

Hosting a UIKit view with data dependencies

Hosting BullsEye in RGBullsEye was pretty easy, but that's because there aren't any data dependencies between the BullsEye view controller and the rest of your SwiftUI app.

In this section, you'll replace the SwiftUI `Slider` view with a `UISlider`. Here's your motivation: the original UIKit RGBullsEye color-coded the sliders by setting their `thumbTintColor` property, but the SwiftUI `Slider` doesn't have this property. So you need to use `UISlider` to access this property.

The process is similar to hosting a view controller, with a few more steps:

1. Create a SwiftUI view that conforms to `UIViewRepresentable`.
2. Implement the `make` method to instantiate the UIKit view.
3. Implement the `update` method to update the UIKit view from the SwiftUI view.
4. Create a `Coordinator` and implement its `valueChanged` method to update the SwiftUI view from the UIKit view.

Conforming to UIViewRepresentable

Start by creating a new **iOS ▸ User Interface ▸ SwiftUI View** file, and name it **ColorUISlider.swift**.

Now start creating `ColorUISlider`. Replace the `struct ColorUISlider` boilerplate with this code:

```swift
struct ColorUISlider: UIViewRepresentable {
  func makeUIView(context: Context) -> UISlider {
    let slider = UISlider(frame: .zero)
    return slider
  }

  func updateUIView(_ uiView: UISlider, context: Context) {

  }
}
```

`ColorUISlider` wraps a `UIView`, not a `UIViewController`, so it conforms to `UIViewRepresentable`, not `UIViewControllerRepresentable`.

This protocol also requires a `make` method and an `update` method. Here, you've implemented the bare minimum, just creating a `UISlider` in `makeUIView(context:)`.

Updating the UIView from SwiftUI

Next, add these properties:

```
var color: UIColor
@Binding var value: Double
```

One of the complications you need to handle is the different *color* types in UIKit and SwiftUI. SwiftUI `Color` is a view, and `UIColor` isn't. Fortunately, you can create a `Color` from a `UIColor` value — `Color(UIColor.red)` — so you declare `color` as `UIColor`.

The other complication is the different *value* types for `UISlider` (`Float`) and `Slider` (`Double`). It's easier to create a `Float` from a `Double` than the other way around, so you declare `value` as a `Double`.

As in `ColorSlider`, `value` is a `@Binding` that references `@State` variables in `ContentView`.

Ignore the error messages about missing arguments in `previews`, while you finish setting up `ColorUISlider`. Add these lines below `let slider = UISlider(...)`, *before* the `return` statement:

```
slider.thumbTintColor = color
slider.value = Float(value)
```

OK, now fix up the the error messages. Down in `ColorUISlider_Previews`, add arguments for `color` and `value`:

```
ColorUISlider(color: .red, value: .constant(0.5))
```

Refresh the preview:

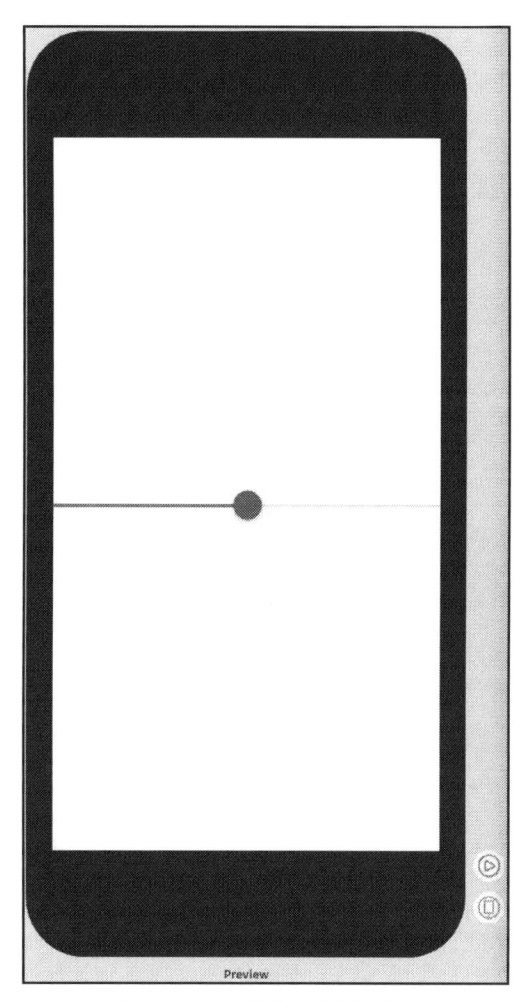

Previewing ColourUISlider.

And there's your color-coded slider thumb! Beautiful, isn't it?

> **Note**: `UISlider` also has `minimumTrackTintColor` and `maximumTrackTintColor` properties, in case you want to dress it up even more.

OK, back to work on `ColorUISlider`. You've completed steps 1 and 2, now move on to step 3.

Coordinating data between UIView and SwiftUI view

Add this line to `updateUIView(_:context:)`:

```
uiView.value = Float(self.value)
```

When the `UISlider` receives a `Double` value from the SwiftUI view, it updates its `Float` value.

And that was the entire step 3.

Step 4 is the longest: You'll create a *coordinator* to keep your SwiftUI view `ColorUISlider` data in sync with the UIKit control `UISlider` data.

Start by adding this **class** *inside* your `ColorUISlider` struct:

```
class Coordinator: NSObject {
  // 1
  var value: Binding<Double>
  // 2
  init(value: Binding<Double>) {
    self.value = value
  }
  // 3
  @objc func valueChanged(_ sender: UISlider) {
    self.value.wrappedValue = Double(sender.value)
  }
}
```

> **Note**: When you create the `Coordinator` class, the protocol requires a `makeCoordinator()` method, so you'll see an error message about not conforming to `UIViewRepresentable`. Don't worry, you'll take care of that very soon.

Here's what your `Coordinator` class is doing:

1. The class property `value` is a binding: It's a reference to the `ColorUISlider` value, which receives a reference to a `@State` variable value in `ContentView`. This `Binding<Double>` syntax for declaring a binding works better in this not-strictly-SwiftUI setting, but this might be a bug.
2. You create the binding when you initialize the `Coordinator`.

3. You create a `valueChanged(_:)` action; you'll soon set up this `Coordinator` as a target for a `UISlider` event. Remember that value is a `Binding<Double>` binding, so `value.wrappedValue` is the value of the binding — a `Double`. And `sender.value` is a `Float`.

Now take care of the does-not-conform error message. Just above `makeUIView(context:)`, add this required `UIViewRepresentable` protocol method:

```
func makeCoordinator() -> ColorUISlider.Coordinator {
  Coordinator(value: $value)
}
```

This creates a `Coordinator` whose value variable is bound to the `ColorUISlider` value variable, which you'll bind to one of the color values in `ContentView`.

So that's how this UIKit control gets the SwiftUI value.

Now add this line to `makeUIView(context:)`, just before the `return` statement:

```
slider.addTarget(context.coordinator,
    action: #selector(Coordinator.valueChanged(_:)),
  for: .valueChanged)
```

You're using the standard UIKit `addTarget(_:action:for:)` method to associate the `UISlider` control with the `Coordinator` target and its `Coordinator.valueChanged(_:)` action. This action method is called whenever the `UIControl` event `valueChanged` occurs.

The only thing `Coordinator.valueChanged(_:)` does is update the `value` of your SwiftUI view `ColorUISlider` with incoming data from the UIKit control `UISlider`.

So now you have two-way communication between `UISlider` and `ColorUISlider`!

Making it all happen!

Finally, put your `ColorUISlider` to work! In `ContentView`, scroll down to `struct ColorSlider`, and replace `Slider` *and all its modifiers* with this view:

```
ColorUISlider(color: textColor, value: $value)
```

Now that you have thumb tint color, you don't need background color. And without background color, rounded corners don't show up.

To fix up the `Color` vs. `UIColor` mismatch, change the type of `textColor` to `UIColor`:

```
var textColor: UIColor
```

Now wrap `textColor` in `Color` in the `foregroundColor` modifier:

```
Text("0").foregroundColor(Color(textColor))
...
Text("255").foregroundColor(Color(textColor))
```

The `foregroundColor` modifier requires a `View` argument, and `Color(textColor)` creates a `Color` view from the `UIColor`.

If Xcode complains about the `VStack` of three `ColorSliders`, specify the type of the `textColor` arguments as `UIColor`:

```
VStack {
  ColorSlider(value: $rGuess, textColor: UIColor.red)
  ColorSlider(value: $gGuess, textColor: UIColor.green)
  ColorSlider(value: $bGuess, textColor: UIColor.blue)
}.padding(.horizontal)
```

This isn't actually necessary — Xcode will *eventually* catch up with `textColor` being of type `UIColor` — but it does no harm. At this point, it's just to prevent the preview refresh from being held up by an out-of-date error message.

Refresh the preview, then build and run:

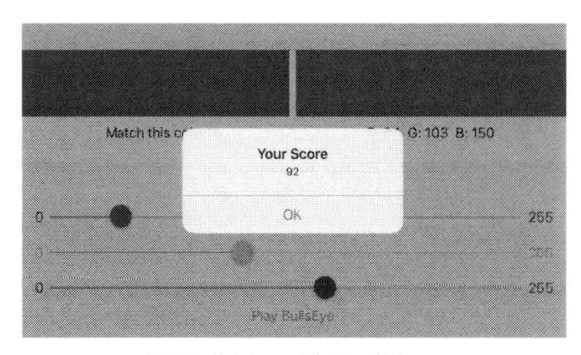

RGBullsEye with UISliders.

Oooh, color-coded slider thumbs! And that's how you overcome the absence of thumb tint color in the SwiftUI `Slider`!

Key points

To host a SwiftUI view in a UIKit project:

1. Add the SwiftUI view file to your project.
2. Add a hosting controller to your storyboard, and create a segue to it.
3. Connect the segue to an `@IBSegueAction` in your view controller code.
4. Set the hosting controller's `rootView` to an instance of your SwiftUI view.

To host a view controller in a SwiftUI project:

1. Add the view controller and storyboard files to the SwiftUI project.
2. In the storyboard's **identity inspector**, set the **Storyboard ID** for the view controller.
3. Create a representation `struct` for the view controller, and implement the `makeUIViewController(context:)` method to instantiate the view controller from **Main.storyboard**.
4. Add a `NavigationLink` to `ContentView`, with the view controller representation as the link's destination.

To host a UIKit view with data dependencies:

1. Create a SwiftUI view that conforms to `UIViewRepresentable`.
2. Implement the `make` method to instantiate the UIKit view.
3. Implement the `update` method to update the UIKit view from the SwiftUI view.
4. Create a `Coordinator`, and implement its `valueChanged` method to update the SwiftUI view from the UIKit view.

Where to go from here?

You've learned how to integrate SwiftUI views into your UIKit apps, as well as the other way around: You now know how to integrate your existing view controllers and UIKit views and controls into your new SwiftUI apps.

So what are you waiting for? The other chapters in this book have loads of ideas for SwiftUI views to add to your existing apps. Or you might see an opportunity to use one of your existing controls, views or view controllers in one of our sample SwiftUI projects. We can't wait to see what you create!

Challenge

Challenge: Data dependency on a UIKit control

The **challenge/starter** folder contains a SwiftUI BullsEye app that changes the slider's background color opacity to provide feedback to the user. Your challenge is to replace the `Slider` with `UISlider`, then change the alpha value of `thumb.tintColor` to provide feedback.

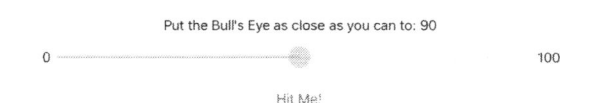

SwiftUI BullsEye with opacity feedback in slider thumb.

> **Hint**: Opacity is the same thing as alpha.

The solution is in the **challenge/final** folder for this chapter.

Chapter 5: The Apple Ecosystem

Audrey Tam

Apple says SwiftUI is the shortest path to building great apps on *every* device. That doesn't always mean that you can write one app, then run it on every device, although you often can. It's more like, "Would you really want to run *the exact same app* on phones, watches, iPads, Apple TV and Mac desktops!?" Each platform is good for some things, but not so good for others.

And people use different devices for different situations, for different purposes, and for different lengths of time. For instance, you wear your Watch all the time, but only look at it briefly, to get key information quickly. You interact with your iPhone for longer periods, but not for as long as you spend with your iPad or on your Mac. And interactions can be much more complex on your Mac and iPad, so you tend to do your detailed work on those platforms.

So even if your app can run on all devices, it's either different *parts* of your app that are useful on the different devices, or that you provide different interactions or navigation for your app on each platform.

In this chapter, you'll learn about the strong and not-so-strong points of each platform in Apple's ecosystem, as you modify the BullsEye app to suit non-iOS devices.

Getting started

Open the **BullsEyePlus** starter project from the chapter materials. Open **ContentView.swift** in the **iOS target**, check that the scheme is an iOS device, and **Live-Preview** the iOS app:

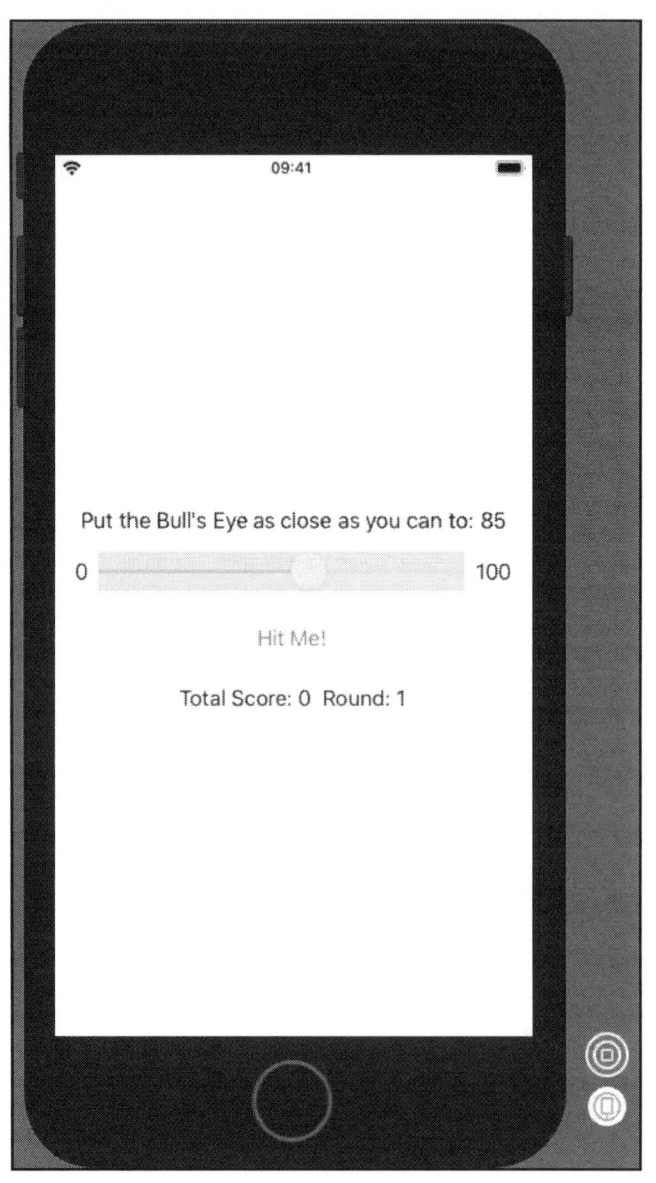

BullsEyePlus iOS app

This app displays a random target value between 1 and 100. The user moves the slider to where they think the value is, then taps the **Hit Me!** button to see their score. Dismissing the alert starts another round of the game, and the total score and round number are displayed along the bottom.

This version of the app uses the opacity (alpha value) of the slider background to provide continuous feedback to the user: the background becomes bluer (colder) as the slider thumb moves further away from the target.

Now open **ContentView.swift** in the **WatchKit Extension**. Change the scheme to **WatchKit App**, pick one of the Apple Watch sizes, then **Live-Preview** the Watch app:

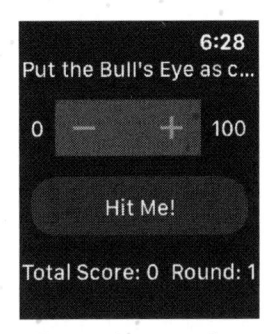

BullsEyePlus Watch app.

> **Note**: If you change the bundle ID of the WatchKit targets, you must also change it in the WatchKit **Info.plist** files: Search for **com.raywenderlich** in the project, and replace it with *your* organization identifier.

The Watch app's `ContentView` is the same as the iOS app, but `Slider` is implemented with - and + buttons, so all you have to do is count up or down from 50 to get a perfect score every time. That is, if you could see what the target value is! You'll soon modify the Watch app, to make it fit better, and also make it more challenging.

The two apps share a `BullsEyeGame` model class, using target membership.

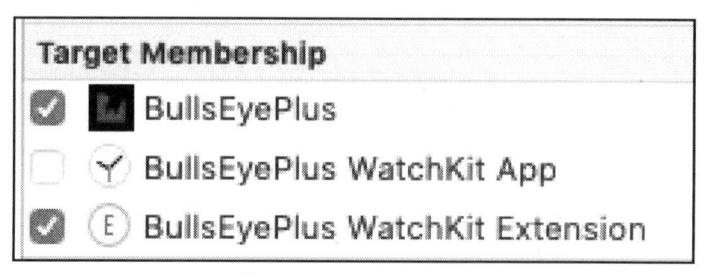

Target membership of BullsEyeGame.swift.

Creating a Swift package

Target membership is adequate when the targets share only one or two files, but it gets cumbersome as you add features. Then it's better to organize the shared files in a **package**. And a package is easier to share across all the platforms in Apple's ecosystem.

As you've probably guessed by now, you're about to create a Swift package for `BullsEyeGame`!

First, create a new Swift package: **File ▸ New ▸ Swift Package…** or **Shift-Control-Command-N**. Name the package **Game**, and add it to the project and to its root group. Create a new folder named **packages**, then click **Create**:

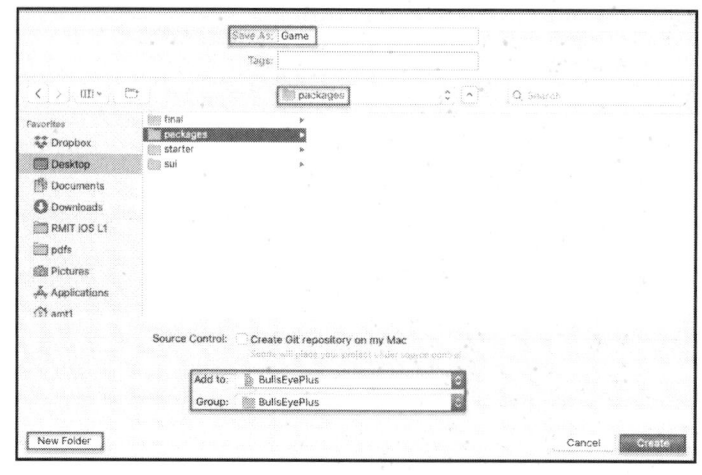

New Swift package dialogue.

The new package already has **Readme** and **Package.swift** files, plus **Sources** and **Tests** groups.

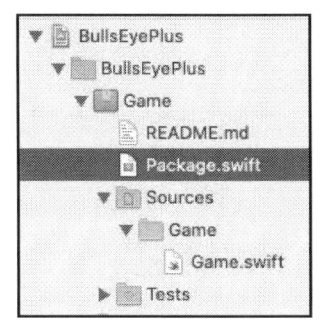

Structure of new package.

And here it is in its own folder in **Finder**:

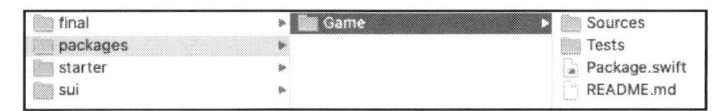

New package in Finder.

> **Note**: **Game** is a local package, which you can add to any project by dragging it into the project navigator. A more common use of Swift Package Manager is to link remote libraries via their repository URL. Check out WWDC 2019 sessions *408 Adopting Swift Packages in Xcode* apple.co/2luxuLJ and *410 Creating Swift Packages* apple.co/2mVg4YX. Or follow our tutorial *An Introduction to Swift Package Manager* bit.ly/2JXL3yD or, if you're a subscriber, our screencast *Creating a Swift Package* bit.ly/2mu3srC

Customizing your Game package

Your **Game** package just needs the `BullsEyeGame` model class. Drag **BullsEyeGame.swift** into **Sources/Game/**.

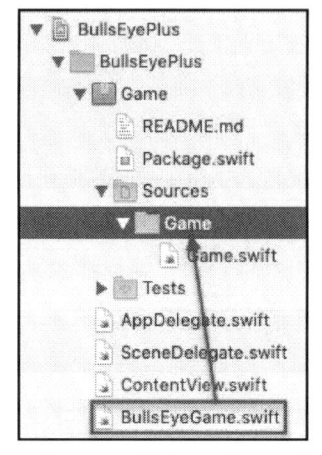

Move Game.swift into the package.

Open **BullsEyeGame.swift**. Now that it's not in the **BullsEye** group, everything in it needs to be `public`, so add that everywhere:

```
public class BullsEyeGame: ObservableObject {

  public let objectWillChange = PassthroughSubject<Void, Never>()

  public var round = 0
  public var startValue = 50
  public var targetValue = 50
  public var scoreRound = 0
  public var scoreTotal = 0

  public init() {
    startNewGame()
  }

  public func startNewGame() {
    ...
  }

  public func startNewRound() {
    ...
  }

  public func checkGuess(_ guess: Int) {
    ...
```

```
    }
  }
```

Versioning your Game package

Next, open the manifest file **Package.swift**; it describes how to build the package. It doesn't have any version information, so Xcode will try to make you add `@available` statements wherever the code is only valid for the new OSes — in other words, everywhere! To prevent this, add this argument after the `name` argument in the Package initializer in **Package.swift**:

```
platforms:
  [.iOS(.v13), .macOS(.v10_15), .watchOS(.v6), .tvOS(.v13)],
```

Linking your Game package library

The **products** argument defines the library that you can link with your app:

```
products: [
  .library(
    name: "Game",
    targets: ["Game"]),
],
```

So, to link this library with your app, go to the iOS app target's **Frameworks, Libraries and Embedded Content** section: Click +, then select **Workspace/Game/Game** from the list:

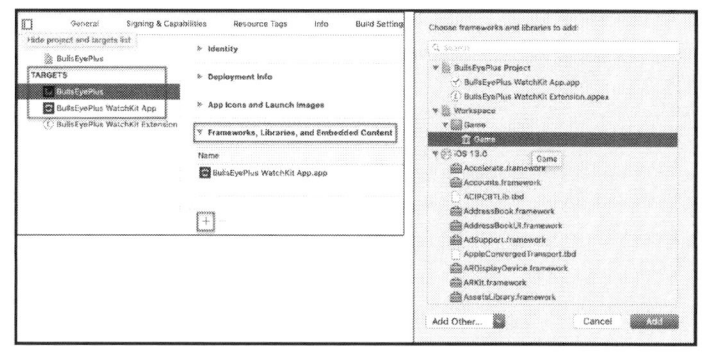

Add BullsEyeGame library to iOS app target.

And do the same for the **WatchKit Extension** target:

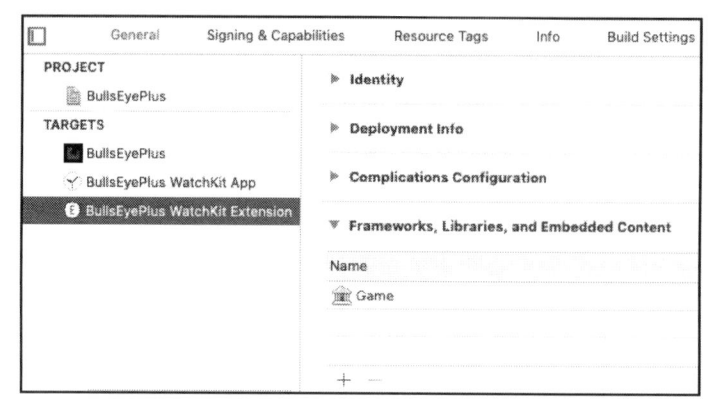

Add BullsEyeGame library to Watch app target.

Importing your Game package module

Finally, you must `import` the **Game** package module into your app, wherever you use it. Add this line to **ContentView.swift** in both the iOS app and the Watch app:

```
import Game
```

Xcode probably pops up the error message **No such module "Game"**.

The first step is to try building the project with **Command-B**. If Xcode is stubborn, try **Product ▸ Clean** (**Shift-Command-K**), **Product ▸ Clean Build Folder…** (**Shift-Option-Command-K**), and delete the project's **Derived Data** folder (Xcode **Preferences ▸ Locations**).

Refresh the preview (**Option-Command-P**), then turn on **Live Preview**, and check that both apps still work:

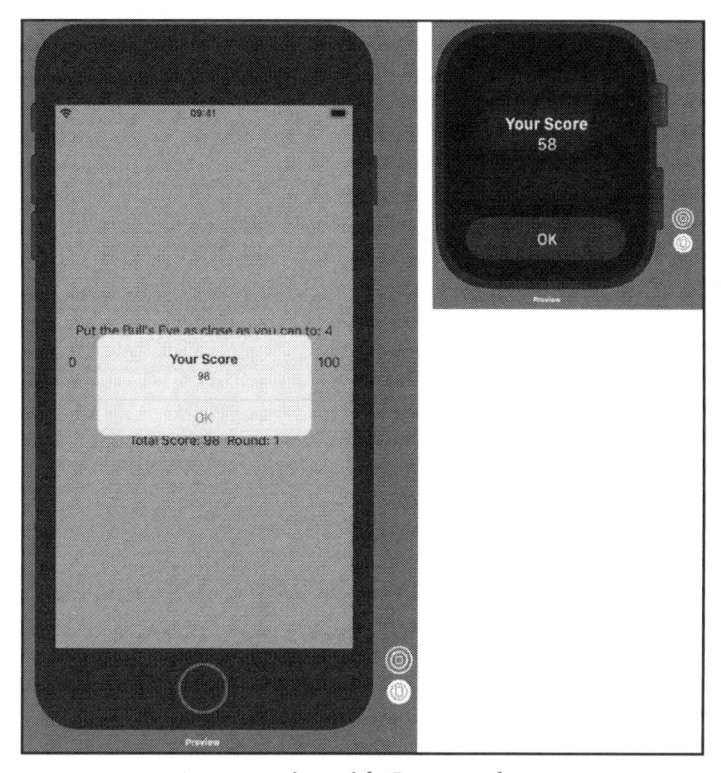

Apps running with Game package.

Both apps work with the **Game** package just as they did with the shared **BullsEyeGame.swift** file. Creating and linking the package was really easy, and Xcode automatically built the package product for each app. You didn't have to configure anything explicitly about platforms, because packages are platform-independent.

Creating a GameView package

Now reinforce your packaging skills by creating a **GameView** package with **BullsEyeGame.swift** and **ContentView.swift**, to use in the macOS app you'll create later in this chapter.

To start, create a new package (**Shift-Control-Command-N**), name it **GameView**, save it in your **packages** folder, and *don't* add it to any project:

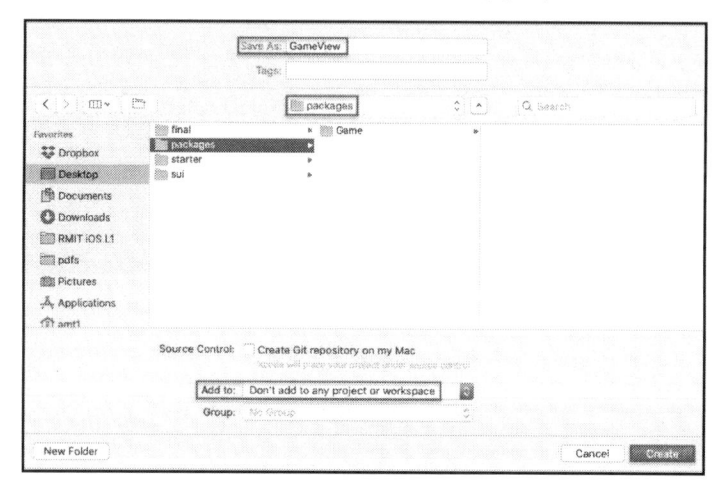

New GameView package.

Dragging files into the project navigator of a package doesn't give you the **Copy items if needed** option, so you'll copy files manually, in **Finder**. Locate your **Game** package in **Finder**, open your new **GameView** folder in another **Finder** window, then *copy* **BullsEyeGame.swift** from **Game/Sources/Game** into **GameView/Sources/GameView**. Also copy **ContentView.swift** from **BullsEyePlus/BullsEyePlus** into **GameView/Sources/GameView**:

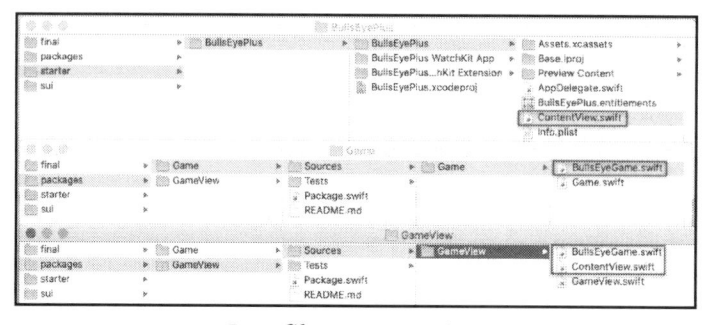

Copy files to GameView.

Now open **GameView/Sources/GameView** in its project navigator. Everything in **BullsEyeGame.swift** is already public, but you need to edit **ContentView.swift** to make `ContentView` and `body` public, like this:

```
public struct ContentView: View {
  ...
  public var body: some View {
```

```
    ...
  }
    ...
}
```

You don't need to `import Game` anymore, so delete this line.

Then add this empty `init` method:

```
public init() { }
```

And finally, add version information after the `name` argument in the `Package` initializer in **Package.swift**:

```
platforms:
  [.iOS(.v13), .macOS(.v10_15), .watchOS(.v6), .tvOS(.v13)],
```

This package is all set for you to use later in this chapter. Go ahead and close it in Xcode.

Designing for the strengths of each platform

SwiftUI provides you with powerful tools for developing apps that run on multiple platforms, such as generic views: Controls like `Toggle`, `Picker` and `Slider` look different on each platform, but have the same relationship to your data, so you can easily adapt them to different platforms. And it has a common layout system as well: You use the same container views to layout your UI.

Each platform has its own strengths, so instead of "write once, run everywhere", it's more like "learn once, apply anywhere".

watchOS

The Watch is the best device for quickly getting the right information at the right time. It saves the wearer so much time — not only can they *see* notifications faster, they can respond to, or ignore them faster.

The screen is very small, so you should show only the most important and relevant information. And navigation should be streamlined, so the user can get any important information within two or three taps.

Remember, it's very tiring to hold your arm up for too long! WatchKit has added more ways to use the **digital crown**, and you'll soon put that into practice.

macOS/iPadOS

People tend to use their Macs and iPads for longer periods, and for more detailed tasks, such as taking notes, searching, and sorting and filtering.

The Mac has a large screen and full keyboard, so many people enjoy saving time by using keyboard shortcuts.

Mac users are accustomed to opening multiple windows. When it's time to declutter your screen, the default **Window** menu includes **Merge All Windows**.

Mac apps often have preferences and inspector windows. And you can also layout touchbar items, using the standard SwiftUI layout system.

tvOS

Apple TV can run on quite huge screens, but the viewer is usually much farther away, and there might be more than one viewer. Like all TV viewing, sessions can be quite long.

Apple TV is best for full-screen experiences of images and video, but not very good for reading or writing a lot of text. It's not mobile, so you can leave out any geofencing features or location-based notifications.

Navigation needs to be streamlined because interaction is via the Siri remote, with swipe-to-browse-and-focus mechanisms to use controls. SwiftUI gives you access to the play, pause and on-exit buttons.

`TabView` is an example of how you would design differently for tvOS than iOS. In an iOS app, `TabView` would be the top level, to keep the tabs visible when the user navigates down the view hierarchy. But you'd embed `TabView` in a `NavigationView` for a tvOS app, so the tabs would disappear when the user drills down so they would get a full-screen experience.

Improving the watchOS app

You saw earlier in this chapter that the iOS `ContentView` works for the Watch app, but the smaller screen causes a few problems.

First, some of the text labels are too long, so you'll shorten them. Go into **ContentView.swift** in the watchOS extension and make the following changes:

- Change "Put the Bull's Eye as close as you can to:" to "Aim for:"
- Change "Total score:" to "Total:"

Next, make the `Slider` more challenging by removing the `step` parameter:

```
Slider(value: $currentValue, in: 1.0...100.0)
```

And finally, take advantage of the Watch's **digital crown** to change the `Slider` value:

```
Slider(value: $currentValue, in: 1.0...100.0)
   .digitalCrownRotation($currentValue, from: 1.0, through: 100.0)
```

> **Note**: The digital crown actually works without adding this modifier, but you first have to tap the slider to give it focus. With the modifier, the digital crown just works, although it also tries to scroll the screen — this might be a bug.

Set the scheme to one of the Watch sizes, then build and run:

Improved watchOS app.

To move the simulator's digital crown, use your usual scrolling action — for me, it's a two-finger drag on the trackpad.

So that's an example of how you could adapt your app to a smaller screen. Now it's time to move on to bigger things: Mac and Apple TV!

Extending the Mac Catalyst app

It's easy to run the iOS app on your Mac as a Mac Catalyst app; you simply need to take care of some administrative details first.

To start, you need to sign the iOS target, in the **Signing and Capabilities** tab: First, personalize the **Bundle Identifier**'s organization identifier to something different from `com.raywenderlich`, then select a **Team** — it doesn't need to be a paid developer account.

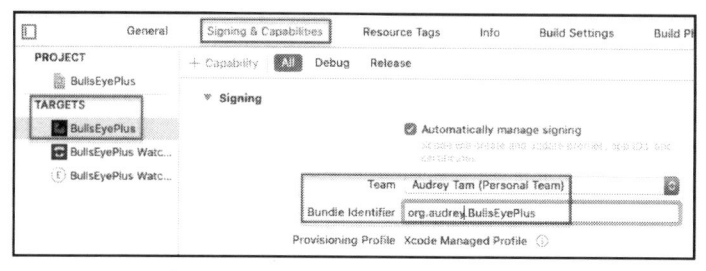

Change bundle ID and select a team.

Next, go back to the **General** tab, and check the **Deployment Info▸Mac** checkbox:

Check the Mac checkbox.

Xcode pops up a dialogue window:

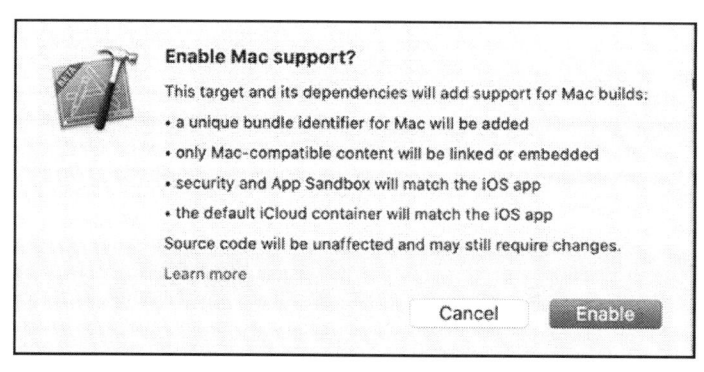

Enable Mac support for this iOS app.

Click **Enable**.

Now check that Xcode has switched to the scheme for your Mac, then build and run. This might take a while, even after the build succeeds.

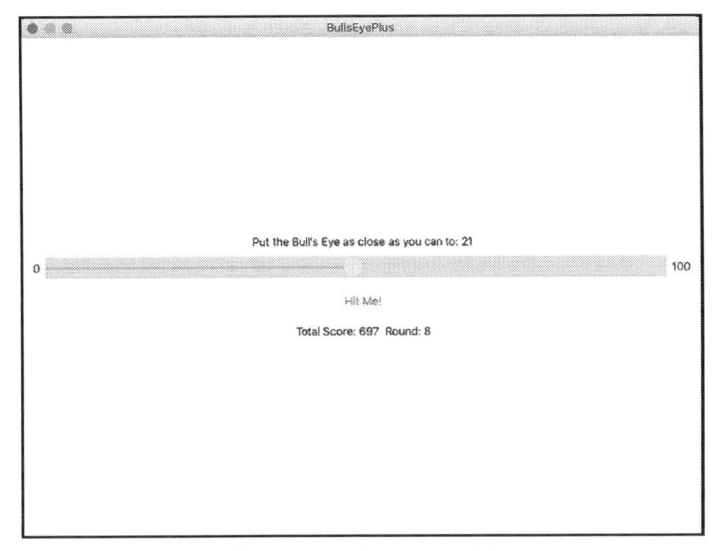

BullsEye running on my Mac.

Wow, you just checked a checkbox, and it works! Next, you'll try out another Mac Catalyst freebie.

iOS Settings == macOS Preferences

Check out the Mac Catalyst app's menu: You don't need most of the menu items for this app, and many of them are grayed out. The **BullsEyePlus** menu doesn't have a **Preferences** menu item:

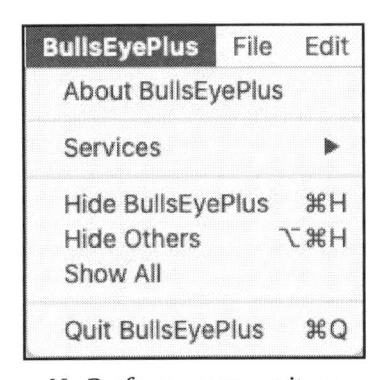

No Preferences menu item.

But if you add **Settings** to the iOS app, you'll get macOS app **Preferences** for free! You're going to add a setting to let the user turn the slider opacity hint on or off.

Stop the Mac Catalyst app, then add a **Settings Bundle** to your app: **Command-N**, then select **iOS ▸ Resource ▸ Settings Bundle**:

Add Settings Bundle.

Leave the name as **Settings**, and make sure the BullsEyePlus target is checked:

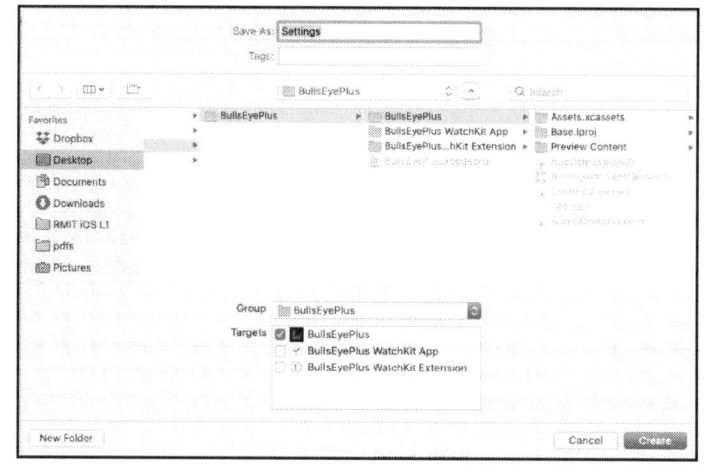

Save Settings Bundle.

And here it is in the project navigator:

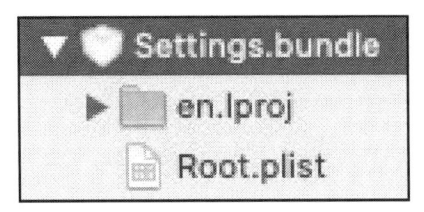

Settings Bundle structure.

Now open **Root.plist**, then delete every item in the **Preference Items** dictionary, except **Toggle Switch — Enabled**:

Toggle Switch Preference Item.

Edit the toggle switch dictionary values: Set **Title** to **Show Hint**, **Identifier** to **show_hint**, and leave **Default Value** set to **YES**:

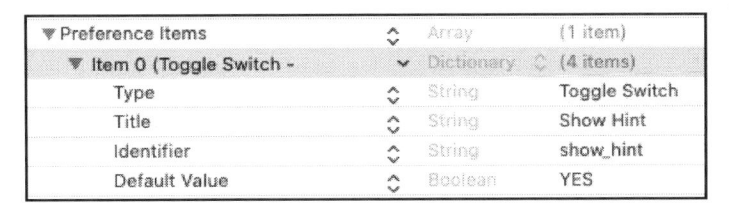

Toggle switch dictionary values.

So that sets up a new `show_hint` key in `UserDefaults`. Next, you'll modify your app to use it.

Open **SceneDelegate.swift**, and add this property:

```
let defaults = UserDefaults.standard
```

Next, pass this to `ContentView` when you create `window.rootViewController`:

```
window.rootViewController = UIHostingController(rootView:
ContentView()
  .environmentObject(defaults))
```

Note that you're modifying the `ContentView()` *argument*, not the `UIHostingController`.

An error message appears: `UserDefaults` doesn't conform to `ObservableObject`. So add this line *outside* the `SceneDelegate` class:

```
extension UserDefaults: ObservableObject { }
```

You're setting up `defaults` to be an `@EnvironmentObject`: All that's needed is for `UserDefaults` to conform to `ObservableObject`!

Now move on to **ContentView.swift**. Add your new `@EnvironmentObject` property:

```
@EnvironmentObject var defaults: UserDefaults
```

Then replace the `Slider` view with the following `if-else` statement. To do this, you'll leverage some new contextual menus in Xcode. First, ensure the canvas is open. **Command-click** on the `Slider`, then select **Make Conditional** from the menu:

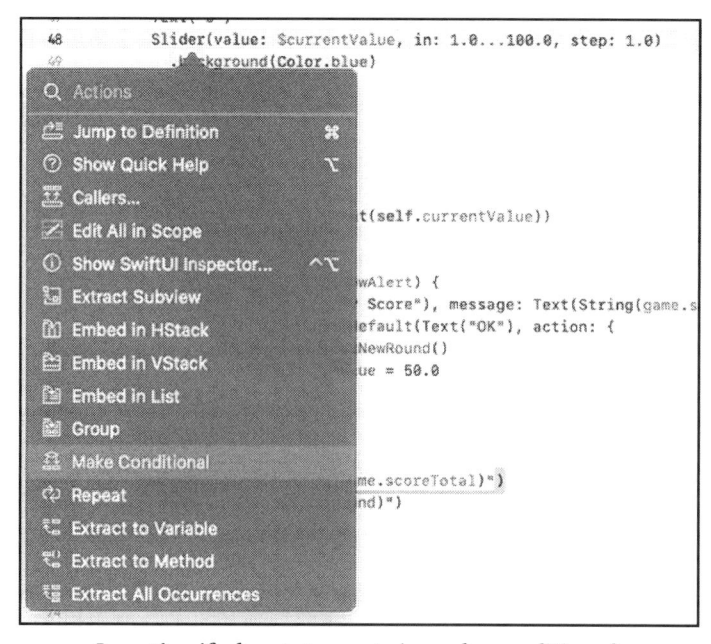

Inserting if-else statement via make conditional.

> **Note:** If your canvas is closed, you won't see the **Make Conditional** option. If **Command-click** jumps to the definition of `Slider`, use **Control-Command-click** instead.

Update the conditional statements to match the following:

```
if defaults.bool(forKey: "show_hint") {
   Slider(value: $currentValue, in: 0.0...100.0, step: 1.0)
     .background(Color.blue)
     .opacity(abs((Double(self.game.targetValue) -
self.currentValue)/100.0))
} else {
   Slider(value: $currentValue, in: 0.0...100.0, step: 1.0)
}
```

If `show_hint` is true, you show the opacity hint; otherwise, you don't.

Now check your scheme is still **Mac**, then build and run. Press **Command-,** to open **Preferences**, and there it is:

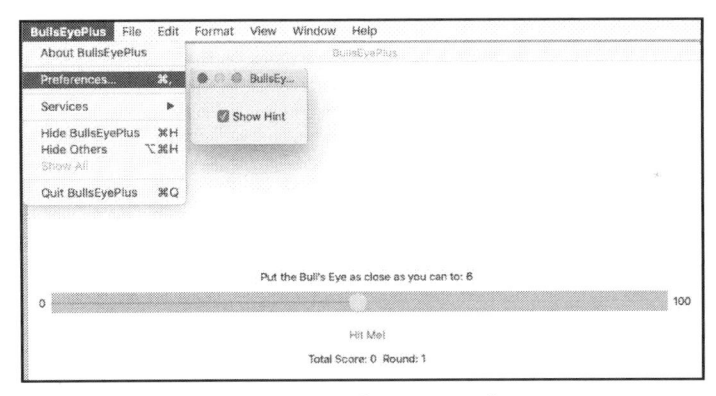

Show Hint preference window.

> **Note:** If the app doesn't respond to the `show_hint` setting, build and run again.

Play around with toggling **Show Hint** on and off: Your preference takes effect as soon as you move the slider!

Creating a MacOS BullsEye app

The Mac Catalyst framework is really convenient for iOS developers—you can continue to use the familiar UI-specific API, and you get a Mac app for free! If you're a macOS developer, you'll be working with macOS knowledge. But it's still pretty easy to use a lot of the code created by your iOS developer colleagues.

In this section, you'll use the **GameView** package you created earlier. It contains the UI as well as the model class. As you'll see, there's not much more work to do!

To start, create a new macOS project: Select **macOS ▸ App**, name it **MacBullsEye**, and check that it's set to **SwiftUI User Interface**:

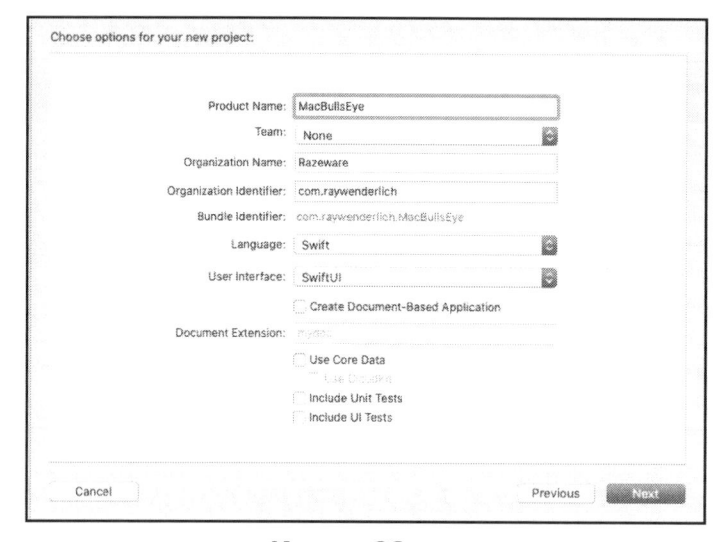

New macOS app.

Actually, you won't need **ContentView.swift**, so delete it in the project navigator.

Now find the **GameView** package you created earlier, and drag it from **Finder** into the project navigator of your new macOS app, above the MacBullsEye group:

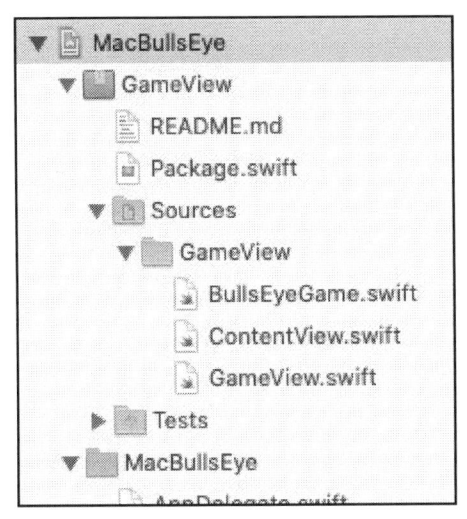

Add GameView package to MacBullsEye.

And now to link it: In your app target's **Frameworks, Libraries and Embedded Content** section, click **+**, then select **Workspace/GameView/GameView** from the list:

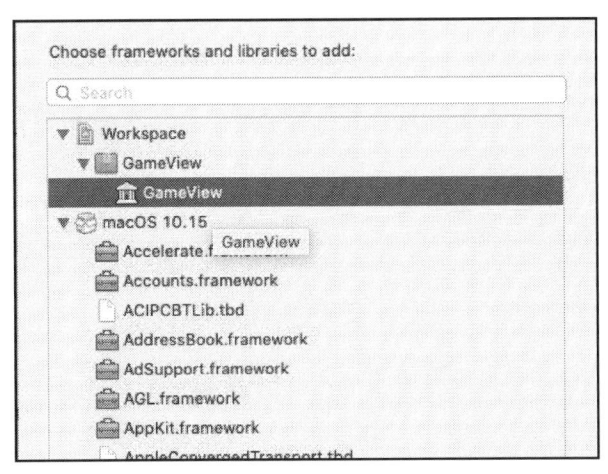

Add GameView library to MacBullsEye.

Then import the module: Add this line to the other imports, at the top of **AppDelegate.swift**:

```
import GameView
```

Now, press **Command-B** to build your new package, then build and run your app:

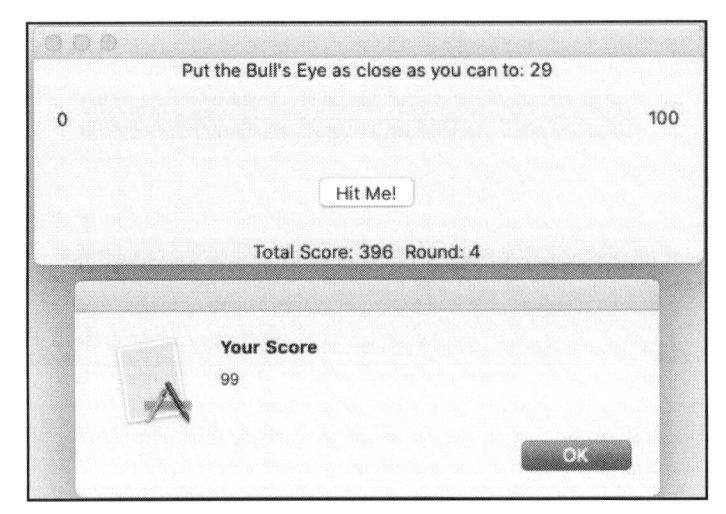

MacBullsEye running from GameView package.

Everything works! How easy was that?

> **Note**: You get an interesting feature with this native macOS app: Clicking on the slider moves its thumb.

Creating a tvOS BullsEye app

And finally, tvOS. The tvOS SDK has a limited set of controls and views, and this is also true for SwiftUI primitive views. The BullsEye app runs into trouble right away — there's no `Slider`! Not even a `Stepper`. What to do?

Well, the `BullsEyeGame` class has a party trick up its sleeve. It's just a random target value, coupled with a way to compute a score from the user's guess. The actual presentation of the game can be flexible. In this case, you can present the target value as a mark on a 1-to-100 line, and ask the user to enter their guess in a text field.

Create a new **tvOS Single View App** with **SwiftUI User Interface**, and name it **TVBullsEye**:

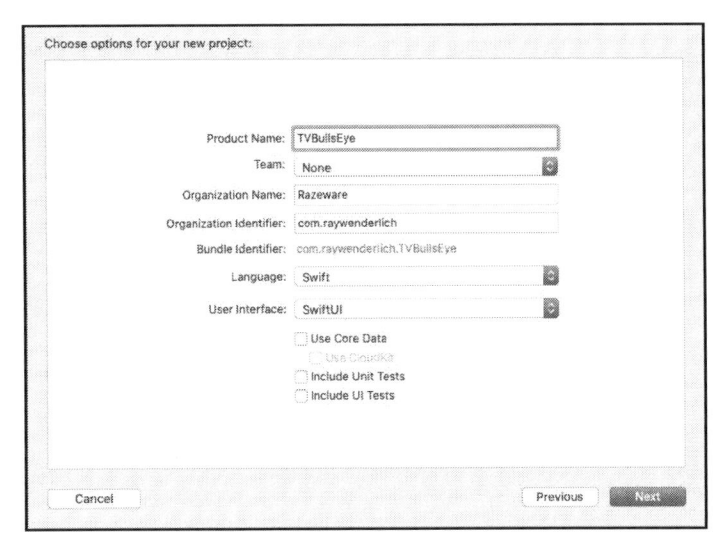

New tvOS app.

Then drag the **Game** package from **Finder** into the project navigator, and link the library on the target page:

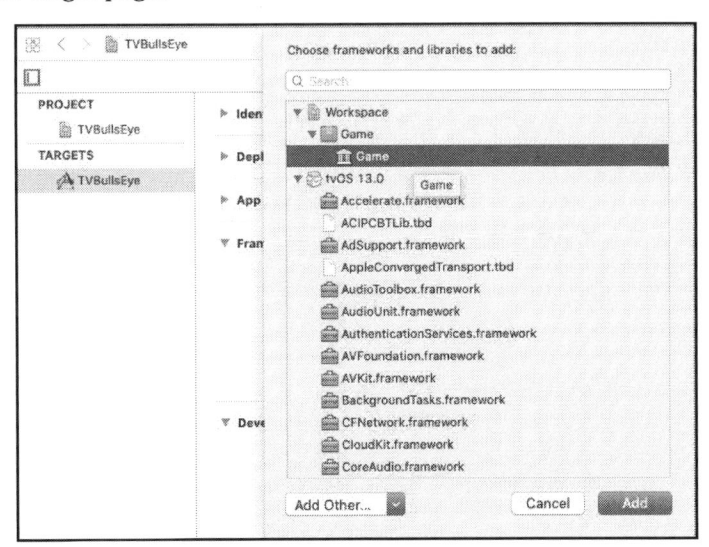

Add Game library to TVBullsEye.

Now import the module in **ContentView.swift**:

```
import Game
```

Build the library (**Command-B**) to get rid of the **No such module "Game"** error, but to be honest, it will probably appear again, whenever you change anything in the project.

Now replace the `ContentView` struct with the following code. I'll break it up so it doesn't span across pages.

First, the data properties:

```
struct ContentView: View {
  @ObservedObject var game = BullsEyeGame()

  @State var currentValue = 50.0
  @State var valueString: String = ""
  @State var showAlert = false
}
```

These are the same as for the regular BullsEye app, but you also need a `String` variable, because of the `TextField`.

Next, start building the body; this first part is very different from the regular app:

```
var body: some View {
  VStack {
    Text("Guess the number:")
    TextField("1-100", text: $valueString, onEditingChanged: { _
 in
      self.currentValue = Double(self.valueString) ?? 50.0
    })
      .frame(width: 150.0)
    HStack {
      Text("0")
      GeometryReader { geometry in
        ZStack {
          Rectangle()
            .frame(height: 8.0)
          Rectangle()
            .frame(width: 8.0, height: 30.0)
            .offset(x: geometry.size.width *
              (CGFloat(self.game.targetValue)/100.0 - 0.5), y:
 0.0)
        }
      }
      Text("100")
    }
    .padding(.horizontal)
  }
}
```

In this game, you ask the user to guess the number that's marked on a horizontal line, and provide a `TextField` to enter their guess as `valueString`. You convert this `String` to a `Double` to get `currentValue`, assigning 50.0 if the `String` doesn't represent a number.

You present the target value as a marker superimposed on a horizontal line — actually, a skinny `Rectangle` on a flat wide `Rectangle`, with the location of the target marker calculated as a fraction of the line's width. The marker's default location is in the center of the line, so a positive offset value moves it above 50, and you need a negative offset value to display a target value that's less than 50.

> **Note**: Learn more about `GeometryReader` in Chapter 13, **Drawing and Custom Graphics**.

Now fill in the rest of the body, which is almost the same as the regular app:

```swift
var body: some View {
  VStack {
    ...
    Button(action: {
      self.showAlert = true
      self.game.checkGuess(Int(self.currentValue))
    }) {
      Text("Hit Me!")
    }
    .alert(isPresented: $showAlert) {
      Alert(title: Text("Your Score"), message: Text(String(game.scoreRound)),
            dismissButton: .default(Text("OK"), action: {
              self.game.startNewRound()
              self.valueString = ""
            }))
    }
    .padding()
    HStack {
      Text("Total Score: \(game.scoreTotal)")
      Text("Round: \(game.round)")
    }
  }
}
```

The **Hit Me!** button and `Text` labels for **Total Score** and **Round** are the same as the iOS game, except to reset the `TextField` text to the empty string.

Using the tvOS simulator

Now build and run: This takes quite a while, the first time. And the simulator can be difficult to use.

When the app starts, you'll see a **Keyboard Connected** message.

Running TVBullsEye app.

Your Mac keyboard's arrow keys move the focus: Press **Down** and **Up** to see the focus move from the text field to the button, then back to the text field. With the focus on the text field, press **Return** to show the software keyboard:

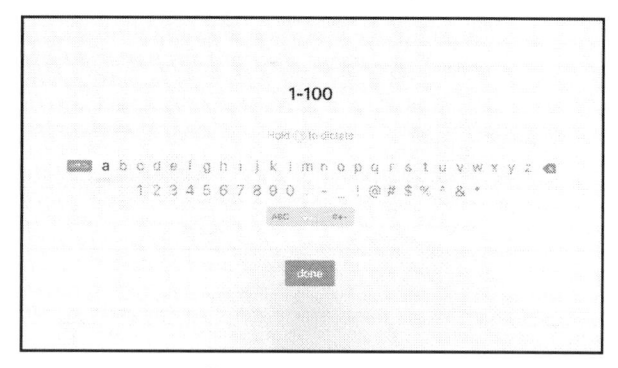

TVBullsEye software keyboard.

The arrow keys work here, too: Use them to focus on a digit, then press **Return**. Huh? You're back on the game screen, with nothing in the text field! Well, there's another tool you can use.

Open the **Hardware** menu, and select **Show Apple TV Remote (Shift-Command-R)**:

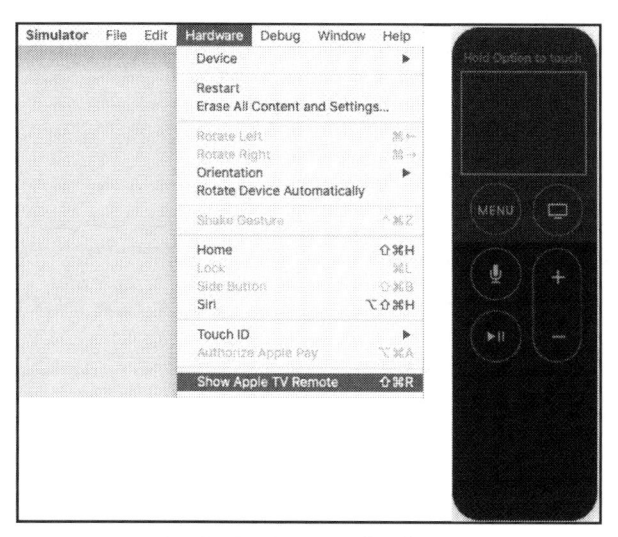

Apple TV Remote simulator.

With focus on the text field, select it by pressing **Return** or by tapping in the center of the remote's *touch surface*, above the **MENU** and **Home** buttons. Again, use the arrow keys to focus on a digit, then *tap the center of the remote's panel*. Success! Your selected digit appears in the text field, and you're still on the text entry screen.

Enter another digit to complete your guess value, then press **Down** to move focus to the **done** button. Press **Return** or tap the remote's panel to select it. And you're back in the game:

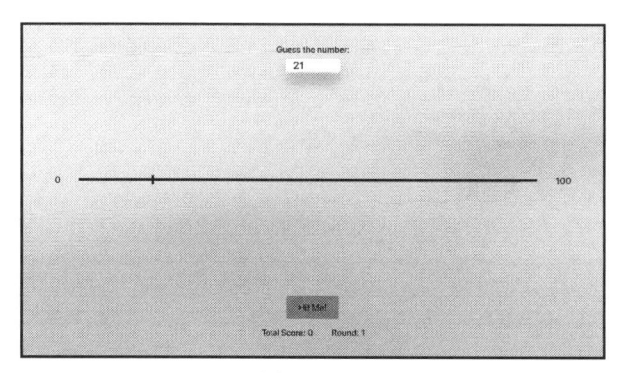

Successful TextField entry.

Move the focus to the **Hit Me!** button, then press **Return**. And there's your score:

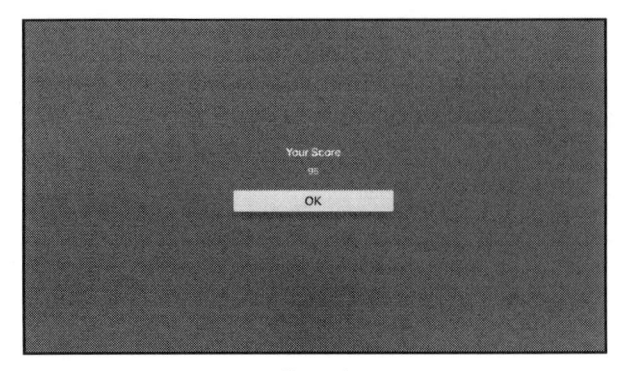

Score!

Press **Return** to dismiss the alert.

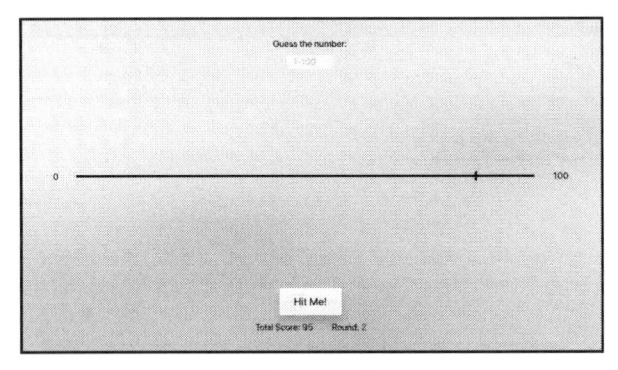

New round

Just like the regular BullsEye game, there are new target, total score and round values. And the text field has reset to the empty string.

So that's one way to port BullsEye to tvOS. With a little more work, you could port RGBullsEye, by creating your own sort-of slider, supplemented by a `TextField` where the user can enter a value between 0 and 255.

Key points

- SwiftUI provides generic views and a common layout system, so you can learn once, and apply anywhere.
- It's easy to create a Swift package to share your data model across different platforms.

- Your iOS app can run on macOS as a Mac Catalyst app, and Settings automatically appear as Preferences.

- You can also share SwiftUI views between iOS and macOS apps.

- Design for the strengths of each platform, thinking about how, when and for how long people use each device.

- Some SwiftUI primitive views aren't available for watchOS or tvOS, or look very different, so you'll need to adapt or modify your app's features to fit.

Chapter 6: Intro to Controls: Text & Image

By Antonio Bello

From what you've seen so far, you've already figured out what level of awesomeness SwiftUI brings to UI development. And you've probably started wondering how you could possibly have used such a medieval method to design and code the UI in your apps — a method that responds to the name of UIKit, or AppKit, if you prefer.

In the previous chapters, you've only scratched the surface of SwiftUI, and learned how to create some basic UI. Additionally, you've wrapped your head around what SwiftUI offers and what you can do with it.

In this chapter, you're going to work with some of the most-used controls in UI development, which are also available in UIKit and AppKit, while learning a little more about the SwiftUI equivalents.

To do so, you'll work on **Kuchi**, a language flash card app, which will keep you busy for the next four chapters. Enjoy!

Getting started

First, open the starter project for this chapter, and you'll see that it's almost empty. There's almost no user interface; only some resources and support files. If you build and run, all you'll get is a blank view.

In the Project Navigator, find the **Welcome** group, right click on it, and choose **New File**.

In the popup that comes next, choose **SwiftUI View**, then click **Next**,

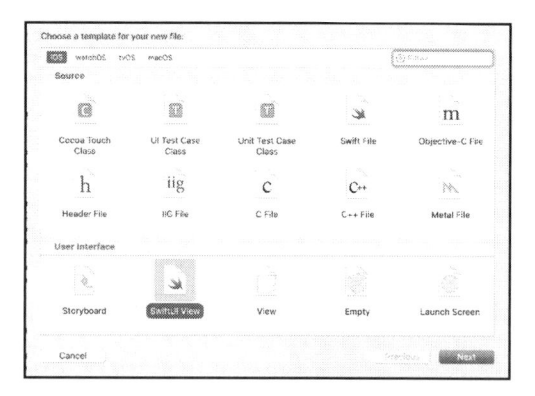

Then type **WelcomeView.swift** in the **Save As** field, and click on **Create**. You now have a blank new view to start with.

Changing the root view

Before doing anything, you need to configure the app to use the new `WelcomeView` as the starting view. Open **SceneDelegate.swift**, and locate the line of code where you create `EmptyView`.

```
window.rootViewController = UIHostingController(
  rootView: EmptyView()
)
```

This code determines the view that's created and displayed when the app is launched. The view currently created is `EmptyView`, which is... well, an empty view: the simplest possible view you could possibly use. Replace it with an instance of the new view you've just created, `WelcomeView`:

```
window.rootViewController = UIHostingController(
   rootView: WelcomeView()
)
```

Now, when the app starts, `WelcomeView` will be your first view.

Welcome, View!

Now, take a look at the newly created view. Open **WelcomeView**, and you will notice there isn't much in it:

- The `WelcomeView` struct, containing the body property and a `Text` component

- A preview provider named `WelcomeView_Previews`

But that's all you need to get started. body is the only thing a view requires — well, besides implementing a great and stylish UI, but that's your job!

In Xcode, ensure that you have the canvas visible in the **assistant** panel, and click the **Resume** button if necessary, to activate or reactivate the preview. You should see a welcome message like this:

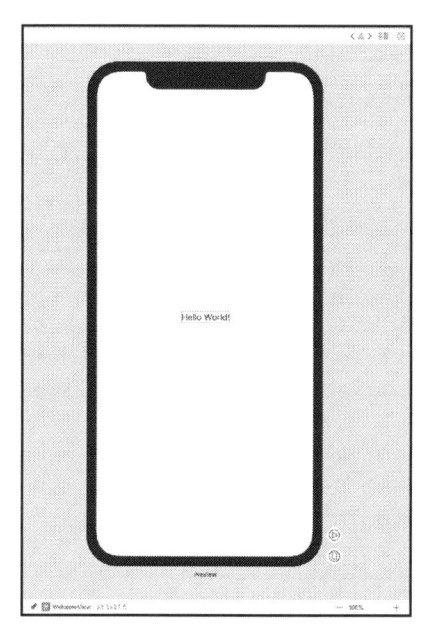

Text

Input requires context. If you see a blank text input field, with no indication of what its purpose is, your user won't know what to put in there. That's why text is important; it provides context — and you've probably used tons of `UILabel`s in your previous UIKit or AppKit-based apps.

As you've already seen, the component to display text is called, simply, `Text`. In its simplest and most commonly used initializer, `Text` takes a single parameter: the text to display. Change the string to `Welcome to Kuchi`:

```
Text("Welcome to Kuchi")
```

Xcode will automatically update the text shown in the preview. Nice! Simple stuff so far, but every long journey always starts with a single step.

Modifiers

Now that you've displayed some text on your screen, the next natural step is to change its appearance. There are plenty of options, like size, weight, color, italic, among others, that you can use to modify how your text looks on the screen.

> **Note:** In the previous chapters, you've already learned how to use a modifier to change the look or behavior of a view. A **modifier** is a view instance method that creates a copy of the view, does something to the view copy (such as changing the font size or the color), and returns the modified view.

To change the look of a Text instance, you use modifiers. But beyond that, more generally, *any* view can be altered using modifiers.

If you want to make the text larger, say, 60 points, add the following font modifier:

```
Text("Welcome to Kuchi")
  .font(.system(size: 60))
```

Then bold the text by adding the next line:

```
Text("Welcome to Kuchi")
  .font(.system(size: 60))
  .bold()
```

Then you can make it a nice red color:

```
Text("Welcome to Kuchi")
  .font(.system(size: 60))
  .bold()
  .foregroundColor(.red)
```

Next, you can split the text onto two lines:

```
Text("Welcome to Kuchi")
  .font(.system(size: 60))
  .bold()
  .foregroundColor(.red)
  .lineLimit(2)
```

And, finally, you can left-align the text:

```
Text("Welcome to Kuchi")
  .font(.system(size: 60))
  .bold()
  .foregroundColor(.red)
  .lineLimit(2)
  .multilineTextAlignment(.leading)
```

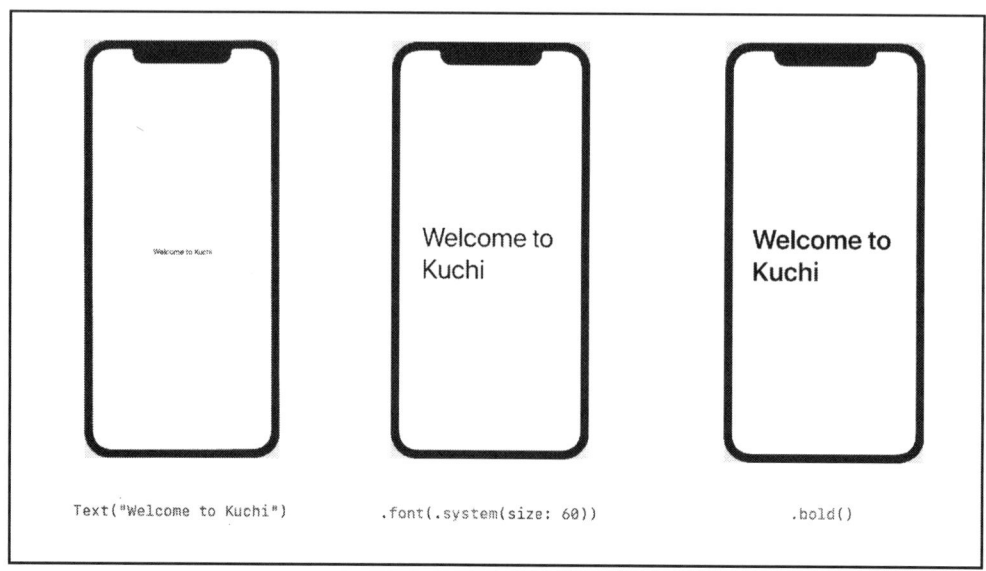

[Three iPhone mockups each showing "Welcome to Kuchi", labeled below:]

`.foregroundColor(.red)`   `.lineLimit(2)`   `.multilineTextAlignment(.leading)`

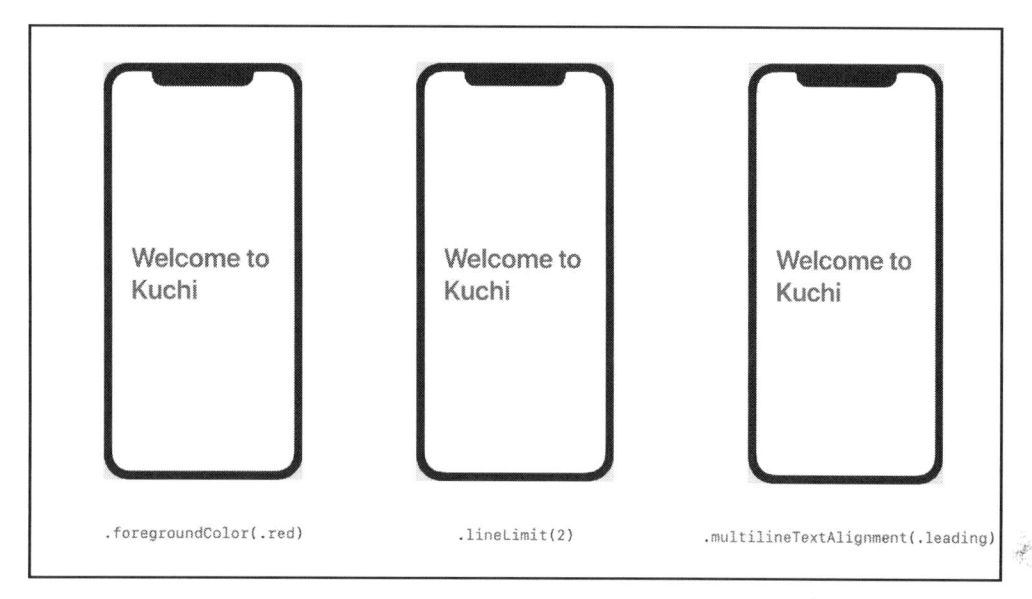

You might have noticed that the final three steps produced no obvious result. In fact, the default value for `.lineLimit` is `nil` (which means no line limit), and for `multilineTextAlignment` the default is `.leading`.

Although it's safe to assume that default values for this UI component won't change, it's possible that they might change in the future, as developers noted during the beta release phases of SwiftUI. Moreover, for the `.lineLimit` case, you might want to restrict the value to 2 at maximum, to preserve screen real estate.

So far you've exclusively used code to add and configure modifiers, but SwiftUI, in tandem with Xcode, offers two alternatives for the lazy, er, I mean *efficient* coders out there:

- A popup canvas inspector, which appears when you **Command-click** on a view component onto the canvas:

- The attributes inspector, which appears by by pressing **Option-Command-4**, and displays the modifiers for the view currently selected in the canvas:

Text is such a simple component, but it has *so* many modifiers. And that's just the beginning.! There are two categories of modifiers that SwiftUI offers:

- Modifiers bundled with the `View` protocol, available to any view.

- Modifiers specific to a type, available only to instances of that type.

`View` has lots of premade and ready-to-use modifiers that are implemented in protocol extensions. For a full list, you can browse the documentation; in Xcode,**Option-click** `View` in the source editor, and then click **Open in Developer Documentation**.

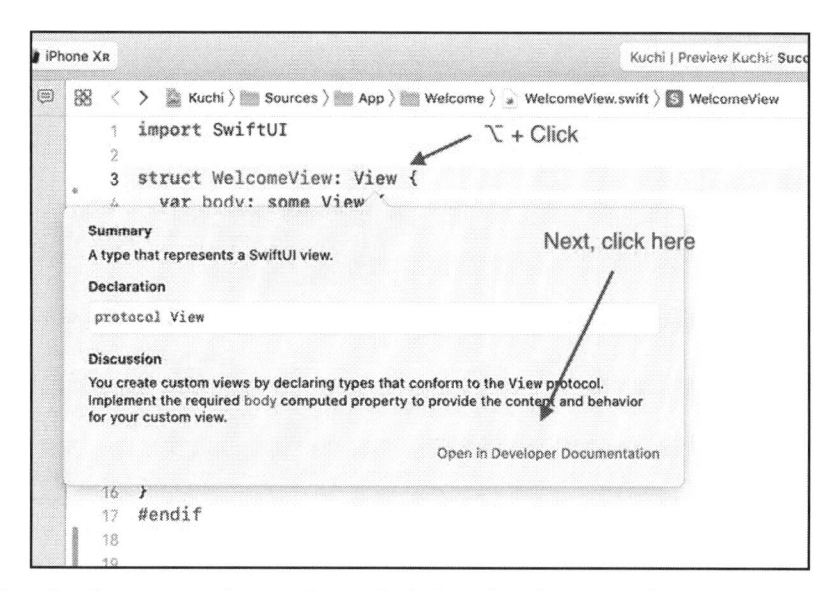

Browsing the documentation is always helpful when learning, but sometimes you need a faster way to search for a modifier. Maybe you don't remember the modifier's name, or maybe you are simply wondering if such a modifier exists.

Again, Xcode and SwiftUI can help with that! Xcode now has a **Modifiers Library**, similar to the **Object Library** available in older versions of Xcode.

To access the library, click the leftmost + button, located at the top-right corner of your Xcode window. The library allows you to browse and search by name, and, most importantly, groups all modifiers by category, so chances are that you'll quickly find what you're looking for, if it actually exists.

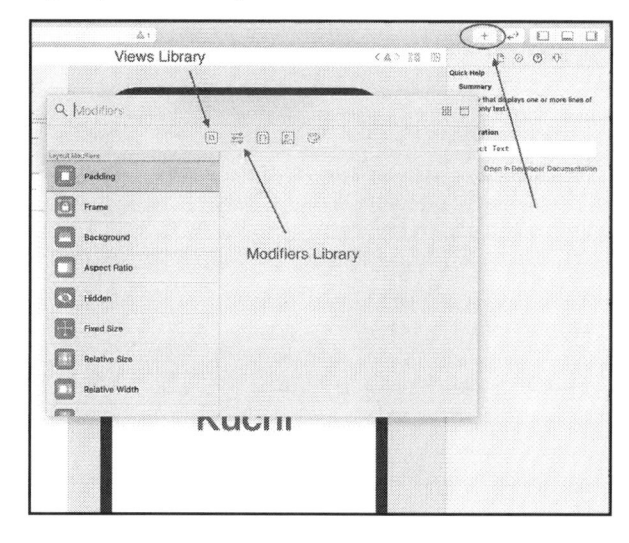

Note that the library also contains the **Views Library**, which you can use to browse and select views, and drag them onto the canvas, for two-way user interface development.

Are modifiers efficient?

Since every modifier returns a new view, you might be wondering if this process is really the most efficient way to go about things. SwiftUI embeds a view into a new view every time you invoke a modifier. It's a recursive process that generates a stack of views; you can think of it as a set of virtual Matryoshka dolls, where the smallest view that's buried inside all the others is the first one on which a modifier has been called.

Intuitively, this looks like a waste of resources. The truth is that SwiftUI flattens this stack into an efficient data structure that is used for the actual rendering of the view.

As a matter of fact, you should feel free to use as many modifiers as you need, without reserve and without fear of impacting the efficiency of your view.

Order of modifiers

Is the order in which you invoke modifiers important? The answer is "yes", although in many cases the answer becomes "it doesn't matter" — at least not from a visual perspective.

For example, if you apply a bold modifier, and then make it red:

```
Text("Welcome to Kuchi")
   .bold()
   .foregroundColor(.red)
```

..or first make it red, and then bold:

```
Text("Welcome to Kuchi")
   .foregroundColor(.red)
   .bold()
```

...you won't notice any difference.

However, if you apply a background color and then apply padding, you *will* get a different result. `.padding` is a modifier that adds spacing between the view the modifier is applied to and the view's parent. Without parameters, SwiftUI adds a default padding in all four directions, but you can configure that padding yourself.

Consider the following configuration below:

```
Text("Welcome to Kuchi")
   .background(Color.red)
   .padding()
```

You add a red background color to the text, and then apply padding. But if you invert that order:

```
Text("Welcome to Kuchi")
   .padding()
   .background(Color.red)
```

You apply the padding first, resulting in a larger view, and then apply the red background. You'll immediately notice that the result is different:

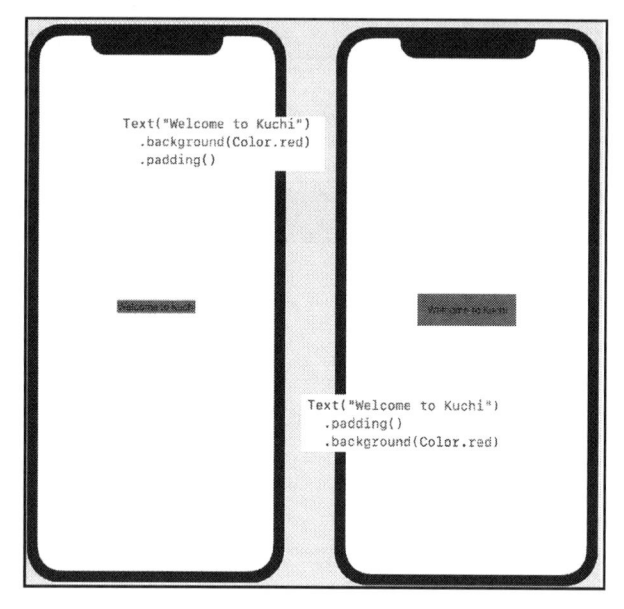

This is because the *view* where you apply the background color is *different* in each case. Another way to look at it is that the view to which you apply the padding is different.

This is clearly visible if you set different background colors before and after applying the padding:

```
Text("Welcome to Kuchi")
   .background(Color.yellow)
   .padding()
   .background(Color.red)
```

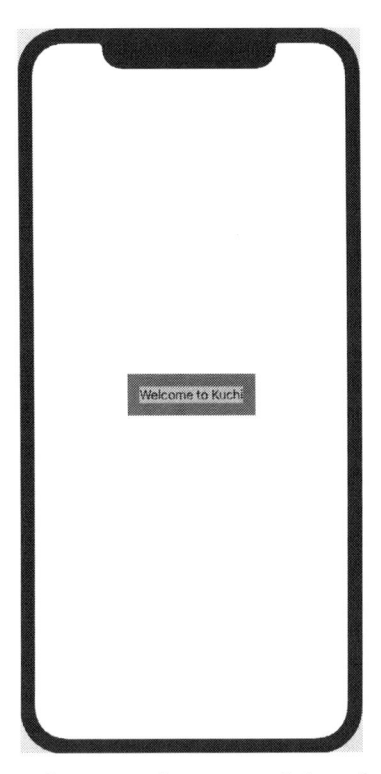

The padding adds some space between the text and the edges of the view. When you apply the background color before the padding, that modification is applied to the view that contains the text, which is a view large enough to contain just the displayed text and nothing more. The `padding` modifier adds a *new* view, to which the *second* background color is applied to it.

Image

An image is worth a thousand words. That may be a cliché, but it's absolutely true when it comes to your UI. This section shows you how to add an image to your UI.

First, remove the welcome `Text` from body and replace it with an `Image` component as shown below:

```
var body: some View {
   Image(systemName: "table")
}
```

This is what you'll see on screen:

Changing the image size

When you create an image without providing any modifiers, SwiftUI will render the image at its native resolution and maintain the image's aspect ratio. The image you're using here is taken from **SF Symbols**, a new set of icons that Apple introduced in the 2019 iterations of iOS, watchOS and tvOS. For more information, check out the links at the end of this chapter.

If you want to resize an image, you have to apply the `resizable` modifier, which takes two parameters: an inset and a resizing mode. The resizing mode can be either `.tile` or `.stretch`. If you don't provide any parameters, SwiftUI assumes no inset for all four directions (top, bottom, leading and trailing) and `.stretch` resizing mode.

> **Note**: If you *don't* apply the `resizable` modifier, the image will keep its native size. When you apply a modifier that either directly or indirectly changes the image's size, that change is applied to the *actual* view the modifier is applied to, but *not* to the image itself, which will retain its original size.

So if images are worth a thousand words, then code examples must be worth a thousand images! To embed an image in a square frame, 60 points wide and high, you simply add the `frame` modifier to the image:

```
var body: some View {
  Image(systemName: "table")
    .frame(width: 60, height: 60)
}
```

The preview won't show any difference; you'll still see the image at its original size. However, if you click the image to select it, Xcode will show the selection highlight as a blue border:

The outermost view has the correct size, but, as you may have expected, the image didn't scale to match.

Now, prepend `frame` with the `resizable` modifier:

```
var body: some View {
  Image(systemName: "table")
    .resizable()
    .frame(width: 60, height: 60, alignment: .center)
}
```

The output should be a lot closer to what you expected:

> **Note:** You've given the image an absolute size, measured in points. However, for accessibility reasons, and to help your app adapt to different resolutions, orientations, devices and platforms, it's always a good idea to let SwiftUI decide how to scale images, and more generally, most of your UI content. You'll cover that briefly in this chapter, but you'll go into scaling more in-depth in in the next chapter.

If you want to transform and manipulate that image to make it look like a bordered and circular red-colored grid with a light gray background, add the following code after `.frame`:

```
// 1
.cornerRadius(60 / 2)
// 2
.border(Color.gray, width: 1)
// 3
.background(Color(white: 0.9))
// 4
.clipShape(Circle())
// 5
.foregroundColor(.red)
```

Here's what you're doing:

1. You set the corner radius to half the size of the image.

2. Next, you add a thin gray border.

3. You then you add a light gray background color.

4. Next, you clip the resulting image using a circle shape, which removes the excess colored background.

5. Finally, you set the foreground color to red.

Here's how the sequence of modifiers affects the resulting image at each step:

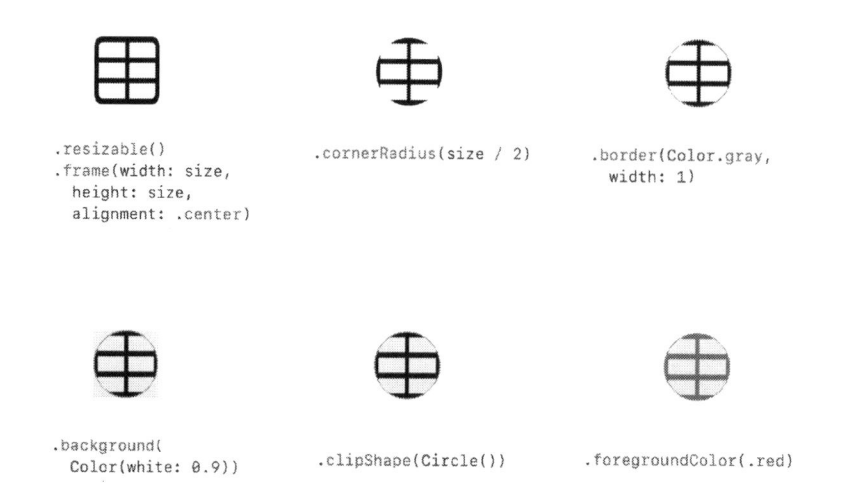

`.resizable()`
`.frame(width: size, height: size, alignment: .center)`

`.cornerRadius(size / 2)`

`.border(Color.gray, width: 1)`

`.background(Color(white: 0.9))`

`.clipShape(Circle())`

`.foregroundColor(.red)`

It turns out one of the modifiers in the previous code is redundant. If you remove that modifier, the resulting image is the same. Can you tell which modifier is redundant?

It might not be obvious at first glance, but the corner radius, which makes the image circular, actually clips the image. But isn't that what the shape clipping at line 4 is doing? Try it out! Delete or comment out the corner radius modifier, and you'll see that the resulting image doesn't change.

You can safely remove that line of code.

Last thought for this section: have you considered how easy it was to manipulate and transform an image with just a few lines of code? How many lines of code would you have written in UIKit or AppKit to achieve the same result? Quite a lot more, I believe.

Brief overview of stack views

Before moving to the next topic, you'll need to recover the code you removed while working on the `Image` in the previous section.

To add the `Text` view again, alter the implementation of body so it looks as follows. Note that this code won't compile at first, but you'll fix that in just a moment:

```
Image(systemName: "table")
    .resizable()
    .frame(width: 60, height: 60, alignment: .center)
    .border(Color.gray, width: 1)
    .cornerRadius(60 / 2)
    .background(Color(white: 0.9))
    .clipShape(Circle())
    .foregroundColor(.red)

Text("Welcome to Kuchi")
    .font(.system(size: 60))
    .bold()
    .foregroundColor(.red)
    .lineLimit(2)
    .multilineTextAlignment(.leading)
```

The reason this code doesn't compile is that body expects a single view at the outermost level, but here you've declared two. To solve this issue, all you have to do is to embed these views into an `HStack`, which is the SwiftUI counterpart of UIKit's `UIStackView` in horizontal layout mode.

Embed the image and text views in an `HStack` as follows:

```
HStack {
  Image(systemName: "table")
    ...

  Text("Welcome to Kuchi")
    ...
}
```

> **Note:** You'll learn about `HStack` in the next chapter. All you need to know right now is that `HStack` a *container view*, which allows you to group multiple views in a horizontal layout.

More on Image

Two sections ago, you played with the Image view, creating an icon at the end of the process. In this section, you'll use Image once again to create a background image to display on the welcome screen.

To do that, you need to know about another container view, ZStack, which stacks views one on top of the other, like sheets of papers in a stack. This is different from HStack (and VStack, which you'll meet later in this chapter) which arranges views next to one another instead.

Since you need to add a background image, ZStack seems to fit the purpose. Embed the HStack of the previous section inside a ZStack:

```
ZStack {
  HStack {
    ...
  }
}
```

Nothing changes in the canvas preview. Now, add this Image view before HStack inside of the ZStack:

```
Image("welcome-background", bundle: nil)
```

The image looks okay, but it has too much presence and color. `View` and `Image` have a comprehensive list of modifiers that let you manipulate the appearance of an image. These include **opacity**, **blur**, **contrast**, **brightness**, **hue**, **clipping**, **interpolation**, and **aliasing**. Many of these modifiers are defined in the `View` protocol, so they're not limited to just images; you could, theoretically, use them on any view.

Use this image as a reference to see what each modifier does. I encourage you to add modifiers one at a time in Xcode, to see the live result build up in the canvas preview:

`Image("welcome-background")`

`.resizable()`

`.scaledToFit()`

`.aspectRatio(1 / 1, contentMode: .fill)`

`.edgesIgnoringSafeArea(.all)`

`.saturation(0.5)`

`.blur(radius: 5)`

`.opacity(0.08)`

Final Result

The final code for the image should look as follows:

```
// 1
Image("welcome-background", bundle: nil)
  // 2
  .resizable()
  // 3
  .scaledToFit()
  // 4
  .aspectRatio(1 / 1, contentMode: .fill)
  // 5
  .edgesIgnoringSafeArea(.all)
  // 6
  .saturation(0.5)
  // 7
  .blur(radius: 5)
  // 8
  .opacity(0.08)
```

Going over this code, here is what you just did:

1. This is the `Image` you've just added.

2. `.resizable`: Make it resizeable. By default, SwiftUI tries to use all of the space at its disposal, without worrying about of the aspect ratio.

3. `.scaledToFit`: Maximize the image so that it's fully visible within the parent, with respect to the original ratio.

4. `.aspectRatio`: Set the aspect ratio, which is `1:1` by default. Setting `contentMode` to `.fill` makes the image fill the entire parent view, so a portion of the image will extend beyond the view's boundaries.

5. `.edgesIgnoringSafeArea`: Ignore the safe area insets, extending the view outside the safe area, so that it occupies the entire parent space. Here, you're ignoring all edges, but it can also be configured on a per-edge basis. To do that, you pass an array of the edges to ignore: `.top`, `.bottom`, `.leading`, `.trailing`, but also `.vertical` and `.horizontal`, which combine the two vertical and the two horizontal edges respectively.

6. `.saturation`: Reduce the color saturation so that the image appears less vibrant.

7. `.blur`: Add some blur. Who doesn't love blur?

8. `.opacity`: Make the image more transparent, which has the side effect of dimming the image to make it a little less prominent.

Once again, there's a redundant modifier in that view. Did you figure out which one it was? Yes, it's the third line: the `.scaledToFit` modifier. You already made the image fit the parent with `.resizable`, and then `.aspectRatio` makes the image fill the parent instead. Comment the `.scaleToFit` modifier, and you'll see that the final result doesn't change.

Can you guess what happens if you switch `scaleToFit` and `aspectRatio`? Would you expect the final result to change?

You've probably figured it out already: `scaleToFit` overrides the fill mode set in the previous line — so now *that* becomes the redundant modifier. However, if you change the aspect ratio, to something like 2:

```
.aspectRatio(2 / 1, contentMode: .fill)
```

The result is quite different in this case, because you're making the width twice as wide, while keeping the height unaltered:

That said, you can revert that aspect radio change, and safely delete the redundant `.scaledToFit`. The code for the background would then look like the following:

```
Image("welcome-background", bundle: nil)
  .resizable()
  .aspectRatio(1 / 1, contentMode: .fill)
  .edgesIgnoringSafeArea(.all)
  .saturation(0.5)
  .blur(radius: 5)
  .opacity(0.08)
```

Splitting Text

Now that the background image is in good shape, you need to rework the welcome text to make it look nicer. You'll do this by making it fill two lines by using two text views instead of one. Since the text should be split vertically, all you have to do is add a VStack around the welcome text, like so:

```
VStack {
  Text("Welcome to Kuchi")
    .font(.system(size: 60))
    .bold()
    .foregroundColor(.red)
    .lineLimit(2)
    .multilineTextAlignment(.leading)
}
```

Next, you can split the text into two separate views:

```
VStack {
  Text("Welcome to")
    .font(.system(size: 60))
    .bold()
    .foregroundColor(.red)
    .lineLimit(2)
    .multilineTextAlignment(.leading)
  Text("Kuchi")
    .font(.system(size: 60))
    .bold()
    .foregroundColor(.red)
    .lineLimit(2)
    .multilineTextAlignment(.leading)
}
```

You may notice that the last three modifiers in each `Text` are the same. Since they are modifiers implemented in `View`, you can refactor the code by applying them to the parent stack view, instead of to each individual view:

```
VStack {
  Text("Welcome to")
    .font(.system(size: 60))
    .bold()
  Text("Kuchi")
    .font(.system(size: 60))
    .bold()
}
.foregroundColor(.red)
.lineLimit(2)
.multilineTextAlignment(.leading)
```

This is a very powerful feature: when you have a container view, and you want one or more modifiers to be applied to all subviews, simply apply those modifiers to the container.

> **Note:** You might be wondering why you didn't do the same thing for the last two modifiers of each contained view. Look at the documentation for `.font` and `.bold`, and you'll see that these are modifiers on the `Text` type. Therefore these modifiers aren't available on `View` and `VStack`.

Wouldn't it be nice if the two lines of text had different font sizes as well? To achieve this, use the `.headline` style on the welcome text, replacing `.font(.system(size: 60))` with the following:

```
.font(.headline)
```

For the Kuchi text, use a `.largeTitle` instead, replacing `.font(.system(size: 60))` with the following:

```
.font(.largeTitle)
```

Finally, you'll style the container slightly to make it a little less cramped. You'll need some padding between the image and the text; you can use the `.padding` modifier and pass `.horizontal`, which adds padding horizontally on both sides. You could alternately pass other edges, such as top or leading, either standalone or as an array of edges. Also you can specify an optional length for the padding. If you don't specify this, SwiftUI will apply a default.

The code for the entire text stack should look like this:

```swift
VStack(alignment: .leading) {
  Text("Welcome to")
    .font(.headline)
    .bold()
  Text("Kuchi")
    .font(.largeTitle)
    .bold()
}
.foregroundColor(.red)
.lineLimit(2)
.multilineTextAlignment(.leading)
.padding(.horizontal)
```

The resulting view should appear as follows:

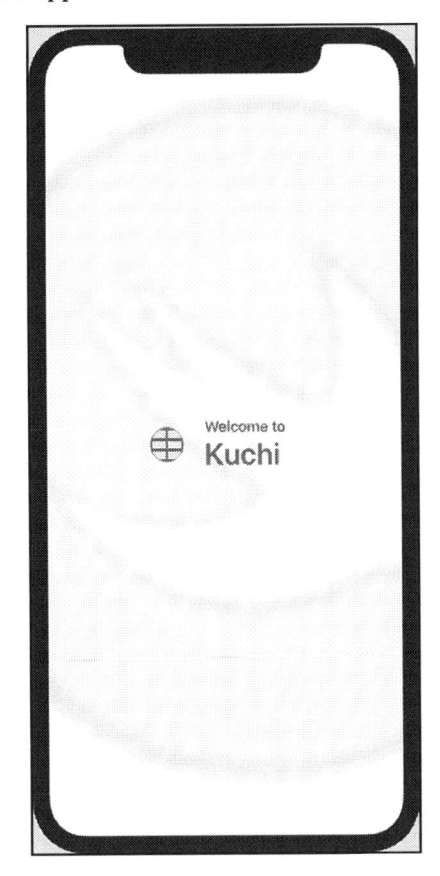

Accessibility with fonts

Initially, all of your views that display text used a `font(.system(size: 60))` modifier, which changed the font used when rendering the text. Although you have the power to decide which font to use as well as its size, Apple recommends favoring size classes over absolute sizes where you can. This is why, in the previous section, you used styles such as `.headline` and `.largeTitle` in place of `.system(size: 60)`

All sizes are defined in `Font` as pseudo-enum cases: They're actually static properties. UIKit and AppKit have corresponding class sizes, so you probably already know a little bit about `title`, `headline`, `body`, or other properties like that.

Using size classes gives the user the freedom to increase or decrease all fonts used in your app relative to a reference size: if the reference size is increased, all fonts becomes larger in proportion, and if decreased, then the fonts become smaller. This is a huge help to people with eyesight issues or visual impairments.

That was a long journey! The concepts here are pretty simple, but necessary to get you started in your SwiftUI development.

Key points

- You use the `Text` and `Image` views to display and configure text and images respectively.

- You use modifiers to change the appearance of your views. Modifiers can be quite powerful when used in combination.

- Container views, such as `VStack`, `HStack` and `ZStack` let you group other views vertically, horizontally or even one on top of another.

Where to go from here?

SwiftUI is brand-new and is still evolving as a technology, even now that it's out of beta. During this period of adjustment, features can change, APIs can be renamed, or even removed altogether. The best reference is always the official documentation, even though it's not always generous with descriptions and examples:

- SwiftUI documentation: apple.co/2MlBqJJ

- The `View` reference documentation apple.co/2LEh5Qs

If you want to take a look and browse through the SF Symbols image library:

- SF Symbols apple.co/2YPtrIx

- SF Symbols App (download) apple.co/30VPAW0

In the next chapter, you'll take a peek at state and data flow, before learning more about more controls available in SwiftUI, in the chapter that follows that.

Chapter 7: State & Data Flow

Phil J. Łaszkowicz

Now that you've gotten a handle on how SwiftUI components are composed visually, you're ready to move on to handling data changes and flow throughout the SwiftUI lifecycle.

Previously, **state and data flow** in Swift would be managed separately from the visual components, with various approaches that were not always necessarily achieved in the most Swift-like manner. You'd typically start with a controller, and you would then delegate events to trickle down changes through your view hierarchy in a prescriptive manner where user-flow informed your controller what needed to be changed, and then the controller would orchestrate changes between our data models and our UI.

Hierarchical changes would require careful orchestration between subview controllers to ensure the source of truth did not go out of sync with the visual representation. A lot to keep in mind, even when building simple features.

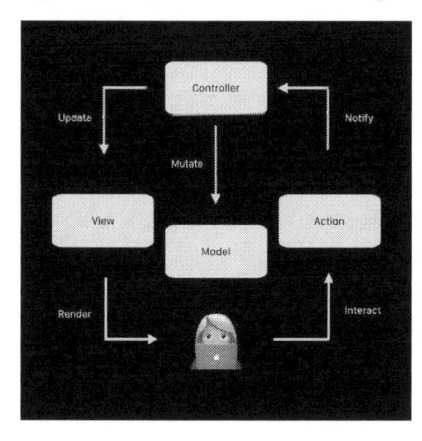

SwiftUI changes this by providing a set of tools and patterns that go far beyond just visual tooling. These provide simple approaches, built upon Swift attributes, to store and update data within your apps effortlessly, removing dependencies on previous KVO observing methodologies and mutating the state rather than the view hierarchy.

With SwiftUI views are a function of state, not a sequence of events, with the app as a constant feedback loop.

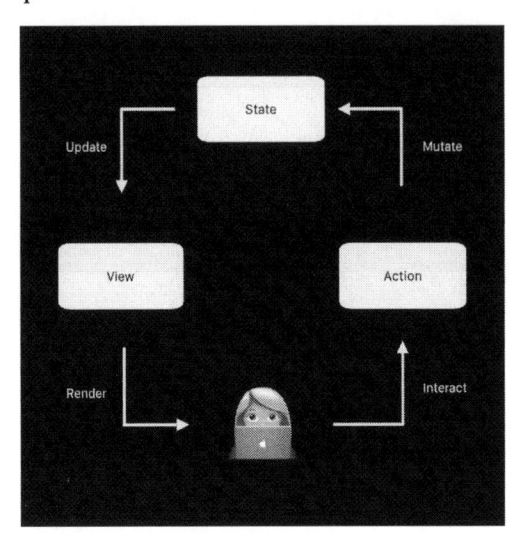

These approaches are reactive, enabling your visual changes to be invoked and your views to be rebuilt automatically after your state mutates. You no longer have to deal with the controller paradigm in SwiftUI and can directly utilize state management within your `View` components. With this, Apple is following the declarative approach that's becoming so familiar in other technologies, such as React, Flutter and more.

The reason this has taken so long to reach Swift is down to the fact Swift inherited much of the UIKit paradigms that were built on its predecessor, Objective-C. Since then, Swift has been evolving and the APIs from AppKit and UIKit have been evolving with it to provide much more imperative and elegant interfaces to UI building.

These tools have been pushed as far as they can until they were no longer suited to the Swift way of building code, and an alternative had to emerge. Essentially, Swift wasn't ready for SwiftUI until Swift 5.1 emerged. We'll explain how Swift 5.1 applies to SwiftUI throughout this book, but for now, focus on how this applies to state.

In this chapter, you'll dive deeper into what state *is*, inside the context of SwiftUI. It's an important and complex topic, so be sure to take your time with the pages to come.

What is state?

As you'll be seeing the term **state** repeatedly, it's probably best to get a clear definition of what state means and how SwiftUI's specific definition applies.

When you design the user interface (UI) of your app, you're often applying state. For example, each time you assign a variable as the value of a UITextField, and then read it back from the UITextField, you've been managing the state of that particular control. When data critical to an app's functionality is read or modified, that's state, whether it's information from a web service, from a local Core Data store, or direct input from the app user — it's all state. So, how does SwiftUI change your existing understanding of state in Swift programming across Apple's ecosystem?

Due mostly to additions to the Swift language in version 5.1, you can now leverage state management boilerplate through the use of property wrappers. State property wrappers use custom attributes to declare persistent storage, due largely to the capabilities brought by the Combine framework. These property wrappers allow value changes to be automatically reflected in your apps without having to write boilerplate state management or binding code.

As state management in SwiftUI is based on property wrapper attributes, you'll start by applying these attributes to your app. Each attribute is tailored for a different use case, so you're going to be selective in where and how you apply them, starting with the simplest: @State.

> **Note**: You've already applied some property wrappers to your code in the previous chapter without having been explained what they're for. So, while you're working through this chapter, you're going to cover the attributes you've already written and modify them for best practice, with explanations of why along the way.

Starting with @State

The intuitively named @State allows you to monitor and read a given persistent value automatically within a local given view. Every @State is a persistent source of truth for a given value, managed by the framework. It's best suited to simple value types (e.g. Bool, Int, or String) with an intended lifetime scope of the view in which you're declaring it.

Although you can use traditional variables in many cases where the `@State` attribute is used, `@State` comes with some nifty benefits that make it compelling for dynamic user interfaces where the data in your views is expected to change, whether by the end-user or by the app itself.

> **Note**: Although this app is based in the one in the previous chapter, some code and functionalities have been added to better explain some of the concepts on this chapter and to allow us to focus on them. Therefore, please **locate the starter project for this chapter and open it up**.

Go back to the `RegisterView` of the language app **Kuchi** to examine how `@State` works in more detail.

In **RegisterView.swift**, you're using `@State` to manage the user's name registration when they first load the app. You declare your state object as so:

```
@State var name: String = ""
```

You then use the `name` variable within your `TextField` by prefixing the variable name with the `$` operator to access the binding property of the state variable. It's important to realize that the attribute is creating a wrapper around your `String` value, with a binding for value changes to occur:

```
TextField("Enter your name", text: $name)
  .multilineTextAlignment(.center)
```

When the user enters a name into the `TextField` control, the value will be updated within the state object and the view will be declared invalid and rebuilt.

You could achieve something similar without the `@State` attribute by referencing the `State` struct directly, and its binding:

```
var name: State<String>
...
name.binding = "Ray"
```

However, that's far less elegant than using the SwiftUI attribute and the `$` prefix operator. The binding is a two-way relationship with the `TextField`: When you modified the value in your `TextField`, it retained a reference to the state wrapper — and the value of your `@State` object is changed without the need for any additional code.

If you wanted to simply add the value of a variable into a read-only `Text` view, you could do this easily without `@State`; you've done this with the title `Text` control as this is a one-way relationship. You simply set the value without modification, like so:

```
private let title = "Welcome to Kuchi"
...
Text(title)
  .font(.title)
  .animation(.spring())
```

This works perfectly fine, and it's the recommended way to manage read-only value updates that are independent of other data, such as labels and titles. After all, the `@State` variable does add an additional, although minor, footprint to variables, so using them with due consideration is important.

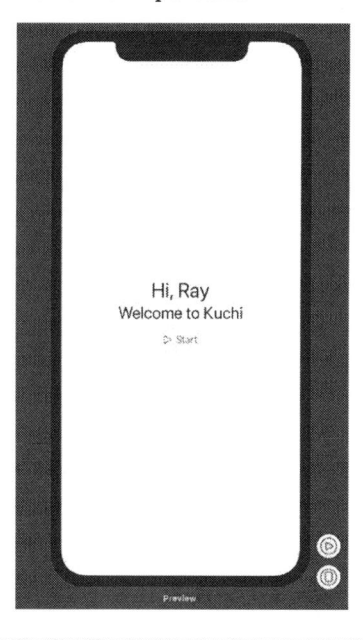

> **Note:** `@State` binding variables are only in memory for the lifetime of the view. When the `View` in which they're declared is no longer available, the `@State` binding values also become unavailable automatically. This frees up precious memory when the value is no longer needed.

To use `@State` effectively, you should limit its use if possible, and use the derived binding or value instead.

@State: Learning to share

Now, what if you want to share a value across multiple views? You have two potential approaches: The first approach is to modify the initializer for your views (`init`) to accept the variable you wish to pass. You do this when passing the score from the `PracticeStore` owner: `ChallengeView`, to its child: `ScoreView`.

As in **ScoreView.swift**:

```
// ScoreView
struct ScoreView {

  @Binding private var answered: Int

  private let questions: Int

  init(answered: Binding<Int>, of questions: Int) {
    self._answered = answered
    self.questions = questions
  }
}
```

You may feel a constant (`let`) is more appropriate for the score (semantically named `answered` in `ScoreView`). However, remembering that the `@Binding` attribute wraps `answered` into a manager object with a bound value, you need to allow it to be mutable.

The value may not change, but the `Binding` state management object that you're passing into the initializer must be allowed to in order to notify the origin `@State` object when a change has occurred. If you do try and make a `@Binding` object a constant, it will result in two errors: one at the declaration ("Property wrapper can only be applied to a `var`"), and when you try and set it during initialization ("Value of type `ScoreView` has no member `answered`").

`@Binding` is a first-class reference to data and is great for reusability. You can access the value of the binding in the same way as you'd access a `@State` value—by using the `$` prefix operator. When setting it in the initializer, the optimal method is to prefix the variable name with an underscore, as illustrated above, as that's the true internal name of your binding. In other words, `answered` is your state wrapper and `_answered` is your state value. If you try and set `answered` to an `Int` value type, you'll receive an error notifying you that `answered` is a `Binding<Int>` and not an `Int`, so coercion is impossible.

Your `questions` variable can be a constant, and a value type, as it'll be set only when the view is built. Score, or `answered`, will also only be set during initialization. So why do you need to bind it, if updates are not required to go two-ways? This is because you need to rebuild the `ScoreView` when the score increments. In `ChallengeView` (**ChallengeView.swift**), which owns the `ScoreView`, this is done using the power of `@State` to force a rebuild of `ScoreView` once the bound value mutates:

```
// In ChallengeView
@State private var score: Int = 0

...
  // In body
  ScoreView(answered: $score,
            of: self.practiceViewModel.assessments.count)
...
```

You *could* raise the hierarchical position of the `PracticeScore` binding to `PracticeView` so that any value change in the model will rebuild all the subviews, but pushing the `PracticeStore` down a layer allows you to have a finer granularity of bindings and updates.

In reality, either way will work just fine, and SwiftUI is clever enough only to rebuild subviews whose values have changed. However, it's always good practice to manage the granularity of state when it requires little developer effort, and `PracticeStore` only needs to know when a session has been completed.

Sharing your variables between views may be more memory efficient, but can also be confusing as you'll need to modify each view that needs access to that value. This is something many developers have become familiar with before SwiftUI, and have contributed countless hours to testing and debugging where values are passed, modifying constructor signatures and maintaining APIs.

`@State` doesn't solve these problems, even though it provides solutions to many others. Data is state, and state is a dependency, and with dependencies comes responsibility.

Being careful when and where you create these dependencies is critical to making SwiftUI work. An important aspect of how state works in SwiftUI is in the single source of truth mechanism: State binding is the declaration of a source of truth within the view hierarchy, and SwiftUI requires that only one source of truth exists. Redeclaring a value elsewhere, which is essentially rebinding a value, creates two sources of truth and invalidates the SwiftUI state model.

If you *did* want to pass the `@State` value down the hierarchy, in a composite view (a parent `View` which combines multiple child `View` objects), you can pass the `@State` in during instantiation as normal:

```
// In RegisterView
if profileViewModel.isRegistered {
  WelcomeView(name: name)
} else {
...
```

However, when you start sending simple values into views through the initializer, it won't be long until you realize you need more complex view models. You should ask yourself, "Does this state need to be owned by the view, or can you lift it or externalize it?"

This brings you to the second option for passing values between views. The `ObservableObject` protocol powers several objects designed to simplify the state management of more complex data types. There are two built-in implementations for `ObservableObject` in SwiftUI, and you're going to start with the one that doesn't require any API changes in your apps: `@EnvironmentObject`.

Environmental state

`@EnvironmentObject` supports the persistence of objects throughout the lifetime of your app, across multiple views. Whenever you declare an `@EnvironmentObject`, you're telling your app to retain a single instance of the object in memory and allow any view you specify to access it. You need to declare it in each desired view for this to work.

Adding a user profile state

You've already decided that your `WelcomeView` and your `RegisterView` need to share some information. Initially, you identified the shared information to be the name of your user:

```
/// RegisterView
struct RegisterView {

  @State var name: String = ""

  @State var isRegistered: Bool = false
```

```
/// WelcomeView
struct WelcomeView {

  @State private var showHome = false
```

```
    private let name: String

    init(name: String) {
      self.name = name
    }
}
```

That's a good start, but you can abstract that idea up and consider a broader data model that represents your entire user throughout your app.

You'll start by representing your user in a `Profile` structure. Add a new **Profile.swift** file to your project, under **Profile**, and write the following code:

```
/// Profile of the learner using the app.
struct Profile {
  /// (Selected) name of the learner.
  var name: String

  /// Initializes a new `Profile` with an empty `name`.
  init() {
    self.name = ""
  }
}
```

With this, you have a fairly basic struct representing a user profile. You have a property —name — but little else. You can easily extend this later to provide more useful profile information, but for now, this is a good start: you have `name`.

If you want to share this `Profile` throughout your SwiftUI app easily, you're going to need to turn this into an `@EnvironmentObject`. Instead of modifying your rather elegant `Profile` struct, you're going to create an object specifically for managing user information across views. You'll call this your `User` object.

Still in the **Profile** group, add a new **User.swift** file and add the following code:

```
import Combine

final internal class User {

  @Published var isRegistered: Bool = false

  var profile: Profile = Profile()

  init(name: String) {
    self.profile.name = name
  }

  init() { }
}
```

You're storing your `Profile` struct as a property in your `User` object. Semantic code is great, and referencing your `name` property through `User.profile.name` is fairly pretty.

Right now, this may seem heavy-handed (a class, with a struct, for a `name` variable), but you want to separate your view state model (`User`) from your general data model (`Profile`). Conflating view state models in SwiftUI with traditional plain-old data models is a habit you don't want to start building at this early stage.

You've also added an `isRegistered` property with a property wrapper named `@Published`. This is a simple way of sending notifications to subscribers of state objects in SwiftUI. In this case, you're using it to notify subscribers that the user has been registered.

You'll extend your `User` object by declaring it as an `ObservableObject`. To keep protocol implementation code clean and easy to find, add a new file named **User+ObservableObject.swift**. This is the Apple way of name extension code files, with the class name following by the plus symbol and the name of the protocol:

```
import Combine

extension User: ObservableObject {

}
```

`User` should conform to `ObservableObject`, to do so, add a new instance variable called `willChange` as a `PassthroughSubject` object in your **User.swift** file:

```
let willChange = PassthroughSubject<User, Never>()
```

> **Note**: Without going too deeply into Combine or `PassthroughSubject`, simply understand that this is how objects notify SwiftUI that they have changed and, therefore, that all bindings should be updated. It's a publisher–subscriber mechanism, not too dissimilar to `NotificationCenter`, but much simpler for managing SwiftUI state. You may be wondering how this compares to `@Published`; the simple answer is to say that they both support similar objectives, but `@Published` provides less control with greater ease of implementation, and `PassthroughSubject` provides better control while requiring additional code.

`PassthroughSubject` is how you send value changes to SwiftUI components. It takes two objects: `Output` and `Failure`.

The first, `Output`, is any object you wish to send as part of our notification. In this case, you're going to send the `User` object itself, but you actually could send *nothing* as your `View` will update regardless as it will hold a reference to the original `User` object.

For consumers of this notification, who have no ready reference to your `User` object, it's useful to specify the object as part of the message. Therefore, you're going to make it easier for future developers of this project by sending the object right from the start.

The second parameter, `Failure`, is designated as an implementation of `Error` and is used in case something goes wrong. There's not really a use case where something could go wrong with your simple user profile, so you're going to leave the `Failure` as `Never` in this example.

> **Note**: This may seem familiar to those of you who have written publisher-subscriber code before, especially with `NotificationCenter`. This will make your `User` object, or any `ObservableObject`, for that matter, a publisher, and any SwiftUI component bound to it, a subscriber. This differs from `NotificationCenter` in that it makes use of the `ObservableObject` protocol to automatically manage subscribers (or "observers") and invalidate any subscribing views who reference the state. This is simpler than `Notification` for UI flow, but doesn't make `NotificationCenter` obsolete by any means.

You now need to use your `PassthroughSubject` object. You do that by sending the changes in the `profile` property's `willSet` closure. Modify it to look like this:

```
var profile: Profile = Profile() {
  willSet {
    willChange.send(self)
  }
}
```

You may see examples elsewhere using `DispatchQueue` to run the notification messaging on a specific thread like below:

```
DispatchQueue.main.async {
  self.willChange.send()
}
```

Combine will optimally run all messages on the main thread by default, so you can omit this in your code: It's unlikely that you'll find performance gains from explicit `DispatchQueue` code when simply sending mutation events.

Your new `willSet` block will now enable `User` to send, or "publish", itself to all subscribers when your `Profile` property changes. You can now declare your `User` object using `@EnvironmentObject` in both `WelcomeView` and `RegisterView`, making it a state object with a `User` binding.

Add the following code inside the main class in **WelcomeView.swift** and **RegisterView.swift**:

```
@EnvironmentObject var user: User
```

If you try and run this, without some additional `@EnvironmentObject` setup code, you will get a fatal runtime error: "No bindable object of type User.Type found". You still need one more change for your `@EnvironmentObject` to work.

Initiating the environment state scope

In **SceneDelegate.swift**, where you instantiate your `UIWindowScene`, you will need to pass the `@EnvironmentObject` into your `StarterView`. All `View` objects support this with the `environmentObject` method which you can call immediately after the `StarterView` constructor.

Change:

```
let practice = PracticeStore()

let window = UIWindow(windowScene: windowScene)
window.rootViewController = UIHostingController(
  rootView: StarterView(isRegistered: false, name: "")
    .environmentObject(practice)
)
```

To:

```
let practice = PracticeStore()
let user = User()

let window = UIWindow(windowScene: windowScene)
window.rootViewController = UIHostingController(
  rootView: StarterView(isRegistered: false, name: "")
    .environmentObject(practice)
    .environmentObject(user)
)
```

After this, all of the `View` ancestor objects will be able to access your `User`'s `BindableObject` by simply declaring it within the `View` with the `@EnvironmentObject` attribute.

SwiftUI is performing some state magic for you here, but you may think that `@EnvironmentObject` feels similar to a global static object in that a single reference exists throughout your app. Such code would look like this:

```
public static class User {
    ...
}
```

This may leave you with a bad taste: Global state is something generally to be avoided. It also becomes inefficient as you extend your app to support more and increasingly complex models.

`@EnvironmentObject` does have scope limitations by design: It cannot simply be accessed unless it's already set up in an ancestor view (with `View.environmentObject(bindable: BindableObject)`). It's only available for those specific views where it's either passed in via the `environmentObject` call or as an ancestor of a view that has had it passed in previously. It also comes with built-in support for Combine, whereas your global static class would need another form of event handling.

If you have a model that needs to exist across non-hierarchical views, where you don't intend to pass the value down from parent `View` objects to child `View` objects, then `@EnvironmentObject` is a good option. User preferences, for example, are needed throughout multiple `View` objects across many apps to adjust the user experience based on settings.

Therefore, setting these up at the beginning of the app's lifecycle as an `@EnvironmentObject` is likely to be beneficial rather than a burden. It doesn't have the data creep of a static object, and it supports live/reactive updates of the views which depend on it.

Configuring the preview environment

As you're using the Xcode canvas feature to see previews of your `View` objects, you also need to ensure you set up regular previews correctly by configuring the appropriate state. Within your `PreviewProvider`, you can do this by passing in a new instance of the `User` object into the `View` object's `environmentObject` method.

Go to **WelcomeView.swift** inside the **Welcome** folder and change the **WelcomeView_Previews** struct accordingly:

```
#if DEBUG
struct WelcomeView_Previews: PreviewProvider {
  static var previews: some View {
    WelcomeView(name: "Ray")
      .environmentObject(User())
  }
}
#endif
```

Note that this is similar to how the **SceneDelegate.swift** file is written to configure the `StarterView`. Each preview that depends on an `@EnvironmentObject` should be configured similarly.

If you ignore the binding and event communication tools provided through Combine and enabled by `ObservableObject`, you'd be correct in discounting `@EnvironmentObject` as little more than a global static state API.

The power of the environment

However, `@EnvironmentObject` is much more efficient and can be used exceptionally well where it makes sense to share an environment state. Apple has some of its environment states available to allow your app to respond to state changes within the user's device itself, such as the following example which monitors the `Locale` environment object:

```
@Environment(\.locale) var locale: Locale
```

Using the `@Environment` will enable access to the system-wide environment settings. By binding it to a `View`, you can ensure your app responds to external changes to settings for language, calendar and locale settings among others.

In those cases where you want to limit the scope of your state — and to be fair, that should be the majority of cases — there is a more efficient tool that fits nicely between `@State` and `@EnvironmentObject`: `@ObservedObject`.

The happy middle-ground: @ObservedObject

Not be confused with the `ObservableObject` protocol, the `@ObservedObject` is an attribute that implements the `ObservableObject` protocol in a manner similar to `@EnvironmentObject`. It provides a way to create state-managed objects that may (or may not) be used in multiple views, but that aren't part of the app environment state. In other words, unlike `@EnvironmentObject`, `@ObservedObject` is not automatically accessible across all views and must be passed down from the parent objects to be usable.

At first glance, the fact that `@State` can be passed down might make you wonder how `@ObservedObject` helps you. `@State` bindings are internally owned by the view in which they're created, and therefore, changes in child views can't be automatically reflected for complex objects. `@State` also only tracks the single value type, or binding, and does not support subscribing to, or messaging from, property changes beyond that.

`@ObservedObject` makes use of Combine to send updates to all subscribers (or bound views) in the same way the `@EnvironmentObject` does, without the required setup or global state concern. It requires management from the developer, and is preferable for externally referenced objects as it's much more powerful than `@State`.

When the view hierarchy requires changes to operate across multiple views based on state changes, hoisting the data into a common ancestor can centralize your source of truth and enable composite views to be rendered efficiently. SwiftUI checks which subviews are invalidated, and it only tears down and rebuilds those as necessary.

In cases where you want to manage state in a single view, you may be tempted to opt for multiple plain old variables to manage multiple state values. For example:

```
struct ProfileView {
    private var sessionsPlayed: Int
    private var name: String
    private var topScore: Int
```

However, due to `View` objects being structs, their properties are immutable. Therefore, the `@State` wrapper is a useful enabler for mutable properties within views. This can often lead to an overdependence on using multiple `@State` objects when you want to update `View` implementations with values.

There is a better way; as you may have guessed, it's @ObservedObject. Consider whether multiple values can be grouped into a new @ObservedObject model instead and raised to a common ancestor.

Moving from environment to hierarchical state

In your app, you lazily made your `PracticeStore` an `@EnvironmentObject` in the beginning because you didn't want to manage scope within your view hierarchy. This isn't good practice as nothing above the `PracticeView` needs to access the `PracticeStore`, and you certainly don't need to instantiate it at the beginning of your app.

Instead, you'd want to create a new `PracticeStore` each time you start a new practice session, such as when you revisit `PracticeView`. This is a perfect application for your new friend `@ObservedObject`.

Start by refactoring your code for a more refined state attachment throughout your view hierarchy. You'll begin with your **SceneDelegate.swift** by removing the call to `environmentObject` in your `scene` function.

Change this code block:

```
let practice = PracticeStore()
let user = User()

let window = UIWindow(windowScene: windowScene)
window.rootViewController = UIHostingController(
  rootView: StarterView(isRegistered: false, name: "")
    .environmentObject(practice)
    .environmentObject(user)
)
```

To:

```
let user = User()

let window = UIWindow(windowScene: windowScene)
window.rootViewController = UIHostingController(
  rootView: StarterView()
    .environmentObject(user)
)
```

This will stop `PracticeStore` from being available to all ancestors throughout the environment. Now you're back to using only one `@EnvironmentObject`, and it's the `User` object you created earlier. That makes more sense.

Your next step is to modify `PracticeView` where you've initially declared the `PracticeStore` state. Open up **PracticeView.swift**. You can modify the declaration line to remove the `@EnvironmentObject` as you're no longer going to rely on the `PracticeStore` as the view state representation.

Modify the following code from this:

```
@EnvironmentObject private var practiceStore: PracticeStore
```

To this:

```
private let practiceStore: PracticeStore
```

> **Note**: You've also made the store a constant as it can be, and *should* be, immutable.

To avoid any errors, update `init()` as well:

```
init() {
  practiceStore = PracticeStore()
}
```

You're now going to push the state down to `ChallengeView`: the view responsible for the current challenge within your practice session. You'll change it from an `@EnvironmentObject` to an `@ObservedObject` state object. Go to **ChallengeView.swift** and modify `practiceStore` to look like this:

```
@ObservedObject private var practiceStore: PracticeStore
```

> **Note**: After changing the practiceStore PropertyWrapper in ChallengeView from an `@EnvironmentObject` to an `@ObservedObject` the init for ChallengeView in PractiveView and in ChallengeView_Previews needs to be updated.

You can ensure the scope is private because you'll have initialized the model in `init()`. Change `init()` to look like this:

```
init(onComplete: @escaping () -> Void, practice: PracticeStore)
{
  self.onComplete = onComplete
```

```
    self.practiceStore = practice
}
```

Your `PracticeView` will now be automatically subscribed to any changes within this instance of the `PracticeStore` model. Unlike `@EnvironmentObject`, you can instantiate multiple `PracticeStore` models independently from your ancestors if you wish, and you don't have to worry about polluting the environment state. When a new `PracticeView` is created, a new `PracticeStore` will also be initialized.

Hierarchical event chaos with state events

It can be incredibly tempting to begin using the power of state in SwiftUI to trigger events. After all, SwiftUI is about state and not user flow: This is a significant differentiator to how you managed apps with view controllers in AppKit and UIKit.

However, SwiftUI still uses actions and callbacks to respond to events just as UIKit did. Not everything needs to be thrown out with SwiftUI, and even `NotificationCenter` has its place within event and data flow management.

This awareness applies to your `PracticeView`: You don't want to depend on your subviews to update your `PracticeScore` to know the practice session has completed. This adds unnecessary state observation, creates unevenness in the responsibility of your views, and can complicate the rendering within your hierarchy.

This is due to the way Combine works, where each change triggers a re-evaluation of the state and the view subhierarchy. If you're not careful, multiple subviews could be forcing a rebuild in the parent view, resulting in inefficient, superfluous subview rebuilds or, sometimes, infinite loops of view rebuilds when a subview updates a parent view state model, which rebuilds the subview model, and so on.

Creating a subview like `ChoicesView`, where there's a single simple action to be taken, means you can treat `ChoicesView` like you'd treat a `Button` in SwiftUI. Within the initializer, you can pass in a closure for the action taken, with any suitable data passed back as part of the closure signature. In the case of our `ChoicesView`, you pass back the selection your user made from the potential answers list:

```
// ChoicesView (no new code added)
private let answer: (_ answer: String) -> Void

init(onSelected action: @escaping (_ answer: String) -> Void,
  answers: [String]) {
    self.answerSubmitted = action
    self.answers = answers
}
```

```
...
// Within the body of the View
Button(action: {
  self.answer(self.answers[index])
}, label: {
  Text(self.answers[index])
    .font(.title)
})
```

And with this, you can leave it up to the parent view to alter the state in `PracticeStore`:

```
// ChallengeView (no new code added)
// Subscribe to the PracticeStore instance
@ObservedObject private var practiceStore: PracticeStore

// Closure for passing up the completion of the session to the
parent view
private let onComplete: () -> Void

// Pass the completion closure into initializer and the practice
session for state binding.
init(onComplete: @escaping () -> Void, practice: PracticeStore)
{
  self.onComplete = onComplete
  self.practiceStore = practice
}

// In the body of ChallengeView
...
  ChoicesView(
    onSelected: answered,
    answers: wordAssessment?.answers ?? [String]()
  )
...

private func answered(_ answer: String) {
  // Check if the PracticeStore session is finished.
  // If so run the onComplete closure.
  if self.practiceStore.finished {
    onComplete()
  }
}
```

Reusable components don't own their own source of truth. That's what binding is for. With `ChallengeView`, you're passing only the values necessary to each subview with `ChallengeView` responsible for managing the binding.

Previously, view controllers were designed to keep views in-sync with the data, and developers were responsible for maintaining this code. `@ObservedObject` provides automatic dependency tracking, while the subview hierarchy has indirect dependencies, minimizing your sources of truth. Compared with your alternative, `@EnvironmentObject` can pass objects indirectly through the hierarchy, allowing the data to apply to the entire ancestor view hierarchy.

Combine and other beasts

You've covered most of what's key to state and data flow in SwiftUI, and you may have noticed much of the power with SwiftUI state flow is due to Combine, which you've only touched upon briefly. Later on, you'll cover the publisher mechanism in Combine and see how Apple's frameworks allow you to reactively update your UI when their state changes by using the `onReceive` closure in the `View` component.

Remember that SwiftUI doesn't remove the power of existing tools like `NotificationCenter` and closures; it simply provides a new set of tools to reduce boilerplate and simplify the flow in your app based on state.

Edging towards immutable access, where possible, is important. It can be all too easy to use `@State` for mutability, but you'll benefit greatly from discipline when managing your data flow and with limited use of `@State`, with `@ObservedObject` preferred in most cases.

And, lastly, understand your data. As with many software development disciplines, understanding your data, and your domain, will help to provide a much richer set of tools with which to build your projects.

Key points

Phew! That was a lot of information about state management. Hopefully, you're now more confident in building larger apps with various forms of state. In this chapter you've learned:

- How SwiftUI state differs from view flow with view controllers in **AppKit** and **UIKit**.
- Various approaches to managing state, including value type, object, and environment state.
- How binding mechanisms work to pass state changes back to parent views.

- How to use Combine's subscriber mechanism to send state objects to subscribing views.

- Introducing state isn't always the answer, and custom event callbacks, such as closures, are still recommended in many cases.

In the next chapter, you'll dive further into SwiftUI controls, focusing more on control flow and navigation.

Where to go from here?

You've only covered the basics of state so far. To get the most out of state with SwiftUI, there's a wealth of material that continues to grow and evolve. These include:

- SwiftUI documentation: apple.co/2MlBqJJ

- State and Data Flow reference documentation: https://developer.apple.com/documentation/swiftui/stateanddataflow

And to become a power SwiftUI developer, you'd do well to check out the **Combine** documentation: https://developer.apple.com/documentation/combine

Chapter 8: Controls & User Input

By Antonio Bello

In Chapter 6, you learned how to use two of the most commonly used controls: Text and Image. In this chapter, you'll learn more about other commonly-used controls, such as TextField, Button,Stepper, and more, as well as the power of refactoring.

A simple registration form

The **Welcome to Kuchi** screen you implemented in Chapter 6 was good to get you started with Text and Image, and to get your feet wet with modifiers. Now, you're going to add some interactivity to the app by implementing a simple form to ask the user to enter her name.

The starter project for this chapter is nearly identical to the final one from Chapter 6 — that's right, you'll start from where you left off. The only difference is that you'll find some new files included needed to get your work done for this chapter.

A bit of refactoring

Often, you'll need to refactor your work to make it more reusable, and to minimize the amount of code you write for each view. This is a pattern that's used frequently and often recommended by Apple.

The new registration view you will be building will have the same background image as the welcome view you created in Chapter 6. Here's the first case where refactoring will come in handy. You could simply copy code from the welcome view and paste it, but that's not very reusable and maintainable, is it?

So, open **WelcomeView.swift**, select the following lines of code, which define the background image, and copy them:

```
Image("welcome-background")
  .resizable()
  .aspectRatio(1 / 1, contentMode: .fill)
  .edgesIgnoringSafeArea(.all)
  .saturation(0.5)
  .blur(radius: 5)
  .opacity(0.08)
```

Then, create a new component view by right-clicking the **Components** group, and creating a new SwiftUI View named **WelcomeBackgroundImage.swift**. Then, paste in the body implementation the code you've copied above (replacing the TextView it contains). The body should now look as follows:

```
var body: some View {
  Image("welcome-background")
    .resizable()
    .aspectRatio(1 / 1, contentMode: .fill)
    .edgesIgnoringSafeArea(.all)
    .saturation(0.5)
    .blur(radius: 5)
    .opacity(0.08)
}
```

Now, go back to **WelcomeView.swift** and replace the lines of code you previously copied with the newly created view, so that it looks like this:

```
var body: some View {
  ZStack {
    WelcomeBackgroundImage()

    HStack {
      ...
```

Ensure that automatic preview is enabled (resume it if necessary), and you'll notice that nothing has changed, which is what you'd expect — because you refactored your code without making any functional changes.

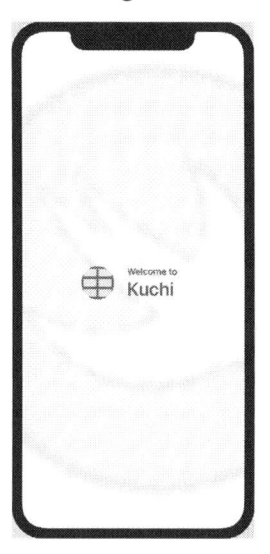

Since the topic of this section is refactoring, you'll go a step further and refactor:

- The icon image that's displayed in the welcome view

- The entire welcome view, composed by the icon and the "Welcome to Kuchi" text

> **Exercise**: Now that you've unlocked the *SwiftUI refactoring ninja* achievement, why don't you try to do the two refactoring on your own, and then compare your work with how it's been done below? You can name the two new views `LogoImage` and `WelcomeMessageView`.

Refactoring the logo image

In **WelcomeView.swift** select the code for the Image:

```
Image(systemName: "table")
    .resizable()
    .frame(width: 60, height: 60, alignment: .center)
    .border(Color.gray, width: 1)
    .background(Color(white: 0.9))
    .clipShape(Circle())
    .foregroundColor(.red)
```

Then:

- Copy the code to your clipboard.
- Replace the code with `LogoImage()`.
- Create a new **LogoImage.swift** file in the **Components** group, using the **SwiftUI** template.
- Replace the body implementation of **LogoImage.swift** with the code you've copied from the welcome view.

If you open **WelcomeView.swift** and resume the preview, once again you won't notice any differences — which means the refactoring worked.

Refactoring the welcome message

In **WelcomeView.swift**, select the entire `HStack` block, then:

- Copy the code to your clipboard.
- Replace the code with `WelcomeMessageView()`.
- Create a new **WelcomeMessageView.swift** file in the **Components** group, using the **SwiftUI** template.
- Replace the body implementation of **WelcomeMessageView.swift** with the code you've copied from the welcome view.

Once again, if you open **WelcomeView.swift** and resume the preview, you won't notice any difference.

Good job! You've just refactored the welcome view making it, and the components it consists of, much more reusable.

Creating the registration view

The new registration view is... well, new, so you'll have to create a file for it. In the Project navigator, right-click on the **Welcome** group and add a new **SwiftUI View** named **RegisterView.swift**.

Next, replace its body implementation with:

```
VStack {
  WelcomeMessageView()
}
```

And with a single line of code, you've just proved how easy and powerful reusable small components can be.

You can also add a background view, which, thanks to the previous refactoring, is as simple as adding a couple lines of code. Replace the body implementation with this code:

```
ZStack {
  WelcomeBackgroundImage()
  VStack(content: {
    WelcomeMessageView()
  })
}
```

Voilà, lunch is served. Faster than a microwave!

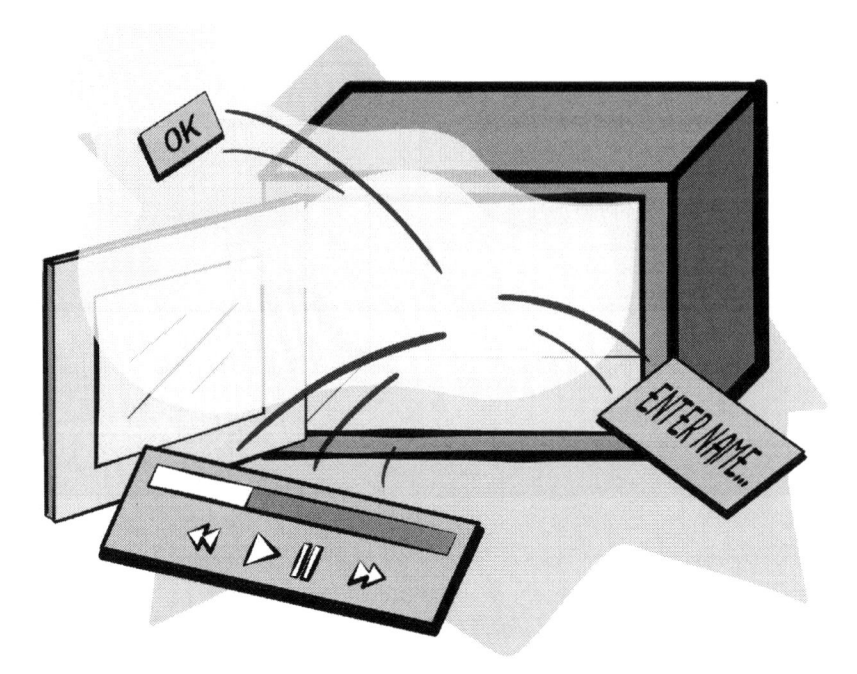

If you try to *run* the app, you'll notice it still displays the welcome view. That's because the app is still configured to display that view on launch. To fix it, open **SceneDelegate.swift**, and in the piece of code where the root view controller is created:

```
window.rootViewController = UIHostingController(
  rootView: WelcomeView()
)
```

Replace `WelcomeView` with `RegistrationView`:

```
window.rootViewController = UIHostingController(
  rootView: RegisterView()
)
```

Power to the user: the TextField

With the refactoring done, you can now focus on giving the user a way to enter her name into the app.

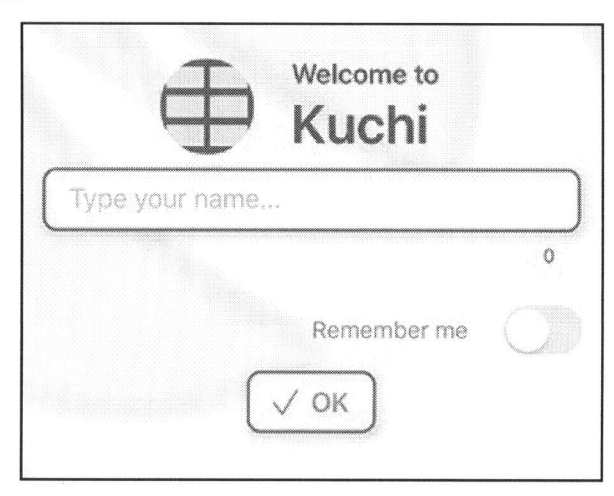

In the previous section, you added a VStack container, and that wasn't a random decision, because you need it now to stack content vertically.

TextField is the control you use to let the user enter data, usually by way of the keyboard. If you've built an iOS or MacOS app before, you've probably met its older cousins, UITextField and NSTextField.

In its simplest form, you can add the control using the initializer that takes a title and a text binding.

The title is the *placeholder* text that appears inside the text field when it is empty, whereas the binding is the managed property that takes care of the 2-way connection bewtween the text field's text and the property itself.

As in Chapter 7, "State and Data Flow", you create a binding by adding the @State attribute to a property, and prefixing the property with $ to pass the binding instead of the property value.

Add this property to RegisterView:

```
@State var name: String = ""
```

And then add the text field after WelcomeMessageView():

```
TextField("Type your name...", text: $name)
```

You'd expect a text field to appear in the preview, but nothing happens — it looks the same as before. What gives?

A closer inspection reveals the problem: if you double-click `TextField` in the code editor, you'll notice that the text field gets selected in the preview — it's just that it's too wide, as you can see from the blue rectangle:

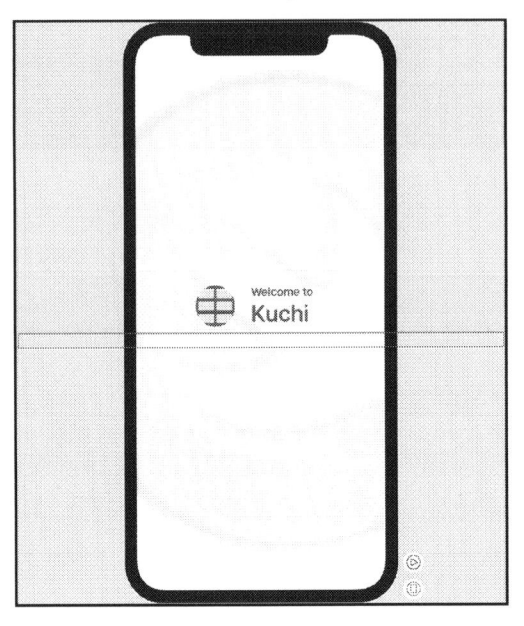

> **Challenge**: can you figure out why is this happening? Hint: it's caused by the background image.

The reason is that the background image is configured with `.fill` content mode, which means that the image expands to occupy as much of the parent view space as possible. Because the image is a square, it fits the parent vertically, but that means that, horizontally, it goes way beyond the screen boundaries.

The way to fix this is to avoid using a `ZStack` and to position the background view behind the actual content using the `.background` modifier on the `VStack` instead.

Remove the `ZStack` from the register view, and then add `WelcomeBackgroundImage()` as a `.background` modifier to the `VStack`:

```
var body: some View {
  VStack(content: {
    WelcomeMessageView()
```

```
        TextField("Type your name...", text: $name)
    })
    .background(WelcomeBackgroundImage())
}
```

> **Note**: In UIKit, views have a `backgroundColor` property, which can be used to specify a uniform background color. The SwiftUI counterpart is more polymorphic; the `.background` modifier accepts any type that conforms to `View`, which includes `Color`, `Image`, `Shape`, among others.

With this change, the text field is now visible.

Styling the TextField

Unless you're going for a very minimalistic look, you might not be satisfied with the text field's styling.

To make it look better, you need to add some padding and a border. For the border, you can take advantage of the `.textFieldStyle` modifier, which applies a style to the text field.

Currently, SwiftUI provides four different styles, which are compared in the image below:

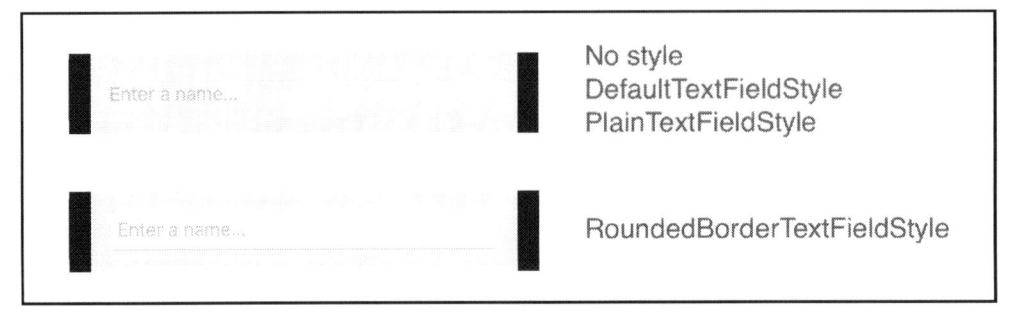

The "no style" case is explicitly mentioned, but it corresponds to `DefaultTextFieldStyle`. You can see that there's no noticeable difference between `DefaultTextFieldStyle` and `PlainTextFieldStyle`. However, `RoundedBorderTextFieldStyle` presents a border with slightly rounded corners. Note that there's also a fourth style, `SquareBorderTextFieldStyle`, but it's available on macOS only.

For Kuchi, you're going to provide a different, custom style. There are two options for this:

- Apply modifiers to the `TextField` as needed.

- Create your own text field style, by defining a concrete type conforming to the `TextFieldStyle` protocol.

At the time of writing, the latter option is not well-documented, and the protocol itself has an empty implementation. So it's not yet clear if or how it can be used for creating custom styles. Instead, you'll implement the custom style using modifiers to the text field.

Apply the following modifiers to the text field:

```
.padding(EdgeInsets(top: 8, leading: 16,
                    bottom: 8, trailing: 16))
.background(Color.white)
.overlay(
  RoundedRectangle(cornerRadius: 8)
    .stroke(lineWidth: 2)
    .foregroundColor(.blue)
)
.shadow(color: Color.gray.opacity(0.4),
        radius: 3, x: 1, y: 2)
```

The figure below shows the effect of each modifier:

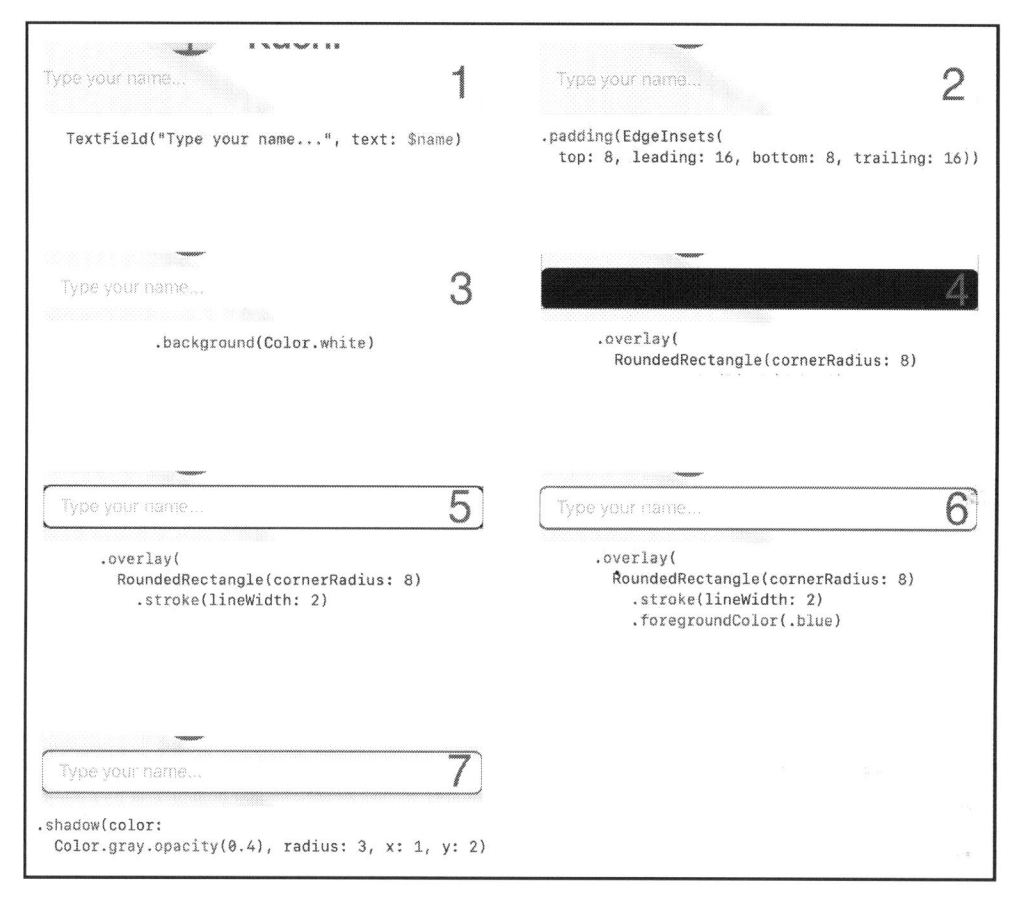

[Figure showing 7 text field variations:
1. `TextField("Type your name...", text: $name)`
2. `.padding(EdgeInsets(top: 8, leading: 16, bottom: 8, trailing: 16))`
3. `.background(Color.white)`
4. `.overlay(RoundedRectangle(cornerRadius: 8))`
5. `.overlay(RoundedRectangle(cornerRadius: 8).stroke(lineWidth: 2))`
6. `.overlay(RoundedRectangle(cornerRadius: 8).stroke(lineWidth: 2).foregroundColor(.blue))`
7. `.shadow(color: Color.gray.opacity(0.4), radius: 3, x: 1, y: 2)`]

This is what each does:

1. Creates an unmodified text field.

2. Adds a padding of 16 points vertically, and 8 points horizontally.

3. Adds a non-transparent white background.

4. Creates an overlay for the border, using a rounded rectangle with corner radius of 8.

5. Adds a stroke effect to keep the border only, leaving the content behind visible.

6. Makes the border blue.

7. Adds a shadow.

You'll notice that the text field has no spacing from the left and right edges; the padding you added in Step 2 adds padding between the actual text field and the view that contains it. To add a padding between the containing view and the parent view, you'll need to add a padding modifier to the view that contains the text field, the `VStack`.

In the containing `VStack`, right before `.background(WelcomeBackgroundImage())`, but after the stack's closing bracket, add the following:

```
.padding()
```

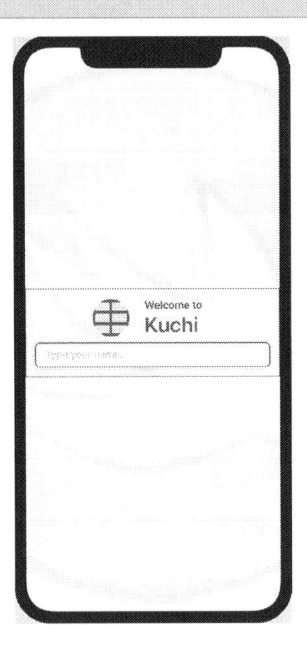

Creating a custom modifier

The border you've just created for the text field will be reused later for a button, so it would be a good idea to move it to a custom modifier that can be applied to any control.

Add a new file to the **Components** group using the **SwiftUI View** template, and name it **BorderedViewModifier**.

First, delete the autogenerated `BorderedViewModifier_Previews` strut. Next, change the protocol it conforms to from `View` to `ViewModifier`:

```
struct BorderedViewModifier: ViewModifier {
```

A `ViewModifier` defines a body member, but instead of being a property, it's a function that takes content — the view the modifier is applied to — and returns another view resulting from the modifier being applied to the content. Replace the property with the following function:

```
func body(content: Content) -> some View {
  content
}
```

The code, as is, returns the same view the modifier is applied to. Don't worry, you're not done yet! :]

Go back to `RegisterView.swift`, then *select and copy* all modifiers applied to the text field:

```
.padding(EdgeInsets(top: 8, leading: 16,
                    bottom: 8, trailing: 16))
.background(Color.white)
.overlay(
  RoundedRectangle(cornerRadius: 8)
    .stroke(lineWidth: 2)
    .foregroundColor(.blue)
)
.shadow(color: Color.gray.opacity(0.4),
        radius: 3, x: 1, y: 2)
```

Next, switch back to **BorderedViewModifier.swift** and paste these modifiers replacing the content of the struct:

```
func body(content: Content) -> some View {
  content
    .padding(EdgeInsets(top: 8, leading: 16,
                        bottom: 8, trailing: 16))
    .background(Color.white)
    .overlay(
      RoundedRectangle(cornerRadius: 8)
        .stroke(lineWidth: 2)
        .foregroundColor(.blue)
    )
    .shadow(color: Color.gray.opacity(0.4),
            radius: 3, x: 1, y: 2)
}
```

Now you can apply your new modifier to the `TextField`. To do that, you use a struct named `ModifiedContent`, whose initializer takes two parameters:

- The content view
- The modifier

Open `RegisterView`, and embed the `TextField` in a `ModifiedContent` instantiation, as follows:

```
ModifiedContent(
    content: TextField("Type your name...", text: $name),
    modifier: BorderedViewModifier()
)
```

After the preview updates, you see that the blue border is correctly applied. But hey, let's be honest, that code doesn't look fantastic. Wouldn't it be better if you could replace it with a simpler modifier call, like any regular modifier call?

Turns out all you need to do is create a convenience method in a view extension. Open `BorderedViewModifier`, and add the following extension at the end of the file:

```
extension View {
    func bordered() -> some View {
        ModifiedContent(
            content: self,
            modifier: BorderedViewModifier()
        )
    }
}
```

Now, you can go back to `RegisterView` and replace the `ModifiedContent` component with the following:

```
TextField("Type your name...", text: $name)
    .bordered()
```

The preview will confirm that the modifier is correctly applied.

A peek at TextField's initializer

`TextField` has two pairs of initializers, with each pair having a localized and non-localized version for the title parameter.

The version used in this chapter is the non-localized version that takes a title and a binding for the editable text:

```
public init<S>(
    _ title: S,
    text: Binding<String>,
    onEditingChanged: @escaping (Bool) -> Void = { _ in },
    onCommit: @escaping () -> Void = {}
) where S : StringProtocol
```

There are two parameters that you haven't used here, and further, that you haven't explicitly provided as they have empty implementation by default. These parameters are two closures that can be used to perform additional processing before and after the user input:

- onEditingChanged: Called when the edit obtains focus (when the Boolean parameter is true) or loses focus (when the parameter is false).

- onCommit: Called when the user performs a commit action, such as pressing the return key. This is useful when you want to move the focus to the next field automatically.

The other pair of initializers take an additional formatter. The non localized version has this signature:

```
public init<S, T>(
    _ title: S,
    value: Binding<T>,
    formatter: Formatter,
    onEditingChanged: @escaping (Bool) -> Void = { _ in },
    onCommit: @escaping () -> Void = {}
) where S : StringProtocol
```

The differences from the other pair are such:

1. The formatter parameter, which is an instance of a class inherited from Foundation's abstract class Formatter. It's usable when the edited value is of a different type than String — for instance, a number or a date — but you can also create custom formatters.

2. The T generic parameter determines the actual underlying type handled by the TextField.

For more information about formatters, take a look at **Data Formatting** apple.co/2MNqO7q.

Showing the keyboard

If you're letting the user type data in, sooner or later you'll have to display the software keyboard. Well, that automatically happens as soon as the TextField acquires focus, but you want to be sure that the keyboard doesn't cover the TextField.

If you change the iOS Simulator to **iPhone 8** and run the app, you'll notice that when the keyboard is visible, it's too close to the text field, although in this case it doesn't actually overlap.

A very basic implementation of a keyboard handler is provided with the project, which you can find in **Utils/KeyboardFollower.swift**.

It uses Notification Center to subscribe for the `keyboardWillChangeFrameNotification` event, which stores a property `keyboardHeight` that contains the keyboard's height. This is equal to zero if the keyboard is hidden, and a value greater than zero if it is visible.

So, you can subscribe for changes and use the keyboard's height to alter the bottom padding of the view containing the `TextField`.

The first thing to do is add a new property directly after name, in `RegisterView`:

```
@ObservedObject var keyboardHandler: KeyboardFollower
```

Next, you need to initialize this property. For this, you can use dependency injection, which means you're passing an instance of `KeyboardFollower` through the initializer.

Add the following to `RegisterView` below the `keyboardHandler` property:

```
init(keyboardHandler: KeyboardFollower) {
  self.keyboardHandler = keyboardHandler
}
```

You need to pass this parameter in all places where `RegisterView` is instantiated. Scroll down to the preview provider, and change the `previews` property implementation to this:

```
RegisterView(keyboardHandler: KeyboardFollower())
```

Next, open **SceneDelegate.swift** and do the same:

```
window.rootViewController = UIHostingController(
  rootView: RegisterView(keyboardHandler: KeyboardFollower())
)
```

Almost done! Lastly, you need to add a bottom padding modifier to the `VStack`, using `keyboardHandler.keyboardHeight` for the length parameter. Add it before all other modifiers in the `VStack`:

```
.padding(.bottom, keyboardHandler.keyboardHeight)
```

With this line, you're telling SwiftUI to apply a dynamic padding, to the bottom of the containing view, that follows the following rules:

- When the keyboard is not visible, `keyboardHandler.keyboardHeight` is zero, so no padding is applied.

- When the keyboard is visible, `keyboardHandler.keyboardHeight` has a value greater than zero, so a padding equal to the keyboard height is applied.

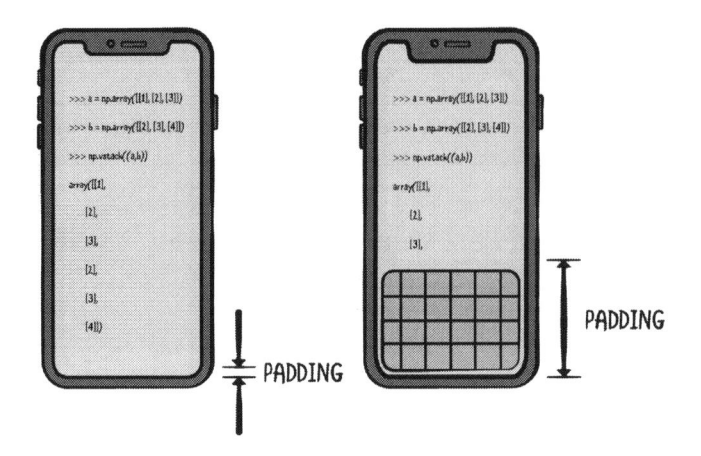

The body implementation should look like this:

```
VStack(content: {
  WelcomeMessageView()

  TextField("Type your name...", text: $name)
    .bordered()
})
  .padding(.bottom, keyboardHandler.keyboardHeight)
  .background(WelcomeBackgroundImage())
  .padding()
```

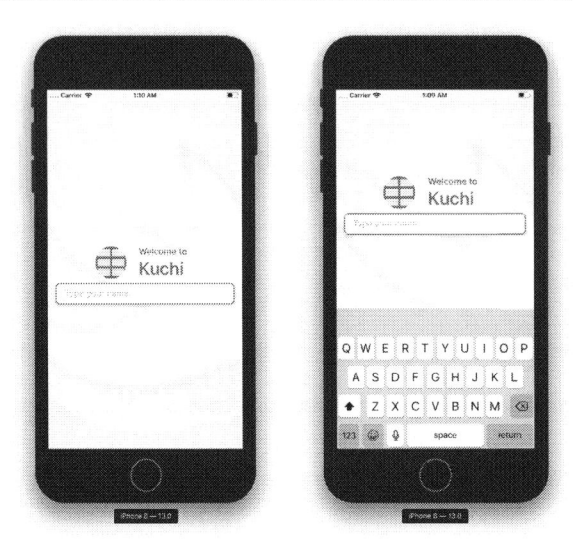

Taps and buttons

Now that you've got a form, the most natural thing you'd want your user to do is to submit that form. And the most natural way of doing *that* is by means of a dear old submit button.

The SwiftUI button is far more flexible than its UIKit/AppKit counterpart. You aren't limited to using a text label alone or in combination with an image for its content.

Instead, you can use anything for your button that's a `View`. You can see this from its declaration, which makes use of a generic type:

```
struct Button<Label> where Label : View
```

The generic type is the button's visual content, which must conform to `View`.

That means a button can contain not only a base component, such as a `Text` or an `Image`, but also any composite component, such as a pair of `Text` and `Image` controls, enclosed in a vertical or horizontal stack, or even anything more complex that you can dream up.

Adding a button is as easy as declaring it: you simply specify a label and attach a handler. Its signature is:

```
init(
    action: @escaping () -> Void,
    @ViewBuilder label: () -> Label
)
```

The initializer takes two parameters, which are actually two closures:

- **action**: the trigger handler
- **label**: the button content

The `@ViewBuilder` attribute applied to the `label` parameter is used to let the closure return multiple child views.

> **Note**: The tap handler parameter is referred to as **action** instead of **tap** or **tapAction** — and if you read the documentation, it's called a **trigger handler**, not **tap handler**.
>
> That's because in iOS it's a tap, in macOS it can be a mouse click, in watchOS a digital crown press, and so forth.

> **Note**: The button initializer takes the tap handler as the first parameter, instead of the last, breaking the common practice in Swift of giving action closures the last position.
>
> This means that you can use *trailing closure syntax*. The reason is very likely because that pattern changes in SwiftUI, and the last parameter is always the view declaration — which, by the way, can use the same trailing closure syntax.

Submitting the form

Although you can add an inline closure, it's better to avoid cluttering the view declaration with code. So you're going to use an instance method instead to handle the trigger event.

In `RegisterView` add the button after the `TextField`:

```
Button(action: self.registerUser) {
  Text("OK")
}
```

Then, add this extension, containing the `registerUser()` event handler:

```
// MARK: - Event Handlers
extension RegisterView {
  func registerUser() {
    print("Button triggered")
  }
}
```

Now run the app, either in the Simulator or by activating the **Live Preview**, and when you press **OK** a message will be printed to the Xcode console. If you've chosen Live Preview, and nothing is displayed, be sure to enable **Debug Preview** from the menu accessible by **right-clicking** the Live Preview button.

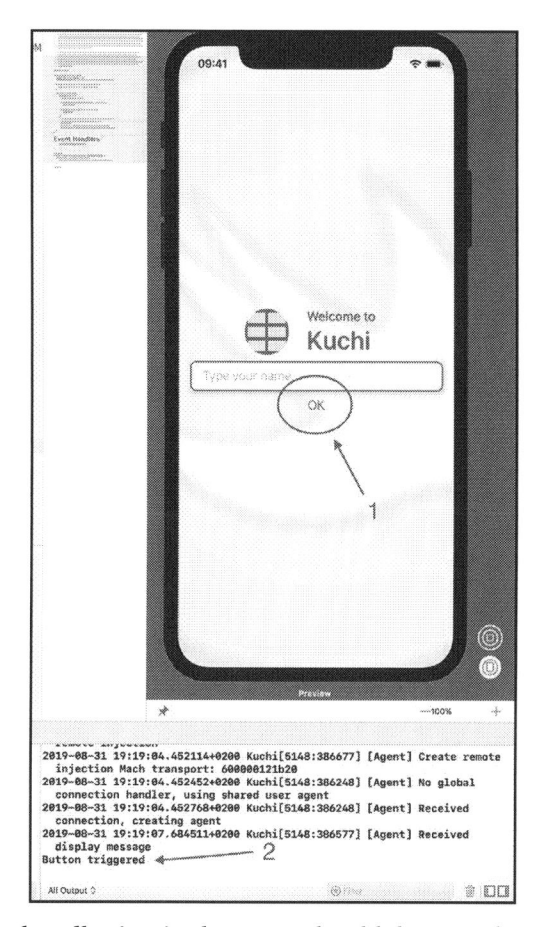

Now that the trigger handler is wired up, you should do something more useful than printing a message to the console. The project comes with a `UserManager` class that takes care of saving and restoring a user and the user settings respectively to and from the user defaults.

`UserManager` conforms to `ObservableObject`, a protocol that enables the class to be used in views. It triggers a view update when the instance state changes. This class exposes two properties — `profile` and `settings` – marked with the `@Published` attribute, which identifies the state that triggers view reloads.

That said, you can delete the name property in RegisterView, and replace with an instance of UserManager:

```
@EnvironmentObject var userManager: UserManager
```

It's marked with the @EnvironmentObject attribute because you're going to inject an instance of it once for the whole app, and retrieve it from the environment anywhere it is needed.

Next, in the TextField, you have to change the $name reference to $userManager.profile.name, so that it looks like the following:

```
TextField("Type your name...", text: $userManager.profile.name)
  .bordered()
```

Lastly, in registerUser() replace the print statement with this more useful implementation:

```
func registerUser() {
  userManager.persistProfile()
}
```

Now, if you try to preview this view, it will fail. That's because, as mentioned above, an instance of UserManager should be injected. You do this in the RegisterView_Previews struct, by passing a user manager to the view via a .environmentObject modifier. Update the RegisterView_Previews implementation so that it looks like:

```
struct RegisterView_Previews: PreviewProvider {
  static let user = UserManager(name: "Ray")

  static var previews: some View {
    RegisterView(keyboardHandler: KeyboardFollower())
      .environmentObject(user)
  }
}
```

Likewise, if you run the app in the Simulator, it will crash. The change you've just made is only for the preview, and it doesn't affect the app. You need to makes changes in SceneDelegate as well. Open SceneDelegate, find func scene(_:willConnectTo:options:) and add these to lines to the beginning of it:

```
let userManager = UserManager()
userManager.load()
```

This creates an instance of `UserManager`, and makes sure the stored user, if available, is loaded. Next, use the `environmentObject` modifier on the `RegisterView` instance to inject it:

```
window.rootViewController = UIHostingController(
  rootView: RegisterView(keyboardHandler: KeyboardFollower())
    .environmentObject(userManager)
)
```

Styling the button

The button is fully operative now; it looks good, but not *great*. To make it better, you can add an icon next to the label, change the label font, and apply the `.bordered()` modifier you created for the `TextField` earlier.

In **RegisterView.swift**, locate the button, and replace it with this code:

```
Button(action: self.registerUser) {
  // 1
  HStack {
    // 2
    Image(systemName: "checkmark")
      .resizable()
      // 3
      .frame(width: 16, height: 16, alignment: .center)
    Text("OK")
      // 4
      .font(.body)
      .bold()
  }
}
// 5
.bordered()
```

You should already be able to discern what this code does, but here's a breakdown:

1. As previously stated, the `label` parameter can return multiple child views, but here you're using a horizontal stack to group views horizontally. If you omit thisz, the two components will be laid out vertically instead.

2. You add a checkmark icon.

3. You make the icon centered, and with fixed 16×16 size.

4. You change the label font, specifying a `.body` type and a bold weight.

5. You apply the `.bordered` modifier, to add a blue border with rounded corners.

If you did everything correctly, this is what your preview should look like:

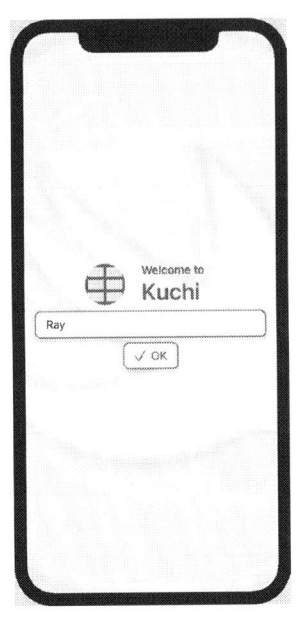

Reacting to input: validation

Now that you've concluded the whole keyboard affair, and you've added a button to submit the form, the next step in a reactive user interface is to react to the user input *while* the user is entering it. It might be quite useful for different reasons, such as:

- Validating the data while it is entered

- Showing a counter of the number of characters typed in

But the list doesn't end there. The old way of monitoring the input entered by the user in UIKit was either by way of a delegate or subscribing to a Notification Center event. You're likely tempted to look for a similar way to react to input changes, such as a modifier that takes a handler closure, which is called every time the user presses a key.

However, the SwiftUI way to monitor for input changes is different.

Say you want to validate the user input, and keep the OK button disabled until the input is valid. In the old days, you'd subscribe for a value changed event, perform a logical expression to determine whether to enable or disable the button, and then update the button state.

The difference in SwiftUI is that you pass the logical expression to a button's modifier, and… there is no "and". That's all. When a status change occurs, the view is rerendered, the logical expression is re-evaluated, and the button's `disabled` status is updated.

In **RegisterView.swift**, add this modifier to the OK button:

```
.disabled(!userManager.isUserNameValid())
```

This modifier changes the `disabled` state. It belongs to the `View` protocol, so it's applicable to any view. It takes one parameter only: a Boolean stating whether the view is interactable or not.

When the user types in the `TextField`, the `userManager.profile.name` property changes, and that triggers a view update. So, when the button is rerendered, the expression in `.disabled()` is re-evaluated, and therefore the button state is automatically updated when the input changes.

In this app, the requirement for a name is that it has to be at least three characters long.

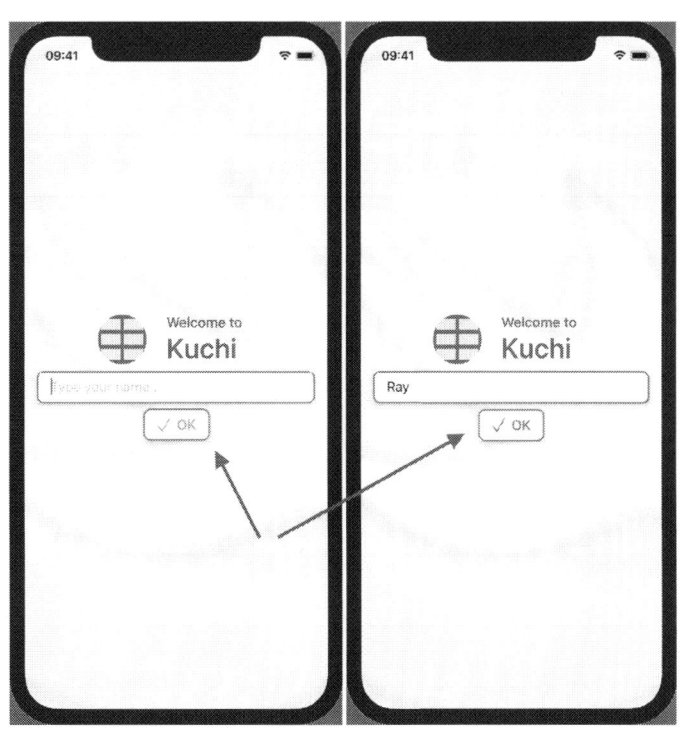

Reacting to input: counting characters

If you'd want to add a label showing the number of characters entered by the user, the process is very similar. After the `TextField`, add this code:

```
HStack {
  // 1
  Spacer()
  // 2
  Text("\(userManager.profile.name.count)")
    .font(.caption)
    // 3
    .foregroundColor(
      userManager.isUserNameValid() ? .green : .red)
    .padding(.trailing)
}
// 4
.padding(.bottom)
```

Going over this line-by-line:

1. You use a spacer to push the Text to the right, in a pseudo-right-alignment way.

2. This is a simple `Text` control, whose text is the count of characters of the `name` property.

3. You use a green text color if the input passes validation, red otherwise.

4. This adds some spacing from the OK button.

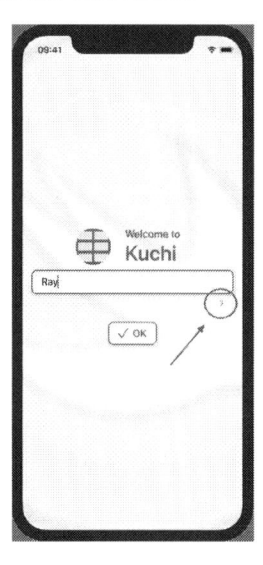

Toggle Control

Next up: a new component. The toggle is a Boolean control that can have an on or off state. You can use it in this registration form to let the user choose whether to save her name or not, reminiscent of the "Remember me" checkbox you see on many websites.

The `Toggle` initializer is similar to the one used for the `TextField`. Its initializer takes a binding and a label view:

```
public init(
    isOn: Binding<Bool>,
    @ViewBuilder label: () -> Label
)
```

For the binding, although you *could* use the state property owned by `RegsterView`, it's better to store it in a place that can be accessed from other views. The `UserManager` class already defines a `settings` property dedicated to that purpose.

After the `HStack` you added earlier for the name counter, and before the `Button`, add the following code:

```
HStack {
    Spacer()

    // 1
    Toggle(isOn: $userManager.settings.rememberUser) {
        // 2
        Text("Remember me")
            // 3
            .font(.subheadline)
            .foregroundColor(.gray)
    }
}
```

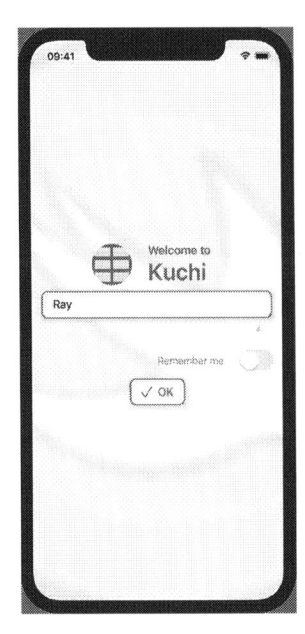

The code is very simple and straightforward:

1. You create the `Toggle` component, binding to `$userManager.settings.rememberUser`.

2. This is the label displayed before the component itself.

3. You alter the default style of the label to make it smaller and gray.

This change alone won't actually add anything functional to the app, besides storing the toggle state as a property. Replace the implementation of `registerUser()` with:

```
func registerUser() {
  // 1
  if userManager.settings.rememberUser {
    // 2
    userManager.persistProfile()
  } else {
    // 3
    userManager.clear()
  }

  // 4
  userManager.persistSettings()
}
```

In this updated version:

1. You check if the user chose whether to remember herself or not.

2. If yes, then make the profile persistent.

3. Otherwise, clear the user defaults.

4. Finally, store the settings.

To see this in effect, you need to run the app. The first time you run it, no user profile will stored. Enter a name, enable the "Remember me" toggle, and press OK; the next time you launch the app, it will prefill the `TextView` with the name you entered.

Other controls

If you've developed for iOS or macOS before you encountered SwiftUI, you know that there are several other controls besides the ones discussed so far. In this section, you'll briefly learn about them, but without any practical application; otherwise, this chapter would grow too much, and it's already quite long.

Slider

A slider is used to let the user select a numeric value using a cursor that can be freely moved within a specified range, by specific increments.

There are several initializer you can choose from, but probably the most used is:

```
public init<V>(
    value: Binding<V>,
    in bounds: ClosedRange<V>,
    step: V.Stride = 1,
    onEditingChanged: @escaping (Bool) -> Void = { _ in }
) where V : BinaryFloatingPoint, V.Stride : BinaryFloatingPoint
```

Which takes:

1. `value`: A value binding

2. `bounds`: A range

3. `step`: The interval of each step

4. `onEditingChanged`: An optional closure called when editing starts or ends

Below is an example of this in action:

```
@State var amount: Double = 0
...

VStack {
  HStack {
    Text("0")
    Slider(
      value: $amount,
      in: 0.0 ... 10.0,
      step: 0.5
    )
    Text("10")
  }
  Text("\(amount)")
}
```

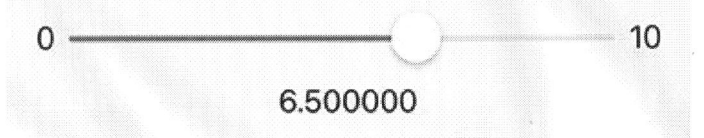

In this example, the slider is bound to the `amount` state property, and is configured with an interval ranging from 0 to 10, and increments and decrements in steps of 0.5.

The `HStack` is used to add two labels at the left and right of the slider, specifying respectively the minimum and maximum values. The `VStack`, instead, is used to position a centered `Text` control below the slider, displaying the currently selected value.

Stepper

`Stepper` is conceptually similar to `Slider`, but instead of a sliding cursor, it provides two buttons: one to increase and another to decrease the value bound to the control.

There are several initializers, with one of the most common ones being this:

```
public init<S, V>(
  _ title: S,
  value: Binding<V>,
  in bounds: ClosedRange<V>,
  step: V.Stride = 1,
  onEditingChanged: @escaping (Bool) -> Void = { _ in }
) where S : StringProtocol, V : Strideable
```

This takes the following arguments:

1. `title`: A title, usually containing the current bound value
2. `value`: A value binding
3. `bounds`: A range
4. `step`: The interval of each step
5. `onEditingChanged`: An optional closure called when editing starts or ends

An example if its usage is:

```
@State var quantity = 0.0
...

Stepper(
    "Quantity: \(quantity)",
    value: $quantity,
    in: 0 ... 10,
    step: 0.5
)
```

Quantity: 2.500000   − │ +

SecureField

`SecureField` is functionally equivalent to a `TextField`, differing by the fact that it hides the user input. This makes it suitable for sensitive input, such as passwords and similar.

It offers a few initializers, one of which is the following:

```
public init<S>(
    _ title: S,
    text: Binding<String>,
    onCommit: @escaping () -> Void = {}
) where S : StringProtocol
```

Similar to the controls described earlier, it takes the following arguments:

1. `title`: A title, which is the placeholder text displayed inside the control when no input has been entered
2. `text`: A text binding

3. `onCommit`: An optional closure called when the user performs a commit action, such as pressing the Return key.

To use it for entering a password, you'd write something like:

```
@State var password = ""
...

SecureField.init("Password", text: $password)
  .textFieldStyle(RoundedBorderTextFieldStyle())
```

Key points

Phew — what a long chapter. Congratulations for staying tuned and focused for so long! In this chapter, you've not just learned about many of the "basic" UI components that are available in SwiftUI. You've also learned the following facts:

- Refactoring and reusing views are two important aspects that should never be neglected or forgotten.
- You can create your own modifiers using `ViewModifier`.
- To handle user input, you use a `TextField` component or a `SecureField` if the input is sensitive.
- When the keyboard is displayed, you must take care of avoiding overlapping the `TextField`. For this, you can use Notification Center and the keyboard's height.
- Buttons are more flexible than their UIKit/AppKit counterparts, and enable you to make any collection of views into a button.
- Validating input is much easier in SwiftUI, because you simply set the rules, and SwiftUI takes care of applying those rules when the state changes.
- SwiftUI has other controls to handle user input, like toggles, sliders, and steppers.

Where to go from here?

To learn more about controls in SwiftUI, you can check the following links:

- Official Documentation: Views and Controls apple.co/2MQgZG1
- WWDC 2019 - SwiftUI Essentials apple.co/2Le3qy6

In the next chapter you'll learn more about view containers. See you there!

Chapter 9: Introducing Stacks and Containers

By Antonio Bello

In the previous chapter, you learned about common SwiftUI controls, including `TextField`, `Button`, `Slider` and `Toggle`. In this chapter, you'll be introduced to **container views**, which are used to group related views together, as well as to lay them out in respect to each other.

Before starting that, though, it's essential that you learn and understand how views are sized.

Layout and priorities

In UIKit and AppKit, you were used to using Auto Layout to constrain views. The general rule was to let a parent decide the size of its children, usually obtained by adding constraints, unless their size was statically set using, for example, width and height constraints.

To make a comparison with a family model, Auto Layout is a conservative model, or patriarchal to both parents, if you prefer.

SwiftUI works in the opposite fashion instead: the children choose their size, in response to a size proposed by the parent. It's more of a modern family model — if you have kids, you know what I mean!

If you have a Text, and you put it in a View, the Text is given a proposed size when the view is rendered, corresponding to the parent's frame size. However, the Text will calculate the size of the text to display, and will choose the size necessary to fit that text, plus additional padding, if any.

Layout for views with a single child

Open the starter project, which is an extension of the project you completed in the last chapter. Open **Practice/ChallengeView.swift**, which is a new view created out of the SwiftUI View template. You can see that it contains a single Text:

```
struct ChallengeView: View {
  var body: some View {
    Text("Hello World!")
  }
}
```

If you reactivate the preview in Xcode, you'll see the text displayed at the center of the screen.

> **Note**: Every view is positioned, by default, at the center of its parent.

This screenshot doesn't give any indication about the Text's frame size. Try adding a red background:

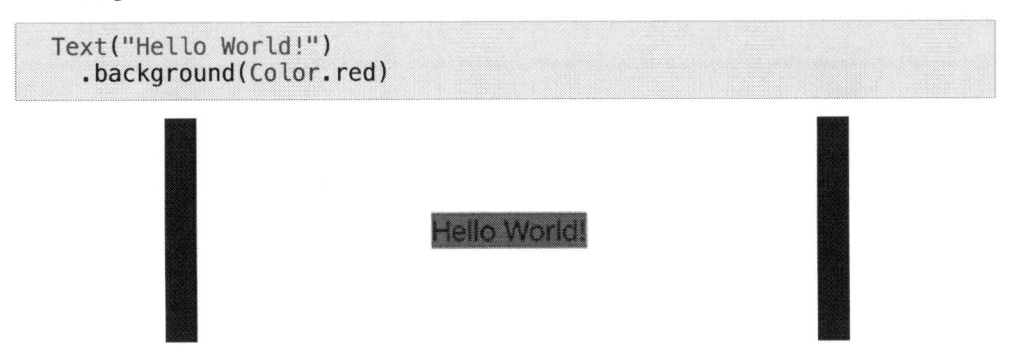

```
Text("Hello World!")
   .background(Color.red)
```

Now you can see that the `Text` sizes itself with the bare minimum to contain the text it renders. Change the text to `A great and warm welcome to Kuchi`:

```
Text("A great and warm welcome to Kuchi")
   .background(Color.red)
```

You'll see that the `Text` resizes its frame to accommodate the new content.

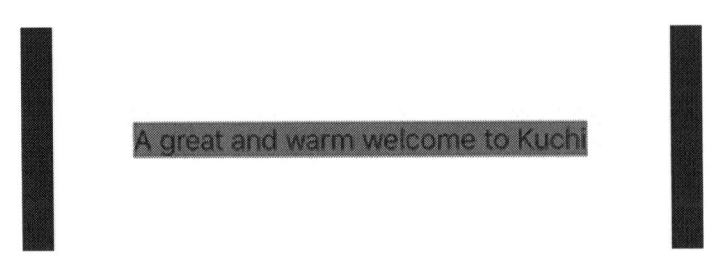

The rules that SwiftUI applies to determine the size of a parent view and a child view are:

1. The parent view determines the available frame at its disposal.
2. The parent view proposes a size to the child view.
3. Based on the proposal from the parent, the child view chooses its size.
4. The parent view sizes itself such that it contains its child view.

This process is recursive, starting at the root view, down to the last leaf view in the view hierarchy.

> **Note**: Each modifier applied to a view creates a new view which embeds the original view. The set of rules described above applies to all the views, regardless of whether they are individual components, or views generated by modifiers.

To see this in action, try specifying a fixed frame for `Text`, plus a new background color:

```
Text("A great and warm welcome to Kuchi")
    .background(Color.red)
    // fixed frame size
    .frame(width: 150, height: 50, alignment: .center)
    .background(Color.yellow)
```

Interestingly, you can see that the `Text` has a size, which differs from the size of the view created by the `.frame` modifier. This shouldn't surprise you, because the four rules described above are applied here:

1. The frame view has a fixed size of 150×50 points.

2. The frame view proposes that size to the `Text`.

3. The `Text` finds a way to display the text within that size, but using the minimum without having to truncate (when possible).

Rule 4 is skipped, because the frame view already has a defined size. The `Text` automatically arranges the text to display in two lines, because it realizes that it doesn't fit in a single line of maximum 150 points without truncation.

If you expand the frame size, you have an additional proof of how views determine their size. Try, for example, a larger 300×100 size:

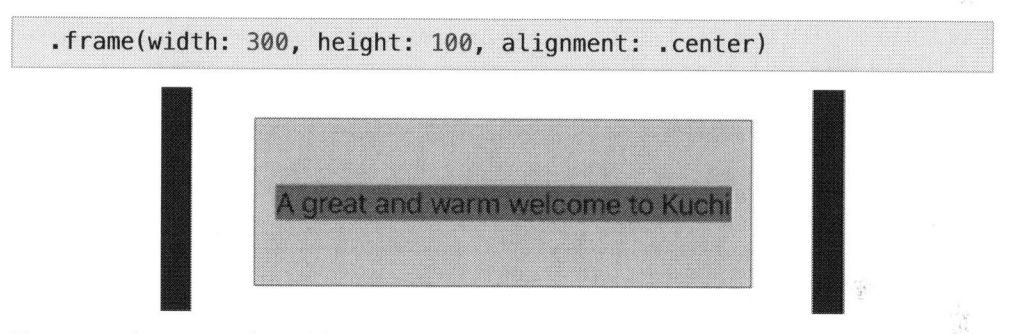

```
.frame(width: 300, height: 100, alignment: .center)
```

Now `Text` has enough width at its disposal to render the text in a single line. However, it still occupies the exact space needed to render the text (in red background), whereas the frame view uses the fixed frame size (in yellow background).

Can you guess what happens if the size of the parent view is not enough to contain the child view? In the case of a `Text`, it will just truncate the text. Try reducing its frame size to 100x50:

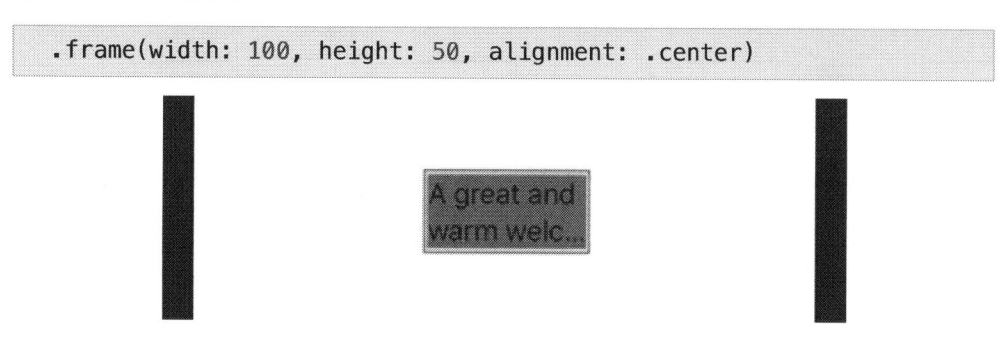

```
.frame(width: 100, height: 50, alignment: .center)
```

This happens in absence of other conditions, such as using
the `.minimumScaleFactor` modifier, which causes the text to shrink to the scale
factor passed as parameter, which is a value between 0 and 1:

```
Text("A great and warm welcome to Kuchi")
    .background(Color.red)
    .frame(width: 100, height: 50, alignment: .center)
    .minimumScaleFactor(0.5)
    .background(Color.yellow)
```

Generally speaking, the component will always try to fit the content within the size proposed by its parent. If the component can't do that because it needs more space, it will apply rules appropriate to, and strictly dependent, from the component type.

This reinforces the concept that, in SwiftUI, each view chooses its own size. It *considers* proposals made by its parent, and it tries to adapt to that suggestion to the best of its ability, but that's always dependent on what type of component the view is.

Take an image, for instance. In the absence of other constraints, it will be rendered at its original resolution, as you can see if you replace the `Text` component with an `Image`:

```
Image("welcome-background")
    .background(Color.red)
    .frame(width: 100, height: 50, alignment: .center)
    .background(Color.yellow)
```

This is the same image you used in Chapter 6, "Intro to Controls: Text and Image".

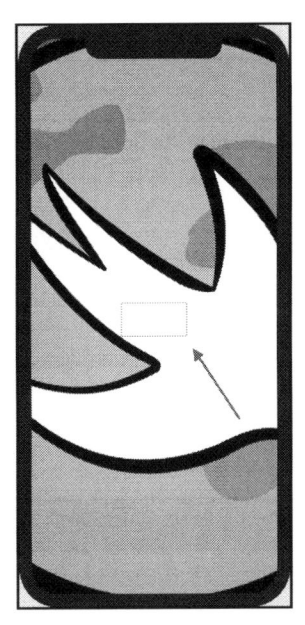

The red arrow highlights the 100×50 static frame, but you can see that the image has been rendered at its native resolution, completely ignoring the proposed size — at least in the absence of any other constraints, such as the `.resizable` modifier, which would enable the image to automatically scale up or down in order to occupy all the available space offered by its parent:

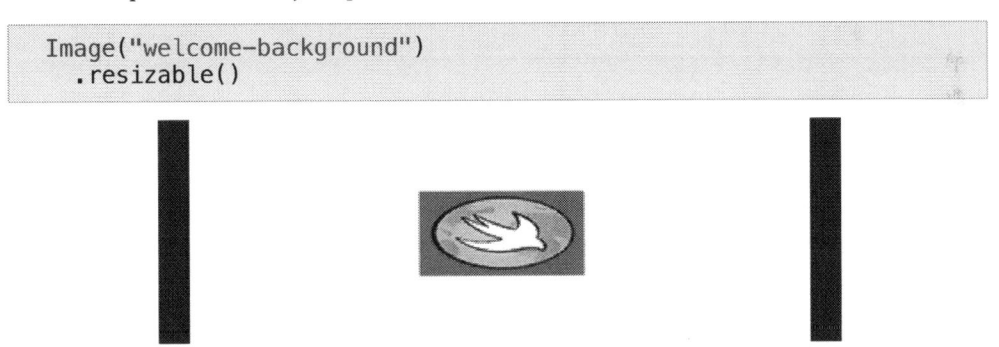

```
Image("welcome-background")
    .resizable()
```

So, in the end, you realize that there's no way for a parent to enforce a size on a child. What a parent *can* do is propose a size, and eventually constrain the child inside a frame of its choice, but that doesn't affect the ability of the child to choose a size that's smaller or larger.

Some components, like `Text`, will try to be *adaptive*, by choosing a size that best fits with the size proposed by the parent, but still with an eye to the size of the text to render. Other components, like `Image`, will instead simply disregard the proposed size.

In the middle, there are views which are more or less adaptive, but also neutral, meaning that they don't have any reason to choose a size. They will just pass that decision to their own children, and size themselves to merely wrap their children.

An example is the `.padding` modifier, which does not have an intrinsic size — it simply takes the child's size, adds the specified padding to each of the four edges (top, left, right, bottom), and uses that to create the view that embeds the child.

Stack views

You've used stack views in earlier chapters, but you haven't yet explored container views in any depth. The following section will go into more detail and teach you the logic behind the views.

Layout for container views

In the case of a container view, i.e., a view that contains two or more children views, the rules that determine children's sizes are:

1. The container view determines the available frame at its disposal, which usually is the size proposed by the parent.

2. **The container view selects the child view with the most restrictive constraints or, in case of equivalent constraints, with the smallest size.**

3. The container view proposes a size to the child view. **The proposed size is the available size divided equally by the number of** (the remaining) **children views.**

4. The child view, based on the proposal from the parent, chooses its size.

5. **The container view subtracts from the available frame the size chosen by the child view, and goes back to step no. 2, until all children views have been processed.**

The differences between this and the case of views with a single child that you've seen in the previous section are highlighted in bold text.

Back to the code! Restore the `Text` as it was before you replaced with the image, and duplicate it inside an `HStack`:

```
HStack {
  Text("A great and warm welcome to Kuchi")
```

```
      .background(Color.red)
    Text("A great and warm welcome to Kuchi")
      .background(Color.red)
  }
  .background(Color.yellow)
```

You've already encountered HStack in the previous chapters, so you should know that it lays out its children views horizontally. Since the two children are equal, you might expect that they have the same size. But this is what you get instead:

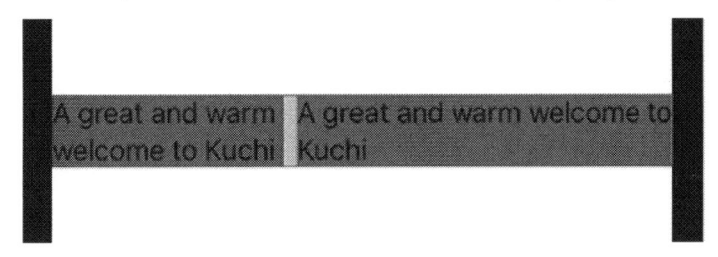

Why is that? A step-by-step breakdown is necessary here:

1. The stack receives a proposed size from its parent, and divides it in two equal parts.

2. The stack proposes the first size to one of the children. They are equal, so it sends the proposal to the first child, the one to the left.

3. The Text finds that it needs less than the proposed size, because it can display the text in two lines, and can format it such that the two lines have similar lengths.

4. The stack subtracts the size taken by the first Text and proposes the resulting size to the second Text.

5. The Text decides to use all the proposed size.

Now try making the second Text slightly smaller, by replacing an m with an n, for example, in the word warm:

```
Text("A great and warm welcome to Kuchi")
   .background(Color.red)
Text("A great and warn welcome to Kuchi") // <- Replace `m` with
                                          //    `n` in `warm`
   .background(Color.red)
```

Being smaller now, the second `Text` takes precedence; in fact, it's the first one to be proposed a size. The resulting layout is this:

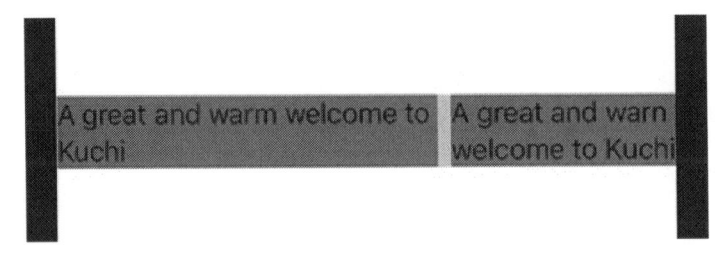

[figure: two Text boxes side by side, each showing "A great and warm welcome to Kuchi"]

You can experiment with the difference between longer and stronger texts in the two `Text` controls if you like.

Layout priority

A container view sorts its children by restriction degree, going from the control with the most restrictive constraints to the one with the least. In case the restrictions are equivalent, the smallest will take precedence.

However, there are cases when you will want to alter this order. This can be achieved in two different ways, usually for different goals:

- Alter the view behavior via a **modifier**.
- Alter the view's layout **priority**.

Modifier

You can use a modifier to make the view more or less adaptive. Examples include:

- `Image` is one of the least adaptive components, because it ignores the size proposed by its parent. But its behavior drastically changes after applying the `resizable` modifier, which enables it to blindly accept any size proposed by the parent.
- `Text` is very adaptive, as it tries to format and wrap the text in order to best fit with the proposed size. But it becomes less adaptive when it's forced to use a maximum number of lines, via the `lineLimit` modifier.

Changes of the adaptivity degree directly affect a control's weight in the sort order.

Priority

You also have the option of changing the layout priority using the `.layoutPriority` modifier. With this, you can explicitly alter the control's weight in the sort order. It takes a `Double` value, which can be either positive or negative. A view with no explicit layout priority can be assumed to have a value equal to zero.

Go back to the **ChallengeView.swift** file, and replace the view content with a stack of three Text copies:

```
HStack {
  Text("A great and warm welcome to Kuchi")
    .background(Color.red)

  Text("A great and warm welcome to Kuchi")
    .background(Color.red)

  Text("A great and warm welcome to Kuchi")
    .background(Color.red)
}
```

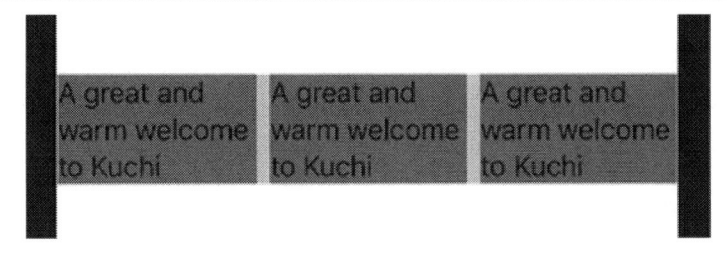

Now try some explicit priorities. You can use any scale when setting priorities; for example, limit to values in the [0, 1] or [-1, +1] range, or go for integer values only, and so forth.

What's important is that **Stack processes views starting from the absolute highest down to the absolute lowest**. If the absolute lowest is below zero, views without an explicitly priority are processed *before* all the ones with negative value.

Add a layout priority of 1 to the second `Text`:

```
HStack {
  Text("A great and warm welcome to Kuchi")
    .background(Color.red)

  Text("A great and warm welcome to Kuchi")
    .layoutPriority(1)
    .background(Color.red)

  Text("A great and warm welcome to Kuchi")
```

```
    .background(Color.red)
}
```

You can see that it is given the opportunity to use as much space as needed.

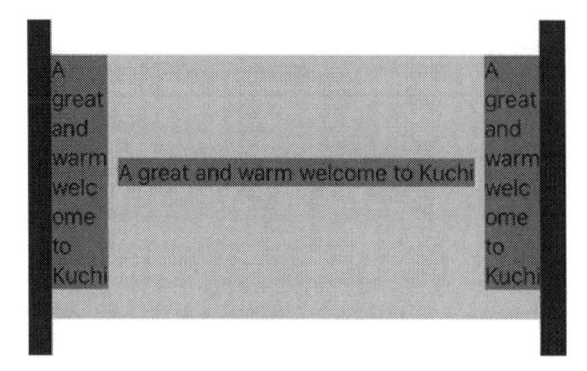

Now try adding a negative priority to the first Text:

```
HStack {
  Text("A great and warm welcome to Kuchi")
    .layoutPriority(-1)
    .background(Color.red)

  Text("A great and warm welcome to Kuchi")
    .layoutPriority(1)
    .background(Color.red)

  Text("A great and warm welcome to Kuchi")
    .background(Color.red)
}
```

With this, you can expect it to be the last element to be processed.

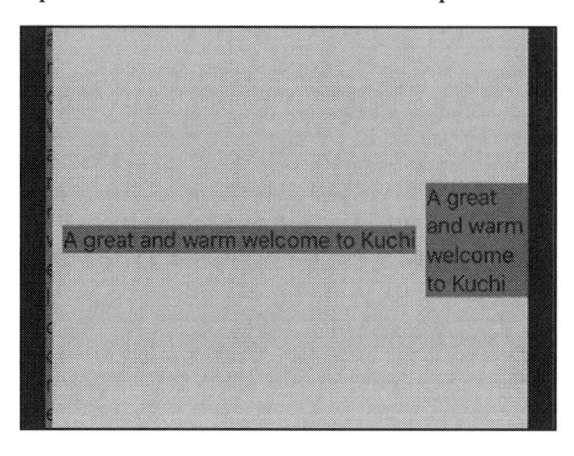

And in fact, it is given a very small width. To counterbalance that, the control expands vertically.

There's an important distinction between the two ways of altering the adaptive degree: **manually setting the layout priority doesn't just alter the sort order, but also the size that is proposed**.

For views with the same priority, the parent view proposes a size that's evenly proportional to the number of children. In the case of different priorities, the parent view uses a different algorithm: **it subtracts the bare minimum size of all children with lower priorities, and proposes that resulting size to the child (or children, if more than one) having the highest layout priority**.

Look again at the result of the previous example. HStack lays out controls horizontally, so width is the most constraining size, because children views compete for width, whereas they have virtually no constraints vertically. So, let's focus on width:

1. HStack calculates the minimum width required by the child view with lower priority. This happens to be the Text at the left, which has priority -1, and whose width is determined by the text displayed vertically. It therefore occupies the minimum possible width, highlighted in blue in the following zoomed-in image:

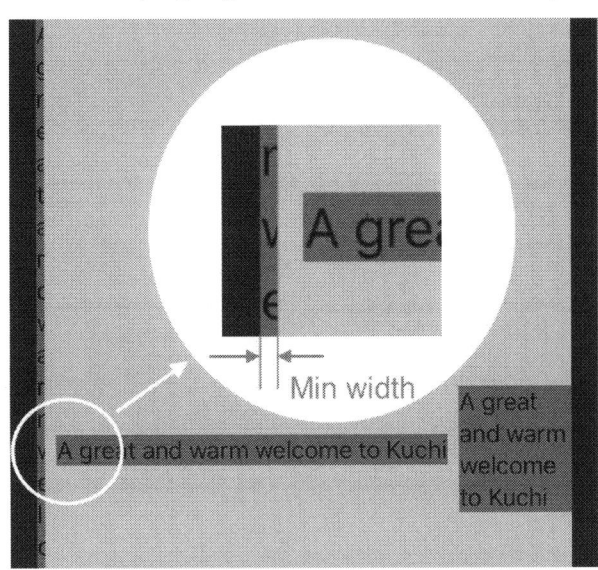

2. `HStack` finds the child view with highest priority, which is the middle `Text`, having priority 1, the highest among its children.

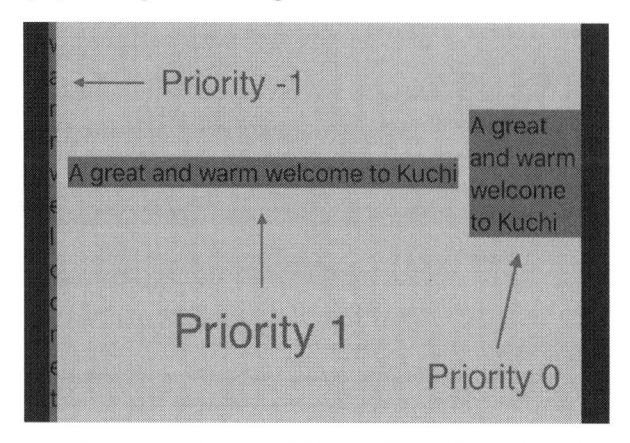

3. `HStack` assigns a virtual minimum width to all children views having a priority lower than the maximum. The minimum width is the one calculated at step 1, and the number of children views having lower priority is two; the `Text`s at left with priority -1 and at right with priority 0.

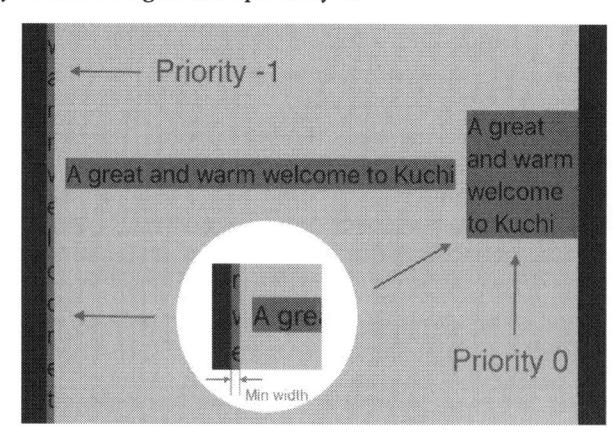

4. Given the width at its disposal, for each child view with lower priority, `HStack` subtracts its minimum width, which in this case is two times the minimum width calculated at step 1. The resulting width is proposed to the child view with the highest priority, the `Text` at center.

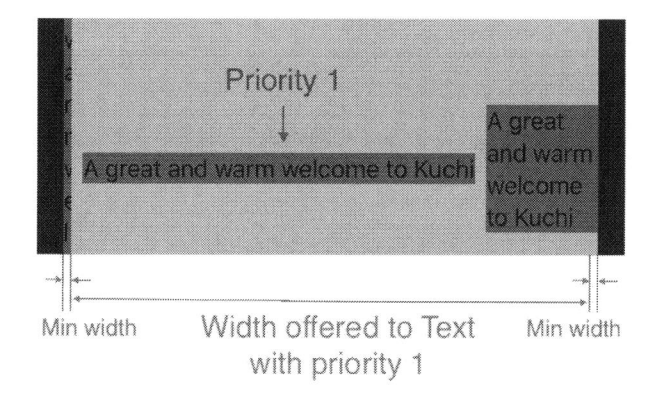

![Priority 1 diagram showing Min width, Width offered to Text with priority 1, Min width]

5. The Text at center decides to take the width necessary to display the text in one line.

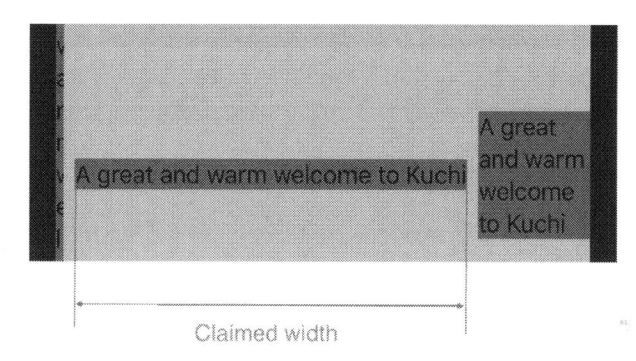

![Diagram showing Claimed width]

At this point, the stack can process the next view, which is the Text with priority 0, at the right side. The algorithm is the same; what's different is that the remaining width is now:

1. The width at HStack's disposal.

2. Minus the size taken by the Text with priority 1.

3. Minus the minimum size required the Text with priority -1.

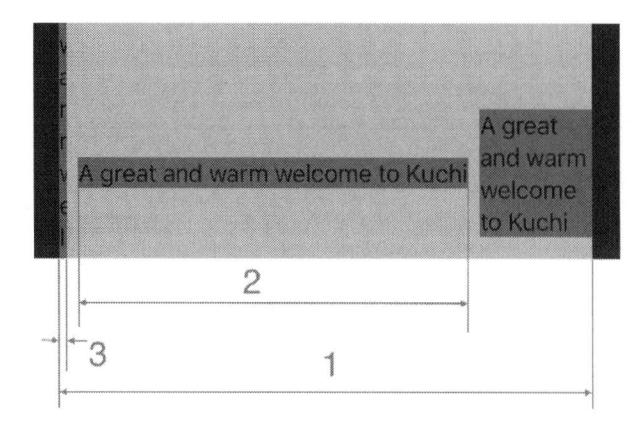

You see that the Text with priority 0 makes best use of the size at its disposal, by wrapping its text across 4 lines. This leaves no size other components can compete for, besides the bare minimum computed at step 1 of the previous list. That's a guaranteed size; it's like having a guaranteed minimum salary, maybe extremely low, but still guaranteed regardless of how greedy your superiors are!

The HStack and the VStack

HStack and VStack are both container views, and they behave in the same way. The only difference is the orientation:

- HStack lays subviews out **horizontally**
- VStack lays subviews out **vertically**

AppKit and UIKit have a similar component, UIStackView, which works in dual mode, having an axis property which determines in which direction its subviews are laid out.

You've already seen HStack and VStack in this and in previous chapters. In many cases, using the initializer that takes the content view only. In reality, it takes two additional parameters, which come with default values:

```
// HStack
init(
  alignment: VerticalAlignment = .center,
  spacing: CGFloat? = nil,
  @ViewBuilder content: () -> Content
)

// VStack
init(
```

```
  alignment: HorizontalAlignment = .center,
  spacing: CGFloat? = nil,
  @ViewBuilder content: () -> Content
)
```

- **alignment** is the vertical and horizontal alignment respectively for HStack and VStack, it determines how subviews are aligned, defaulted to `.center` in both cases.

- **spacing** is the distance between children. When `nil`, a default, platform-dependent distance is used. So if you want zero, you have to set it explicitly.

The `content` parameter is the usual closure that produces a child view. But containers can usually return more than one child, as you've seen in the example of this section where the `HStack` contains three `Text` components.

The `@ViewBuilder` attribute is what enables that: It enables a closure which returns a child view to provide multiple children views instead.

A note on alignment

While the `VStack` alignment can have three possible values — `.center`, `.leading` and `.trailing` — the `HStack` counterpart is a bit richer. Apart from center, bottom and top, it also has two very useful cases:

- **firstTextBaseline**: Aligns views based on the topmost text baseline view.

- **lastTextBaseline**: Aligns views based on the bottom-most text baseline view.

These come in handy when you have texts of different sizes and/or fonts, and you want them to be aligned in a visually appealing fashion.

An example is worth a thousands words so, still in `ChallengeView`, replace its body property with:

```
var body: some View {
  HStack() {
    Text("Welcome to Kuchi").font(.caption)
    Text("Welcome to Kuchi").font(.title)
    Button(action: {}, label: { Text("OK").font(.body) })
  }
}
```

This renders as a simple `HStack` with two `Text`s and a `Button`, each having a different font size. If you preview it as-is, you see that the three children are centered vertically:

Welcome to Kuchi **Welcome to Kuchi** OK

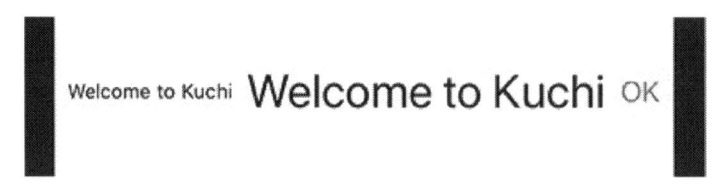

But that doesn't look very good, does it? To make it look nicer, it would be better to have the text aligned at bottom, which you can do by specifying the `HStack` alignment in its initializer:

```
HStack(alignment: .bottom) {
```

But again, this isn't very pleasing to the eye:

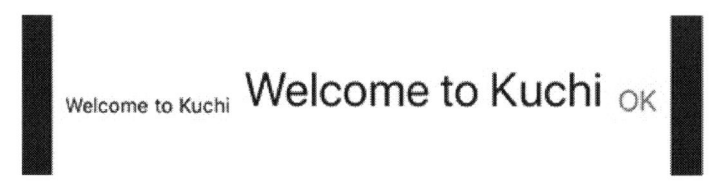

Welcome to Kuchi **Welcome to Kuchi** OK

And this is where the two baseline cases can come to the rescue. Try using `.firstTextBaseline`:

```
HStack(alignment: .firstTextBaseline) {
```

The smaller text and the button are now moved up slightly to match the larger text's baseline. That looks much better, right?

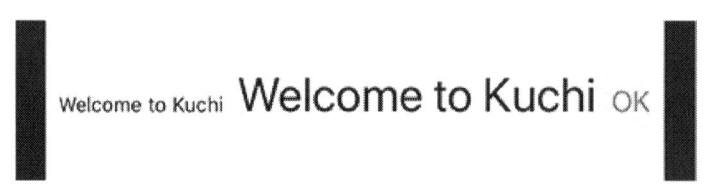

Welcome to Kuchi **Welcome to Kuchi** OK

The ZStack

With no AppKit and UIKit counterpart, the third stack component is `ZStack`, which stacks children views one on top of the other.

In `ZStack`, children are sorted by the position in which they are declared, which means that the first subview is rendered at the bottom of the stack, and the last one is at the top.

Interestingly, `.layoutPriority` applied to children views doesn't affect their Z-order, so it's not possible to alter the order in which they are defined in the `ZStack`'s body.

As with the other container views, `ZStack` positions its children views at its center by default.

Speaking of size, if the `HStack` has its height determined by its tallest subview, and the `VStack` has its width determined by its widest subview, both the width and height of a `ZStack` are determined respectively by its widest and the tallest subviews.

You'll use `ZStack` in a moment to build a portion of the congratulations view in the Kuchi app.

Other container views

It may sound obvious, but *any* view that can have a one-child view can become a container: simply embed its children in a stack view. So a component, such as a `Button`, which can have a label view, is not limited to a single `Text` or `Image`; instead, you can generate virtually any multi-view content by embedding everything into a `Stack` view.

Stack views can also be nested one inside another, and this is very useful for composing complex user interfaces. Remember, however, that if a view becomes too complex, it could (and should!) be split into smaller pieces.

> **Note**: Rumor has it that `Stack` cannot contain more than 10 children. This is not documented, but is, at the time of writing, easily verifiable by creating a stack with 11 children. The compiler will issue one of those cryptic errors messages to tell you you've strayed too far.

Back to Kuchi

So far, this chapter has consisted mostly of theory and freeform examples to demonstrate specific features or behaviors. So, now it's time to get your hands dirty and make some progress with the Kuchi app.

The Congratulations View

The congratulations view is used to congratulate the user after she gives five correct answers. Open **CongratulationsView.swift** and take a look at its content.

```
struct CongratulationsView: View {
  init(userName: String) {
  }

  var body: some View {
    EmptyView()
  }
}
```

If this is the first time you encounter `EmptyView`, it's just… an empty view. You can use it as a placeholder everywhere a view is expected, but you don't yet have any view for it, either by design, or because you haven't built it yet.

Content in this view will be laid out vertically — so a good kick-off is adding a `VStack`, replacing the empty view:

```
var body: some View {
  VStack {
  }
}
```

You'll see that the compiler is complaining. A `VStack` must have at least one child view. So, you'll add a static congratulations `Text` inside, using a large font size of gray color:

```
VStack {
  Text("Congratulations!")
    .font(.title)
    .foregroundColor(.gray)
}
```

Congratulations!

Right after that congratulations `Text`, add another smaller `Text`:

```
Text("You're awesome!")
  .fontWeight(.bold)
  .foregroundColor(.gray)
```

Congratulations!
You're awesome!

The bottom of this view should contain a button to close the view and go back. Add the following to the bottom of the stack:

```
Button(action: {
  self.challengesViewModel.restart()
}, label: {
  Text("Play Again")
})
  .padding(.bottom)
```

The button label shows a simple "Play Again" message, and the action is to reset the challenges status in the `challengesViewModel` property. But there's a problem: This property doesn't yet exist in the view. So, you'll need to add it.

It's an environment object, created and initialized in `SceneDelegate`, so you simply need to declare it using the proper attribute. Add it before the initializer:

```
struct CongratulationsView: View {
  // Add this property
  @EnvironmentObject
  var challengesViewModel: ChallengesViewModel

  init(userName: String) {
    ...
```

And this is how it looks:

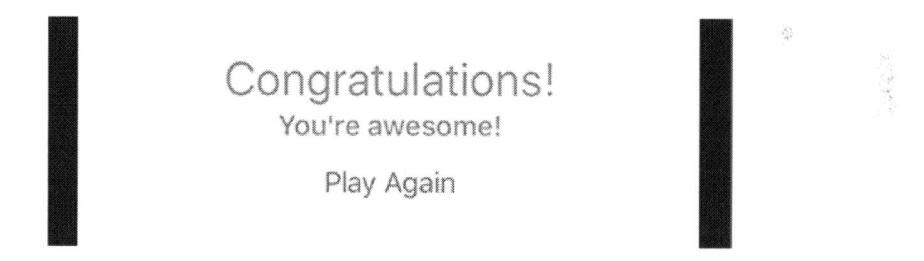

Congratulations!
You're awesome!

Play Again

User avatar

But let's not stop there — surely you can make this look even better! How about adding the user's avatar and their name on a colored background, but split vertically in two halves of different color? Something like this:

It might look complicated at first glance, but it only consists of three layers:

1. The background, split in two halves of different colors
2. The user avatar
3. The name of the user

You might already have figured out that you need a `ZStack` to implement it.

Between the two `Text`s in the `VStack`, add the following code:

```
// 1
ZStack {
  // 2
  VStack(spacing: 0) {
    Rectangle()
      // 3
      .frame(height: 90)
      .foregroundColor(
        Color(red: 0.5, green: 0, blue: 0).opacity(0.2))
```

```
      Rectangle()
        // 3
        .frame(height: 90)
        .foregroundColor(
          Color(red: 0.6, green: 0.1, blue: 0.1).opacity(0.4))
    }

    // 4
    Image(systemName: "person.fill")
      .resizable()
      .padding()
      .frame(width: avatarSize, height: avatarSize)
      .background(Color.white.opacity(0.5))
      .cornerRadius(avatarSize / 2, antialiased: true)
      .shadow(radius: 4)

    // 5
    VStack() {
      Spacer()
      Text(userName)
        .font(.largeTitle)
        .foregroundColor(.white)
        .fontWeight(.bold)
        .shadow(radius: 7)
    }.padding()
  }
  // 6
  .frame(height: 180)
```

Phew — that's a lot of code! But don't be intimidated — it's just a bit long. Here's what's happening:

1. You use a `ZStack` to layer content on top of one another

2. The bottom layer (the one added first) is the background, which is split into two halves.

3. Each of the two halves has a fixed height of 90 points and different background colors. This tells the `VStack` how tall it should be.

4. This is the user avatar, configured with a predefined size, and with a semi-transparent background color, rounded corners and some shadow. Notice how easy it is to customize an image!

5. The final `VStack` contains the name of the user, aligned to the bottom. The `Spacer` makes sure that the `Text` showing the name of the user is pushed to the bottom. More on `Spacer` in a moment.

6. This entire ZStack is set to a fixed height.

The resulting view should look like this:

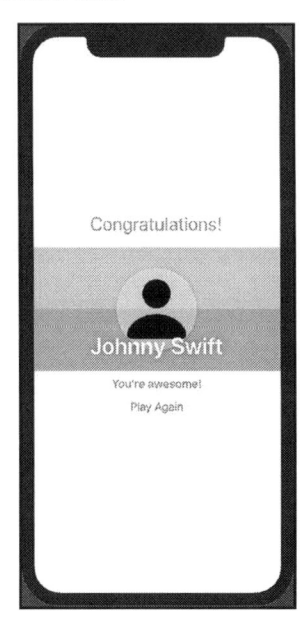

Much nicer, right?

The Spacer view

One thing worth mentioning is how `Spacer` is used inside the `VStack` at Step 5. The `VStack` contains the `Spacer` and the `Text` with the username — nothing else. So you might wonder why it's even necessary?

If you remove both the `Spacer` and the `VStack`, the user name would still be displayed, but it would be centered vertically:

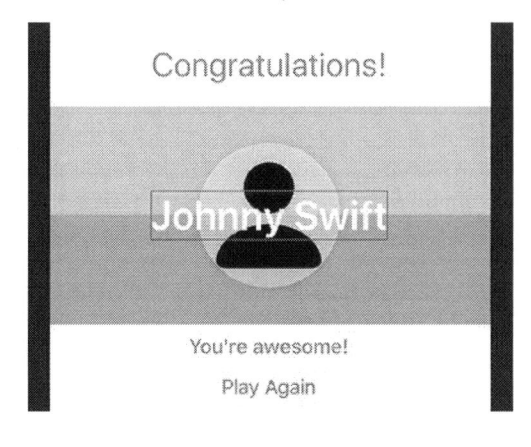

In order to push it down, you use a VStack, containing a Spacer at top and the Text at bottom. The Spacer expands along the major axis of its containing stack (or in both directions, if not in a stack) — so, as a side effect, it pushes the Text down.

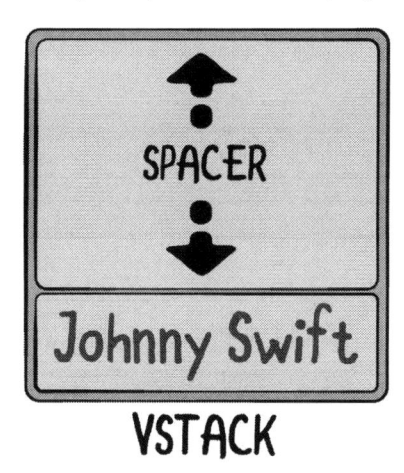

Following the layout rules described at the beginning of this chapter, this is how it works:

1. The VStack is proposed a size by its parent, the ZStack.

2. VStack finds that the child view with less layout flexibility is the Text, so it proposes a size. In the absence of layout priority, as in this case, the proposed size is half the size at its disposal.

3. The Text computes the size it needs, and sends the ticket back to the VStack.

4. The VStack subtracts the size claimed by the Text from the size at its disposal, and proposes that to the Spacer.

5. The Spacer, being flexible and unpretentious, accepts the proposal.

> **Challenge**: The view would look much better if the button were aligned to the bottom of the screen. How could you do that?

There are probably several ways of achieving that result, but it can be done with Spacers alone.

In order to push the button down, you need to add a `Spacer` between the button and the text above it:

```
Text("You're awesome!")
  .fontWeight(.bold)
  .foregroundColor(.gray)

Spacer() // <== The spacer goes here

Button(action: {
  self.challengesViewModel.restart()
}, label: {
  Text("Play Again")
})
```

However, although you've achieved the desired result, something's not quite right:

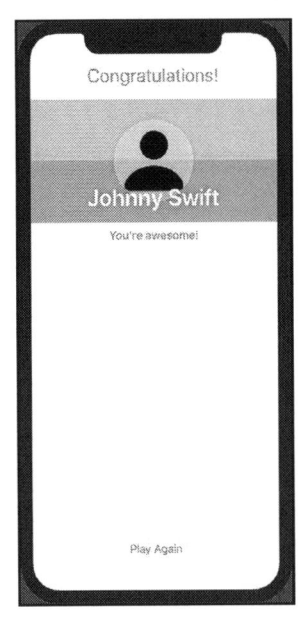

The button is now anchored to the bottom, but everything else has been pushed toward the top. To fix that, all you have to do is add another `Spacer` before the first `Text` in the `VStack`:

```
VStack {
  Spacer() // <== The spacer goes here

  Text("Congratulations!")
  ...
```

Mission accomplished!

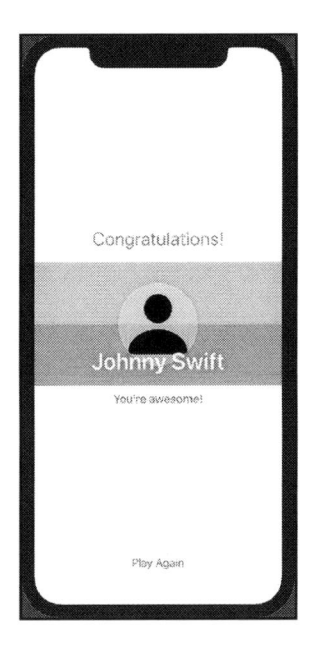

Completing the challenge view

Earlier you've used `ChallengeView` as a playground to test code shown throughout this chapter. Now you need to fill it with more useful code. The challenge view is designed to show a question and a list of answers.

Both use views defined in **QuestionView.swift** and **AnswersView.swift**. The answer's view, however, is hidden the first time the challenge view is shown, and it appears when the user taps anywhere on the screen.

First up, you need to add some properties that the view will need later. Open **ChallengeView.swift** and add the following two properties:

```
let challengeTest: ChallengeTest
@State var showAnswers = false
```

As with previous examples, the preview is complaining about something. In `ChallengeView_Previews`, replace its entire implementation with:

```
// 1
static let challengeTest = ChallengeTest(
  challenge: Challenge(
    question: "おねがい します",
    pronunciation: "Onegai shimasu",
    answer: "Please"
  ),
  answers: ["Thank you", "Hello", "Goodbye"]
)

static var previews: some View {
  // 2
  return ChallengeView(challengeTest: challengeTest)
}
```

Straightforward stuff here:

1. You create a challenge test to use in preview mode.

2. You pass that test to the view initializer.

`ChallengeView` is used inside `PracticeView`, and again, `ChallengeView` expects a parameter that you need to pass in. Open **PracticeView.swift**, and replace the `ChallengeView()` line with:

```
ChallengeView(challengeTest: challengeTest!)
```

Force unwrapping is fine in this instance, as you're checking for `nil` on the line above.

With all that setup out of the way, you're ready to build the actual challenge view. As previously mentioned, the view is designed to show a question and a list of answers. To achieve this, replace the body of **ChallengeView.swift** with:

```
var body: some View {
  // 1
  VStack {
    // 2
    Button(action: {
      self.showAnswers = !self.showAnswers
    }) {
      // 3
      QuestionView(question: challengeTest.challenge.question)
        .frame(height: 300)
    }
```

```
    // 4
    if showAnswers {
      Divider()
      // 5
      ChoicesView(challengeTest: challengeTest)
        .frame(height: 300)
        .padding()
    }
  }
}
```

Here's what's going on:

1. The two views are stacked vertically, so you use a `VStack`.

2. This button wraps the `QuestionView`, and on tap, it toggles the visibility of the `ChoicesView`.

3. This is `QuestionView` which, as mentioned, is implemented in its own file.

4. There's some conditional logic here to display `ChoicesView` only when `showAnswers` is `true`.

5. This is `ChoicesView`, implemented in its own file too. It receives a challenge test as parameter, which you provide via an instance property.

With all this done, you can run the app and try out a few challenges.

Congratulations for the achievement! Here's a few screenshots of how the app looks.

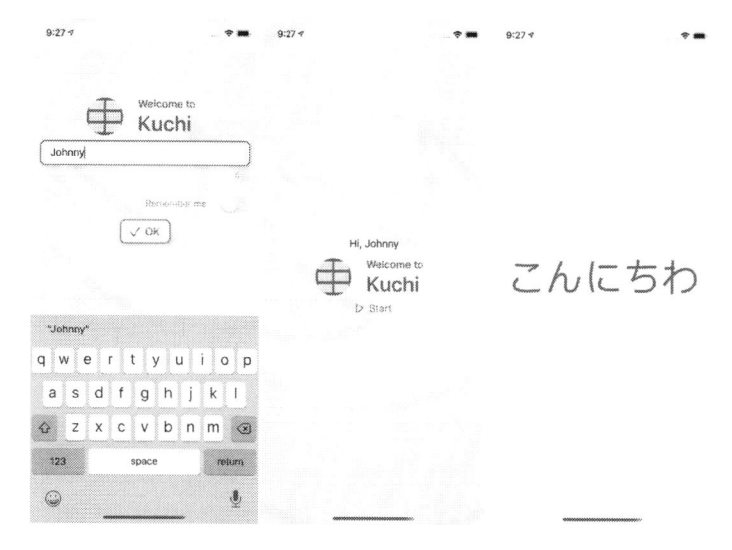

Key points

Another long chapter — but you did a great job at getting through it! A lot of concepts have been covered here, the most important ones being:

- SwiftUI handles layout in a different and easier way (at least, from the developer's point of view) than Auto Layout.

- Views choose their own size; their parents cannot impose size but only propose instead.

- Some views are more adaptive than others. For instance, `Text` tries to adapt to the size suggested by its parent, while `Image` simply ignores that and displays the image at its native resolution.

- There are three types of stack views; `VStack` for vertical layouts, `HStack` for horizontal layouts, and `ZStack` for stacking content on top of another.

- Stack views propose sizes to their children starting from the least adaptive to the most adaptive.

- The order in which children are processed by stack views can be altered by using the `layoutPriority` modifier.

Where to go from here?

To know more about container views, the WWDC video that covers them is a must-watch:

- WWDC 2019: Session 237 **"Building Custom Views with SwiftUI"** apple.co/2lVpSSc

Also recommended is the official documentation, which currently is a bit lacking in the verbosity department, but hopefully that will improve in the near future.

- Stack Views: Official documentation apple.co/2lXlbr1

There are a few other container views that have not been covered in this chapter:

- `Form`
- `Group`
- `GroupBox`

You can check out the documentation for more information on these. Good luck in your adventures with SwiftUI stack and container views!

Chapter 10: Lists & Navigation

By Bill Morefield

It's a rare app that can work with only a single view; most apps use many views and must provide a way for the user to navigate between them smoothly. The navigation you design has to balance many needs: you need to display data in a logical way to the user, you need to provide an easy way to move between views, and you need to make it easy for the user to figure out how to perform a particular task.

SwiftUI provides a unified interface to manage navigation while also displaying data. In this chapter, you'll explore how to display data to the user, while also building several types of navigation between views.

Getting started

Open the starter project for this chapter; you'll find a very early version of an app for an airport. In this chapter, you will build out the app to display today's flight arrivals and departures. In a real-world app, you would likely get this information from an API through Combine. For this app, though, you'll be using mock data.

Open the **Models** folder in the app, and you'll see two files. The first is **FlightInformation.swift**, which encapsulates information about flights. It contains a static method `generateFlight()` that generates test data for one flight, and another static method `generateFlights()` that generates an array of thirty flights. The other is **ContentView.swift**, which contains a variable `flightInfo` in which the app stores a new set of flights each time the app runs.

Navigating through a SwiftUI app

When designing the navigation for your SwiftUI app, you must create a navigation pattern that helps the user to move confidently through the app and perform tasks in an intuitive manner. Your users will hardly ever notice navigation that's done really well, but they won't stand for an app that's hard to navigate, or one that makes it hard to find information. SwiftUI is a cross-platform framework, but takes its primary design inspiration from iOS and iPadOS. Therefore, SwiftUI integrates patterns and design guidelines that are common on those platforms.

SwiftUI navigation organizes around two styles: flat and hierarchical. In SwiftUI, you implement a flat hierarchy using a `TabView`. A flat navigational structure works best when the user needs to move between different views that divide content into categories. The view layout will be broad, with many top-level views. Each view has little depth below. This kind of navigational structure makes it easier for users to discover as the path between the starting view and any view in the app is as short as possible. Too many categories, or indiscernable categories, can overwhelm the user.

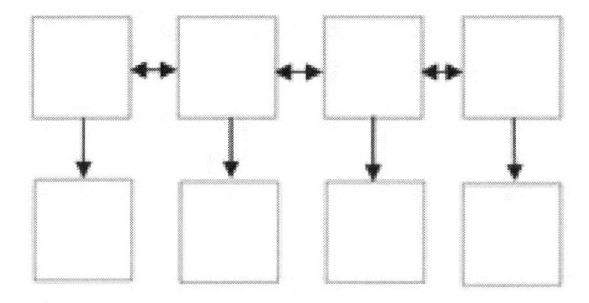

Flat navigation

Hierarchical navigation provides the user with fewer options at the top, and a deeper structure underneath. In SwiftUI, you implement hierarchical navigation using a `NavigationView`. Compared to a flat layout, a hierarchical layout has fewer lop level views, but each contains a deeper view stack beneath. The user may also have to backtrack through several layers of the navigation stack to find another view. Hierarchical navigation works well when the user has little need to switch laterally between view stacks, and for view stacks that move from broader to more specific information at each level.

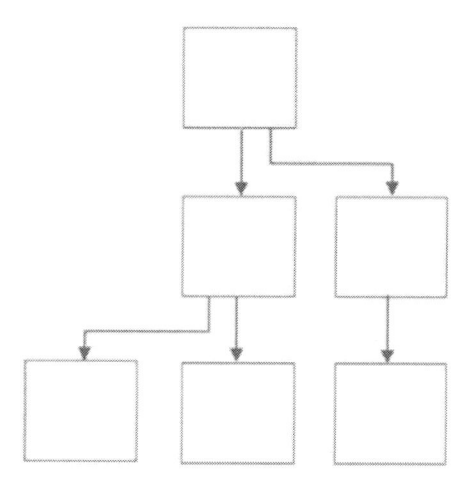

Hierarchical navigation

The layout of your views — or view stack — in your app will likely be a combination of these two categories. You might have a top-level using `TabView` to show several views. Each of those views might then contain a `NavigationView` that lets the user dive deeper into the app. No matter what your navigation design looks like, your overarching goal should be to keep the navigation consistent within the app. Switching between different navigation paradigms without warning or context can confuse your users.

Creating navigation views

You'll first set up a tab view in the sample app. Open **ContentView.swift** and change the view as follows:

```swift
// 1
TabView {
  // 2
  FlightBoard()
  // 3
    .tabItem({
      // 4
      Image(systemName: "icloud.and.arrow.down").resizable()
      Text("Arrivals")
    })
  FlightBoard()
    .tabItem({
      Image(systemName: "icloud.and.arrow.up").resizable()
      Text("Departures")
    })
```

```
    })
}
```

Here's how the tab view code works:

1. You first declare that you're creating a tab view using the `TabView` control.

2. You provide a set of views to the enclosure of `TabView`. Each view becomes the contents of a tab, and modifiers on the views define the information about the tab.

3. You apply the `tabItem(_:)` method to the view contents, for each tab, to set an image, text, or combination of the two.

4. Each tab displays a system image and a text label. You can only use `Text`, `Image`, or an `Image` followed by `Text` views as the tab label. If you use anything else, then the tab will show as visible but empty.

Since the views are identical, it's a bit hard to see any difference as this uses the default SwiftUI view. You're going to change that. Open **FlightBoard.swift** and add the following code above the body of the view:

```
var boardName: String
```

You also need to update the preview to provide the expected values. Change the preview to read:

```
FlightBoard(boardName: "Test")
```

Also, replace the view with the following code to show the passed in the name parameter.

```
Text(boardName).font(.title)
```

Go back to **ContentView.swift**. Change each call to `FlightBoard` to add the appropriate name. The first one should read:

```
FlightBoard(boardName: "Arrivals")
```

And the second call should read:

```
FlightBoard(boardName: "Departures")
```

Build and run the app, or open **ContentView.swift** and start **Live Preview**, and click on each tab to see the appropriate view.

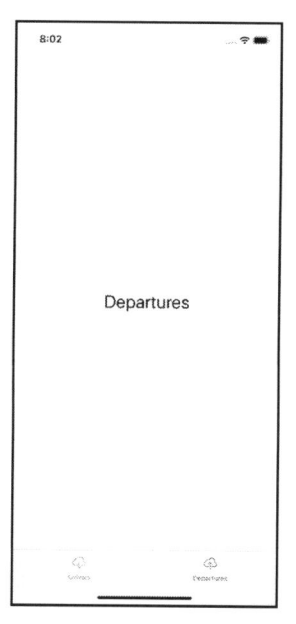

Many apps work well with the flat navigation style provided by a tab view, and this app presents data that fits well into a master-detail flow. In the next section, you'll change the app to use a navigation view layout.

Using navigation views

A navigation view arranges multiple views into a stack, transitioning from one view to another. In each view, the user makes a single choice that continues to a new view in the stack. You can go backward in the stack, but you can't jump between different children in the stack. On a large-screen device, SwiftUI also supports a split-view interface, which separates the main views of the app into separate panes. One view generally remains static, while the second changes as the user navigates through the view stack.

You'll now change the navigation in your app to a hierarchical style using a `NavigationView`. You'll add links to the two flight boards as buttons on the home view. Open **ContentView.swift** and replace the view body with the following:

```
// 1
NavigationView {
  ZStack {
    Image(systemName: "airplane").resizable()
      .aspectRatio(contentMode: .fit)
      .frame(width: 250, height: 250, alignment: .center)
```

```
        .opacity(0.1).rotationEffect(.degrees(-90))
      VStack(alignment: .leading, spacing: 5) {
        // 2
        NavigationLink(destination: FlightBoard(boardName:
  "Arrivals")) {
          // 3
          Text("Arrivals")
        }
        NavigationLink(destination: FlightBoard(boardName:
  "Departures")) {
          Text("Departures")
        }
        Spacer()
      }.font(.title).padding(20)
    Spacer()
    // 4
    }.navigationBarTitle(Text("Mountain Airport"))
  }
```

Here's how this code sets up the app navigation:

1. `NavigationView` defines the starting point of the stack of views that represent a path in the navigation hierarchy. You'll usually use this to handle data with a master-detail flow. Here, you start with two broad options that each show a list of items the user can select. The navigation view also provides a toolbar and a link to back out of these views.

2. This `NavigationLink` struct creates a button to let the user move deeper into the navigation stack. The `destination:` parameter provides the view to show when the user presses the button to go to the next step in the view stack.

3. The enclosure for the `NavigationLink` becomes the view displayed as the link. In this case, you're using static text.

4. You use the `navigationBarTitle(_:)` method to provide a title for the `NavigationView` to display at the top.

It might seem odd that you call `navigationBarTitle(_:)` on the `ZStack` and not the `NavigationView`. But remember, you're defining a hierarchy of views. A view's title typically changes when migrating through the view stack. The method finds the navigation view this control resides in and changes that title accordingly. All methods that change the current navigation view operate on views within the stack — not the stack itself. This also means these settings won't show on the preview or Live View.

The preview shows your progress and the two links.

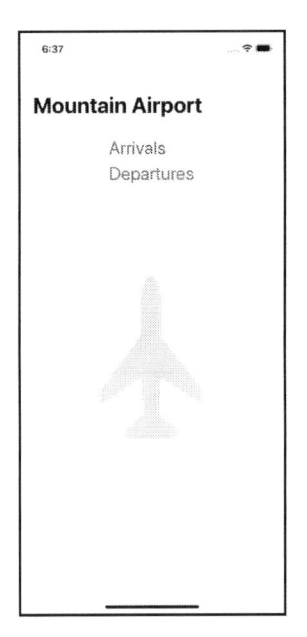

On the iPhone and Apple TV, SwiftUI uses a navigation stack by default. On the iPad and Mac, Apple defaults to a split-view styled navigation. That's great, except that — at least in the current beta implementation — you must swipe in from the leading edge to show the initial view.

You can override the default behavior by adding a call to `.navigationViewStyle(_:)`. To set the default to a stack on all platforms, you can add `.navigationViewStyle(StackNavigationViewStyle())` after `navigationBarTitle(_:)`.

Next, you need to implement the views to show the flights arriving and departing from the airport. You'll also learn more about working with data in your SwiftUI views.

Displaying a list of data

Open the file **FlightBoard.swift**. Right now, this is a default SwiftUI view. You will update it to display the flight information for arriving or departing flights, depending on what's passed in as arguments.

Open the new file and add the following code after the `boardName` variable:

```
var flightData: [FlightInformation]
```

This variable holds information about flights to display on the page.

You also need to update the preview to provide the expected values. Change the preview to read:

```
FlightBoard(boardName: "Test", flightData:
FlightInformation.generateFlights())
```

You can also update the navigation links you created in the previous step. Open **ContentView.swift** and change the navigation links to:

```
// 2
NavigationLink(destination: FlightBoard(boardName: "Arrivals",
              flightData: self.flightInfo
                .filter { $0.direction == .arrival })) {
  // 3
  Text("Arrivals")
}
NavigationLink(destination: FlightBoard(boardName: "Departures",
              flightData: self.flightInfo
                .filter { $0.direction == .departure })) {
  Text("Departures")
}
```

You've added the two parameters to be the views SwiftUI should transition to when the user taps the button. Here, you also use the `filter(_:)` method on the array to pass only the flights going in the direction matching the link.

Go back to **FlightBoard.swift**. Having an array of data to display is a pretty common task, and each platform provides a way to work with this data in the array. SwiftUI provides a couple of ways to loop through data in your view.

The first SwiftUI method to loop through data is `ForEach`. Change the body of the view to:

```
VStack {
  Text(boardName).font(.title)
  ForEach(flightData, id: \.id) { fl in
    Text("\(fl.airline) \(fl.number)")
  }
}
```

In the canvas, you'll see a new preview window for each flight that shows the airline and flight number. If you start **Live View**, you'll see a stack of views.

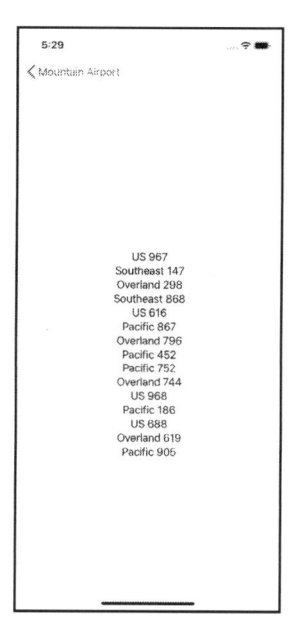

[Screenshot of iPhone showing "Mountain Airport" screen with a list of flights: US 967, Southeast 147, Overland 298, Southeast 868, US 616, Pacific 867, Overland 796, Pacific 452, Pacific 752, Overland 744, US 968, Pacific 186, US 688, Overland 619, Pacific 905]

`ForEach` iterates over the items in the passed data, calling the closure for each element and passing in the current element. In the closure, you define the view to display for the element. In this code, a `Text` view shows the flight airline and number.

The `id:` parameter hints that SwiftUI has expectations for the data passed to `ForEach`. In the next section, you'll explore making your data work with SwiftUI.

Making your data more compatible with iteration

The data passed into `ForEach` must provide a way to identify each element of the array as unique. In this loop, you use the `id:` parameter to tell SwiftUI to use the `\.id` property as the unique identifier for each element in the array. The only requirement for the unique identifier is to implement the `Hashable` protocol, which the native Swift `String` and `Int` types do already. You can also use the Foundation `UUID` and `URL` types if need be. As `.id` is an `Int`, it works just fine as the unique identifier.

If your class implements `Hashable`, you can also use the entire object as the unique identifier. To do so, pass `\.self)` as the `id:` parameter. You can also use this technique to iterate over a set of integers or other objects that implement the `Hashable` protocol.

You can remove the need to specify the unique identifier by making your type conform to the `Identifiable` protocol. This protocol, new in Swift 5.1, provides a defined mechanism by which SwiftUI knows how to determine the unique identifier for a piece of data. The only requirement for this protocol is to have a property named `id` that conforms to the `Hashable` protocol. Since you already have such a property on the `FlightInformation` class, you simply have to let SwiftUI know this, and it can figure everything else out.

Open **FlightInformation.swift**. At the end of the file, add the following code:

```
extension FlightInformation: Identifiable {
}
```

Adding the extension tells SwiftUI that `FlightInformation` implements `Identifiable`. Since `FlightInformation` already meets the protocol requirements, you don't need to make any other changes.

Since you no longer need to specify the identifier for SwiftUI, open **FlightBoard.swift** and change the `ForEach` declaration to:

```
ForEach(flightData) { fl in
```

You'll see the list works as before:

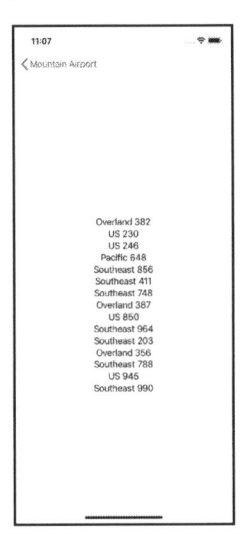

As the amount of data you display increases, it can become challenging to display it all in a single view. SwiftUI gives you tools to handle this situation, and you'll explore one in the next section — the `ScrollView`.

Showing scrolling data

Open **FlightBoard.swift** and change the body of the view to:

```swift
VStack {
  Text(boardName).font(.title)
  ForEach(flightData) { fl in
    VStack {
      Text("\(fl.airline) \(fl.number)")
      Text("\(fl.flightStatus) at \(fl.currentTimeString)")
      Text("At gate \(fl.gate)")
    }
  }
}
```

Build and run the app. Navigate to a flight board, and you'll immediately see the problem. There is so much data to display, that part of it runs off the bottom of the screen.

There are several ways to handle large collections of data that don't fit neatly into your view. The first approach is to use a `ScrollView` to wrap data. Wrap the `ForEach()` iterator inside a `ScrollView` so it looks like this:

```
ScrollView {
  ForEach(flightData) { fl in
    VStack {
      Text("\(fl.airline) \(fl.number)")
      Text("\(fl.flightStatus) at \(fl.currentTimeString)")
      Text("At gate \(fl.gate)")
    }
  }
}
```

The `ScrollView` wraps the enclosed view within a scrollable content region. This region allows the user to scroll through the data without affecting the rest of the view.

Build and run the app, and navigate to a flight board. You'll see the title for the board no longer disappears off the view. If you drag over the list, you'll see that you can scroll through the vertical list and no longer lose content off of your screen.

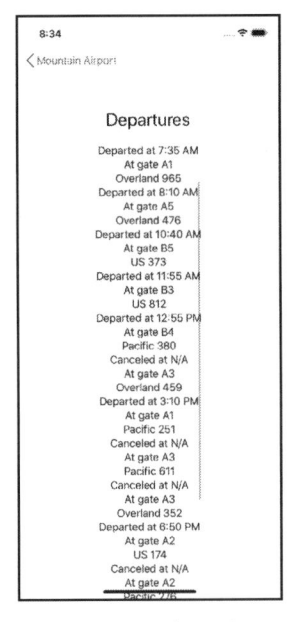

SwiftUI notices you've wrapped a `VStack` and applies vertical scrolling, and not horizontal. This means that if a line of text within the view became longer than the width of the view, SwiftUI wouldn't automatically add horizontal scrolling.

You can override this default by passing in the desired scroll axes to `ScrollView`. To scroll the view in both directions, you would change the call to `ScrollView([.horizontal, .vertical]) {`.

`ScrollView` provides a useful, generic way to let a user browse through a view. There's another option for displaying a single column list of data, though — the appropriately named `List` struct, which also provides built-in scrolling. In the next section, you'll convert the flight board to use a `List`.

Creating lists

`ForEach` iterates over the elements of the array, but it relies on you to figure out what to *do* with that data. Since iterating through data and displaying it to the user is such a common task, all platforms have a built-in control for this task. SwiftUI provides the `List` struct, in addition to `ForEach`, that does the heavy lifting for you.

Using the `List` struct displays rows of data arranged in a single column, using a platform-appropriate control.

Open **FlightBoard.swift**. Delete the body of the view and replace it with:

```
VStack {
  Text(boardName).font(.title)
  List(flightData) { fl in
    Text("\(fl.airline) \(fl.number)")
  }
}
```

You'll see there are no changes here, other than changing the name of the struct. `List` uses the platform's built-in list format to provide functionality without much work on your part. If you start **Live View**, you'll see the list automatically supports scrolling, out of the box. If you've ever had to use `UITableView` in iOS, you can easily see that you've just created the same result in Swift UI — with a lot less effort.

The preview now shows a list of flights:

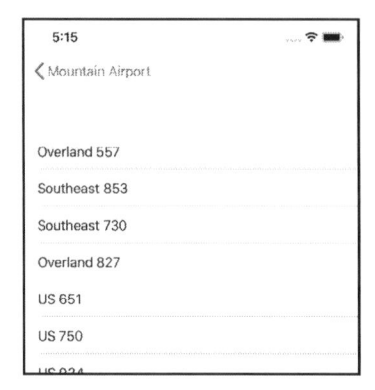

Think of `List` as a specific case of `ForEach` you use to display rows of one-column data. Almost every framework and platform provides a version of this control, as it's a pretty common UX use case. When you need more flexibility to work with the data in the collection, you can use `ForEach`.

When the user selects a flight from the list, you want to show more information about that flight on a new view. Your first thought might be to wrap the list in **FlightBoard.swift**, so your code would look like this:

```
NavigationView {
  List(flightData) { fl in
    Text("\(fl.airline) \(fl.number)")
  }
}
```

If you made this change, this would cause a problem because this view is already part of a navigation stack from the `NavigationView` you added in **ContentView.swift**. If you added another `NavigationView`, you would end up with a view that looked like this when arriving on the page:

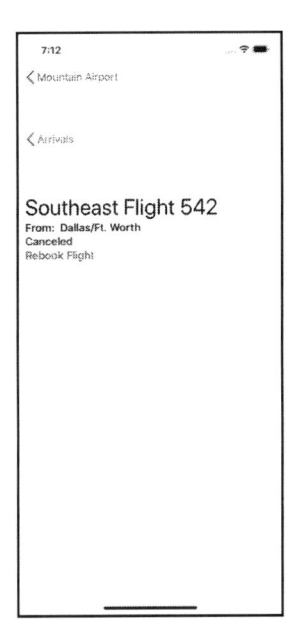

Having two backlinks breaks the concept of a navigation view. A navigation view creates a stack of views starting with the initial view. You should only ever have a single `NavigationView` in your app's view hierarchy, or odd behavior will ensue.

You now need to set the title for this view in the view stack. Remove the `Text(boardName).font(.title)` from the beginning of the `VStack`. Add the following after the `List` element to set the title for this view:

```
.navigationBarTitle(boardName)
```

You'll see the title doesn't appear above the list in the preview. If you start **Live Preview**, you'll see the title also doesn't show. That's because the view doesn't have any way of knowing that it's part of a view stack. Preview and Live Preview both only work on the view related to the current code.

Build and run the app so you can see this in action. Navigate to one of the board pages, and you'll see the title appear as expected.:

This shows that when you're working through views deeper down in your navigation stack, you can't simply rely on the preview alone to ensure your view looks right.

You're now going to create a separate view to display the information for each flight in the row. Create a new SwiftUI View named **FlightRow.swift**. Above the body, add a variable to pass information for the flight to the view:

```
var flight: FlightInformation
```

Now replace the view in **FlightRow.swift** with:

```
HStack {
  Text("\(self.flight.airline) \(self.flight.number)")
    .frame(width: 120, alignment: .leading)
  Text(self.flight.otherAirport).frame(alignment: .leading)
  Spacer()
  Text(self.flight.flightStatus).frame(alignment: .trailing)
}
```

Update the preview for this view to:

```
FlightRow(flight: FlightInformation.generateFlight(0))
```

Each row now shows the city and status for the flight in addition to the airline and flight number.

Go back to **FlightBoard.swift**. Change the enclosure of the list to use the new view:

```
FlightRow(flight: fl)
```

You'll now see the preview shows your more complex row. Separating views in SwiftUI helps reduce the clutter and length of code; this makes your view more comfortable to read and to update in the future.

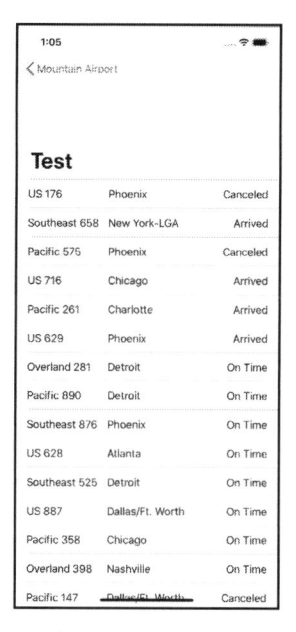

Next, you'll need to add a view to show more details about a flight and connect the rows to this new view.

Adding navigation links

Create a new SwiftUI view named **FlightBoardInformation.swift**. You'll use this view to provide more detailed information about the flight to the user.

In the new view, add a variable you'll use to pass in the flight for which you want to display information for:

```
var flight: FlightInformation
```

Now change the view body to:

```
VStack(alignment: .leading) {
  HStack{
    Text("\(flight.airline) Flight \(flight.number)")
      .font(.largeTitle)
    Spacer()
  }
  Text("\(flight.direction == .arrival ? "From: " : "To: ") \
(flight.otherAirport)")
  Text(flight.flightStatus)
    .foregroundColor(Color(flight.timelineColor))
  Spacer()
}.font(.headline).padding(10)
```

Also change the preview to provide a flight as follows:

```
FlightBoardInformation(flight:
  FlightInformation.generateFlight(0))
```

The primary flow of a navigation view is a type of master-detail. This navigation follows the flow from more general information, to more specific information. Displaying details about a flight from a list of flights is a good use case for this navigation style. To create this navigation flow, you can add the link between the rows in **FlightBoard.swift** and this new view.

Go to **FlightBoard.swift** and change the view to:

```
List(flightData) { fl in
  NavigationLink(destination: FlightBoardInformation(flight:
fl)) {
    FlightRow(flight: fl)
  }
}.navigationBarTitle(boardName)
```

This code should look familiar; it's similar to the navigation links you added to the app's start page at the beginning of this chapter. Again, you pass the view to display as the `destination:` parameterwhen the user taps the button. You also define what to show in the enclosure; in this case, it's a `FlightRow` view. Wrapping the navigation link inside a `List` means SwiftUI renders each item in the list as a separate navigation item. On iOS, you'll get the small right disclosure arrow at the end of each row that you're probably familiar with.

Build and run the app. Tap either of the two flight board choices, and then tap on a flight. You'll see the flight details displayed:

Adding items to the navigation bar

Each view in the navigation view stack has a navigation bar. By default, the navigation bar contains a link back to the previous view. You can add additional items to the navigation bar if you need to, although you want to avoid overcrowding it with too many controls.

You'll add a toggle to the navigation bar to hide cancelled flights from the list. Open **FlightBoard.swift** and add the following code after the declaration of `flightData`:

```
@State private var hideCancelled = false
```

You set this state variable to hide cancelled flights. Now, add a computed property after the new state variable to filter flights based on this variable:

```
var shownFlights: [FlightInformation] {
  hideCancelled ?
    flightData.filter { $0.status != .cancelled } :
    flightData
}
```

Change the variable passed to `List` to use the computed property, instead of the passed flights.

```
List(shownFlights) { fl in
```

With those changes, you can now filter the list of flights by changing the `showAll` state variable using a toggle on the navigation bar. Add the following code after the `navigationBarTitle(_:)` method.

```
.navigationBarItems(trailing:
  Toggle(isOn: $hideCancelled, label: {
    Text("Hide Cancelled")
  }))
```

The `navigationBarItems(trailing:)` method adds a button to the trailing edge of the navigation bar. There's a corresponding method to add the button to the leading edge, should you ever need that. The toggle takes a binding to the `hideCancelled` state variable. Using the state variable lets SwiftUI handle refreshing and updating the list when the value changes.

Build and run the app, navigate to one of the flight boards, and try out the toggle to see it in action.

You'll find many places to use this master-detail view hierarchy in apps. There's another common way to display a new view in response to a user action, and that's a modal view.

Displaying a modal sheet

The other common way to display information in response to a user action is by using a modal sheet. These are useful when you want to focus the user's attention on the current view. You'll now change the navigation so that the flight details show as a modal sheet.

The modal sheet slides the view up over the current view. Since the sheet no longer needs to sit in the view hierarchy, you no longer need to wrap the rows as NavigationLinks. Open **FlightBoard.swift** and change the view to:

```
List(flightData) { fl in
    FlightRow(flight: fl)
}.navigationBarTitle(boardName)
```

SwiftUI provides two ways to display a modal based on a @State variable. The first method uses a Bool variable that you set to true when the sheet should display. The second method works off an optional state variable that displays when the variable becomes non-nil. You'll use the `Bool` method for this modal. All modals provide these two options, and you'll see an example using an optional variable later in this chapter.

Open **FlightRow.swift** and add the following new variable after the `flight` variable:

```
@State private var isPresented = false
```

This line defines a `@State` variable that indicates when to show the modal sheet. Now change the view to:

```
Button(action: {
  // 1
  self.isPresented.toggle()
}) {
  HStack {
    Text("\(flight.airline) \(flight.number)")
      .frame(width: 120, alignment: .leading)
    Text(flight.otherAirport).frame(alignment: .leading)
    Spacer()
    Text(flight.flightStatus).frame(alignment: .trailing)
    // 2
  }.sheet(isPresented: $isPresented, onDismiss: {
    // 3
    print("Modal dismissed. State now: \(self.isPresented)")
  }) {
    // 4
    FlightBoardInformation(flight: self.flight)
  }
}
```

Here's the new wrapping for the modal sheet:

1. You now wrap the `HStack` for the row inside a button. The button's action toggles the `isPresented` state variable.

2. To tell SwiftUI you want to display a modal, you call `sheet(isPresented:onDismiss:content:)`. Here, you pass the `isPresented` state variable telling SwiftUI to show the modal when the variable becomes `true`. When the user dismisses the modal, SwiftUI sets the state back to `false`.

3. The optional `onDismiss:` includes a closure you can use to execute code after the user dismisses the modal. Here, you print a message to the console and show that the value of the state variable is now `false`.

4. You provide the view to show on the modal sheet as the closure for `sheet(isPresented:onDismiss:content:)`.

Go to **FlightBoard.swift**, activate **Live View**, and tap any row to see the modal appear. Swipe down on the modal to dismiss it, and in the debug console you'll see the state variable become `false` after you dismiss the modal:

Programmatically dismissing a modal

You've probably noticed that the navigation view has disappeared. That's because a modal sheet takes over the whole screen, and no longer wraps the view in any existing navigation view. You can create a new navigation view on the modal, but doing so creates a whole new navigation view stack.

You should also add a button to dismiss the modal, which will provide a method to dismiss the modal on platforms where the swipe gesture isn't supported, such as in Catalyst apps.

Open **FlightBoardInformation.swift**. First, you'll need a variable to store a `@Binding` to the passed display flag from the `FlightRow` view. Add the following code after the `flight` variable at the top of the struct:

```
@Binding var showModal: Bool
```

In the initial `HStack`, add the following code after the spacer:

```
Button("Done", action: {
    self.showModal = false
})
```

Since the view now expects the caller to pass in the state, you also need to update the preview to do so. Change the preview to read:

```
FlightBoardInformation(flight:
FlightInformation.generateFlight(0),
                  showModal: .constant(true))
```

The `.constant(true)` value provides a pseudo-state that lets the preview behave correctly.

Now, go back to **FlightRow.swift** and change the `sheet(isPresented:onDismiss:content:)` enclosure to `FlightBoardInformation` to pass in the state:

```
FlightBoardInformation(flight: self.flight, showModal: self.
$isPresented)
```

Start **Live Preview** and you'll see tapping on the row now bring up the modal with a **Done** button in the navigation bar. Tapping the button dismisses the modal, just as swiping down does.

Master-detail and modal views handle most of your needs for displaying user information. Sometimes, though, you don't need something that complex. In the next section, you'll see how to implement other modal views that can also provide information and capture input from the user.

Using alerts, action sheets and popovers

A modal is a great choice when your view needs the user's full attention. In the right spots, they help your user focus on relevant information and improve the app experience. However, modal views interrupt the app experience, and you should use them sparingly. SwiftUI provides three more specialized modal views to help you capture user attention: alerts, action sheets and popovers. You'll check out each of those now.

Creating an alert

Alerts are useful to bring something important to the user's attention, such as warning about a severe problem, or confirming actions with severe consequences.

You're going to add a button to help the user rebook a cancelled flight. It won't do anything right now — you're waiting on the backend team to finish that API. Instead, you'll display an alert telling the user to contact the airline.

Open **FlightBoardInformation.swift**. You can set alerts, like modals, to display based on a state variable. Add the following state to the top of the struct:

```
@State private var rebookAlert: Bool = false
```

Now after the code to display the flight status, add the following code for the alert:

```
// 1
if flight.status == .cancelled {
  // 2
  Button("Rebook Flight", action: {
    self.rebookAlert = true
  })
    // 3
    .alert(isPresented: $rebookAlert) {
      // 4
      Alert(title: Text("Contact Your Airline"),
            message: Text("We cannot rebook this flight. Please contact the airline to reschedule this flight."))
    }
}
```

Here's what you're doing with this code:

1. The view only shows when the flight status is `.cancelled`.

2. The button sets the `rebookAlert` state variable to `true` when tapped.

3. You call `alert(isPresented:content:)` on the `Button` struct to create the alert. You also pass in the state variable telling SwiftUI to show the alert when `rebookAlert` becomes `true`.

4. In the enclosure, the `Alert` struct defines the alert message to show the user. You don't provide any additional buttons, so the user's only option is to tap the **OK** button to dismiss the alert.

Run the app. Tap on the **Departures**, then tap on any **Cancelled** flight. Tap on the **Rebook Flight** button, and the alert will appear.

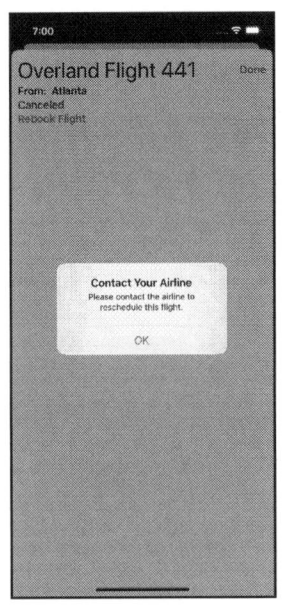

If you're familiar with iOS and iPadOS development, you'll see that the `Alert` method in SwiftUI has some limitations. The current SwiftUI alert doesn't support adding a text field for feedback as `UIAlertController` in iOS did. You'll need to create a modal sheet instead to perform the same task.

You can also attach multiple alerts to a view. They must have different triggers, or SwiftUI will only show the last alert. As with a modal sheet, you can also have the alert triggered by binding to an optional variable. You'll use this method and implement an action sheet in the next section.

Adding an action sheet

You display an action sheet in response to a user action, and the user should expect the action sheet to appear. You can use it to get confirmation of the action, or also let the user select from multiple options. In this section, you'll add a button to let the user check-in for a flight and display an action sheet to confirm the request.

Instead of a Boolean state variable that you've used for the modal sheet and alert, you'll use an Optional variable. You can use either of these methods with all of the modal views in this chapter.

The primary reason to use the Optional variable over the Boolean is that you can access the Optional variable inside the enclosure. The variable must implement the `Identifiable` protocol discussed earlier in this chapter.

You'll create a simple struct implementing the `Identifiable` protocol for this action sheet. Open **FlightBoardInformation.swift**. Add the following code after the `import SwiftUI` line:

```swift
struct CheckInInfo : Identifiable {
  let id = UUID()
  let airline: String
  let flight: String
}
```

You define a new `CheckInInfo` struct that implements the `Identifiable` protocol. To meet the requirements of the protocol, you include an `id` member of type `UUID`. By definition, a `UUID` provides a unique value and implements the `Hashable` protocol, making it a perfect unique identifier. You then add `airline` and `flight` strings that you provide when creating the message.

Now add the following state variable to hold the `CheckInInfo` after your current state variables at the top of the View:

```swift
@State private var checkInFlight: CheckInInfo?
```

Now add the following code after the alert you added in the last section:

```swift
// 1
if flight.direction == .departure &&
   (flight.status == .ontime || flight.status == .delayed) {
  Button("Check In for Flight", action: {
    // 2
    self.checkInFlight =
      CheckInInfo(airline: self.flight.airline, flight:
self.flight.number)
```

```
    })
    // 3
    .actionSheet(item: $checkInFlight) { flight in
      // 4
      ActionSheet(title: Text("Check In"),
        message: Text("Check in for \(flight.airline) Flight \
(flight.flight)"),
        // 5
        buttons: [
          // 6
          .cancel(Text("Not Now")),
          // 7
          .destructive(Text("Reschedule"), action: {
            print("Reschedule flight.")
          }),
          // 8
          .default(Text("Check In"), action: {
            print("Check-in for \(flight.airline) \
(flight.flight).")
          })
        ])
    }
}
```

A lot of the code looks the same as what you've done with a modal sheet and alert. The action sheet uses the optional variable in place of a `Bool`. It also requires information on the buttons to display. Here's how the new elements in this code work:

1. You only show this button for a flight that's departing this airport, and whether it's on time or delayed.

2. The button's action sets the `checkInMessage` state variable to a new instance of `CheckInMessage` that stores the airline and number of the flight.

3. As you did with the alert, you add the action sheet to the button. Here you use the `actionSheet(item:content:)` and not `actionSheet(isPresented:content:)`. The optional variable is passed as the `item:` parameter. When the variable becomes non-nil, as it will when the button's action executes, SwiftUI displays the action sheet. The variable becoming non-nil acts as a trigger the same way the alert's Boolean binding told SwiftUI to display the alert. You also provide a parameter inside the enclosure; when SwiftUI shows the sheet, this parameter contains the contents of the bindable value that triggered it.

4. You create an action sheet using the contents of the passed-in variable to display the name of the flight to the user on the action sheet.

5. An alert provides a limited ability to gather feedback. You have many more options with an action sheet, though all must be buttons. Here, you pass an array of `ActionSheet.Button` items to the `buttons:` parameter for those you wish to use in this action sheet.

6. The first defined button is the cancel button. Providing a cancel button gives the user a clear back-out option. You do nothing when the user selects this option, so there is no need for any parameter other than text for this button.

7. You use the `.destructive` type method for actions that have destructive or dangerous results. SwiftUI displays the text in red to highlight the seriousness of this action. The `action:` parameter provides code that SwiftUI executes when the user selects this option. Here, you display a message to the debug console.

8. The default button for the action sheet used uses the `action:` parameter to display a message to the debug console.

Build and run the app. Select **Departures** and then tap any **On Time** or **Delayed** flight. Now tap the **Check In** button. You'll see the action sheet appear.

If you tap the **Not Now** button, then nothing happens since you provided no `action:` parameter. Tap either the **Check In** or **Reschedule** button, and the appropriate message appears in the console window in the debug area of Xcode.

```
Make a symbolic breakpoint at UIViewAlertForUnsatisfiableConstraints to
    catch this in the debugger.
The methods in the UIConstraintBasedLayoutDebugging category on UIView
    listed in <UIKitCore/UIView.h> may also be helpful.
Do check-in for Southeast Flight 784.
```

Closely related to the action sheet is the final type of final type transient view in SwiftUI: the popover. In the next section, you'll add a popover to the app.

Showing a popover

Like the action sheet, you usually display a popover in response to a user action. You'll find popovers most useful on larger screen devices such as iPads and Macs. On smaller screen devices, your needs are better served with a full-screen view such as a modal sheet. If the screen is too small, SwiftUI will render the popover as a modal sheet instead. Your popover should save state immediately when shown, as the user could dismiss it at any time.

Creating and using a popover works much like an alert and action sheet. You can use a Boolean or Optional type as with the other modal views. For this example, you'll use a `Bool` state variable as you did with the alert. You'll add a button that will popover a new `FlightTimeHistory` view that shows the recent history of the flight in a list. Open **FlightBoardInformation.swift** and add the code for a new state variable after the existing ones.

```
@State private var showFlightHistory = false
```

Now add the following code to the view just before the `Spacer()` at the end of the `VStack`.

```
Button("On-Time History") {
  self.showFlightHistory.toggle()
}
.popover(isPresented: $showFlightHistory, arrowEdge: .top) {
  FlightTimeHistory(flight: self.flight)
}
```

The code looks much like when you added an alert to the view earlier. Alerts, action sheets and popovers all perform the same task — to provide a temporary view to inform the user and optionally gather a response. As a result, they operate in similar ways. The `popover(isPresented:arrowEdge:)` method sets the `showFlightHistory` state variable to watch to show the popup.

Popovers traditionally show an arrow pointing back to the control that initiated the popover. The `arrowEdge:` parameter defines the direction the popover the arrow comes from the control. Here the `.top` value asks for the popover sheet to have an arrow at its top, pointing to the control. That means the popover shows below the control.

Otherwise, this code should look familiar. The button toggles the `showFlightHistory` state variable to `true`, causing the popover to appear.

Build and run the app with an iPad target. Navigate to the details for a flight and then tap the new **On-Time History** button. Don't forget that SwiftUI defaults to a split view on the iPad, so you'll need to swipe in from the left to see the initial view in the navigation.

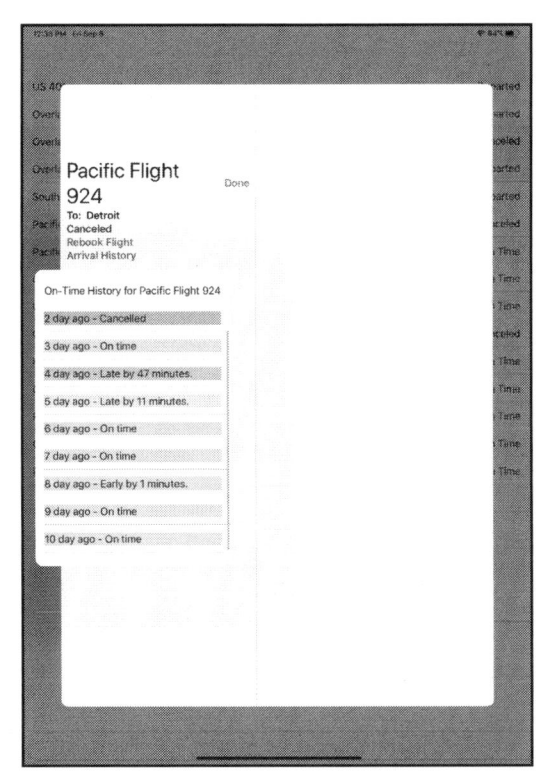

Key points

- App navigation generally combines a mix of flat and hierarchical flows between views.
- Tab views display a flat navigation that allows quick switching between the views.
- Navigation views create a hierarchy of views as a view stack. The user can move further into the stack, and can back up from within the stack.
- A navigation link connects a view to the next view in the view stack.
- You should only have one `NavigationView` in a view stack. Views that follow should inherit the existing navigation view.
- You apply changes to the navigation view stack to controls in the stack, and not to the `NavigationView` itself.
- A `ScrollView` wraps a section of a view within a scrollable region that doesn't affect the rest of the view.
- SwiftUI provides two ways to iterate over data. The `ForEach` option loops through the data allowing you to render a view for each element.
- A `List` uses the platform's list control to display the elements in the data.
- Data used with `ForEach` and `List` must provide a way to uniquely identify each element. You can do this by specifying an attribute that implements the `Hashable` protocol, have the object implement `Hasbable` or have your data implement the `Identifiable` protocol.
- Modal sheets pop on top of the view. You can use either a `Bool` state variable or an optional state variable that implements the `Identifiable` protocol to tell SwiftUI to display them.
- The alert, action sheet and popover views provide a standard way to display information to the user. All of these views can also get feedback from the app user.
- Alerts generally display information about unexpected situations, or confirm actions that have severe consequences.
- Action sheets and popovers display in response to a user action. You use action sheets for smaller screen devices and popovers on larger screens.

Where to go from here?

The first stop when looking for information on user interfaces on Apple platforms should be the Human Interface Guidelines:

- https://developer.apple.com/design/human-interface-guidelines/.

You won't yet find SwiftUI specific information there, but you'll find information for all the platforms that SwiftUI supports.

The WWDC 2019 SwiftUI Essentials video also provides an overview of Apple's guidelines on how views, navigation and lists fit together:

- https://developer.apple.com/videos/play/wwdc2019/216/

Section II: Intermediate SwiftUI

Build on what you learned in Section I to begin using SwiftUI in more complex ways in your apps. Specifically, you will learn:

Chapter 11: Testing & Debugging: We all know how important testing is in modern application development. See how to apply UI Testing to your SwiftUI apps in this very simple, yet powerful course.

Chapter 12: Handling User Input: Learn how to trigger updates on the interface, including how to easily test a SwiftUI interface, how to manage the flow of screens throughout a complex app, and how to deal with gestures, including the development of a custom gesture.

Chapter 13: Drawing & Custom Graphics: Learn how to draw with the use of paths, shapes, and geometry. Follow along to design your own element and bring it to life by applying some basic animations.

Chapter 14: Animations: Learn the basic concepts for animating views using SwiftUI. Learn how to apply animations to view transitions, how to animate state changes and how to combine and chain those animations.

Chapter 11: Testing and Debugging

By Bill Morefield

Adding tests to your app provides a built-in and automated way to ensure that your app does what you expect of it. And not only do tests check that your code works as expected, but it's also some assurance that future changes won't break existing functionality.

In this chapter, you'll learn how to implement UI tests in your SwiftUI app, and what to watch out for when testing your UI under this new paradigm.

Different types of tests

There are three types of tests that you'll use in your apps. In order of increasing complexity, they are: base tests, integration tests, and user interface tests.

The base of all testing, and the foundation of all other tests, is the **unit test**. Each unit test ensures that you get the expected output when a function processes a given input. Multiple unit tests may test the same piece of code, but each unit test itself should only focus on a single unit of code. A unit test should take milliseconds to execute. You'll run them often, so you want them to run fast.

The next test up the testing hierarchy is the **integration test**. Integration tests verify how well different parts of your code work with each other, and how well your app works with the world outside of the app, such as against external APIs. Integration tests are more complex than unit tests; they usually take longer to run, and as a result, you'll run them less often.

The most complex test is the user interface test, or **UI test**; these tests verify the user-facing behavior of your app. They simulate user interaction with the app and verify the user interface behaves as expected after responding to the interaction.

As you move up the testing hierarchy, each level of test checks a broader scope of action in the app. For example, a unit test would verify that the `calculateTotal()` method in your app returns the correct amount for an order. An integration test would verify that your app correctly determines that the items in the order are in stock. A UI test would verify that after adding an item to an order, the amount displayed to the user displays the correct value.

SwiftUI is a new visual framework, so this chapter focuses on how to write UI tests for SwiftUI apps. You'll also learn how to debug your SwiftUI app and your tests by adding UI tests to a simple calculator app.

Debugging SwiftUI apps

Open the starter project for this chapter, and build and run the app; it's a simple calculator. The app also supports Catalyst, so it works on iOS, iPadOS and the Mac. Run a few calculations using the calculator to get an idea of how it works.

Debugging SwiftUI takes a bit more forethought and planning than most tests, because the user interface and code mix together under the SwiftUI paradigm. Since SwiftUI views are nothing but code, they execute just like any other code would.

Go to **ContentView.swift** and look for the following lines of code. They should be near line 118:

```
Button(action: {
    self.display = "\(self.memory)"
}) {
    Text("MR")
        .frame(width: 45, height: 45)
}
```

This code defines a button for the user interface. The first block defines the action to perform when the user taps the button. The next block defines what the button looks like in the view. Even though the two pieces of code are adjacent, they won't always execute at the same time.

Setting breakpoints

To stop code during execution of an app, you set a breakpoint to tell the debugger to halt code execution when it reaches a particular line of code. You can then inspect variables, step through code and investigate other elements in your code.

To set a breakpoint, you put your cursor on the line in question and then press **Command + ** or select **Debug ▸ Breakpoints ▸ Add Breakpoint at Current Line** from the menu. You can also click on the margin at the line where you want the breakpoint.

Use one of these methods to set two breakpoints; one on the button, and then one on the first line of code in the `action:` for the **M+** button as shown below:

```
135     Button(action: {
136         if let val = Double(self.display) {
137             self.memory = self.memory + val
138             self.display = ""
139             self.pendingOperation = .none
140         } else {
141             // Add Bug Fix Here
142             self.display = ""
143         }
144     }) {
145         Text("M+")
146             .frame(width: 45, height: 45)
147             .addButtonBorder(Color.gray)
148     }
```

You can start the app in the simulator, but you can also run the app in the preview in debug mode. To do this, hold down **Control** and click the **Play** button on the preview.

You'll see a menu that lets you choose between the standard **Live Preview** and **Debug Preview**.

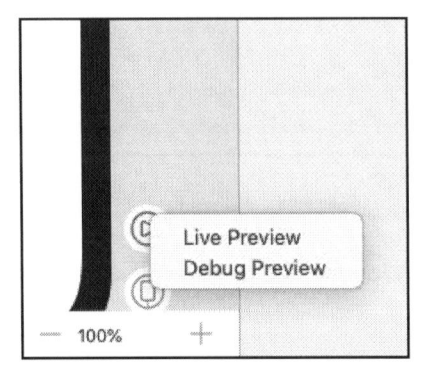

Select **Debug Preview** from the menu to start the app. Debug Preview runs your app in debug mode using the simulator in the background. After a moment, the app reaches the breakpoint at the `Button` control. SwiftUI executes the code in the view to create your UI. When it reaches the breakpoint, execution pauses just as it would with any other code.

When execution reaches a breakpoint, the app pauses and Xcode returns control to you. At the bottom of the Xcode window, you'll see the **Debug Area** consisting of two windows below the code editor. If you don't see the Debug Area, go to **View ▸ Debug Area ▸ Show Debug Area** or press **Shift + Command + Y** to toggle the Debug Area.

The left pane of the Debug Area contains the Variables View. It shows you the current status and value of active variables in your app. The right pane contains an interactive Console, the most complex and powerful tool for debugging in Xcode.

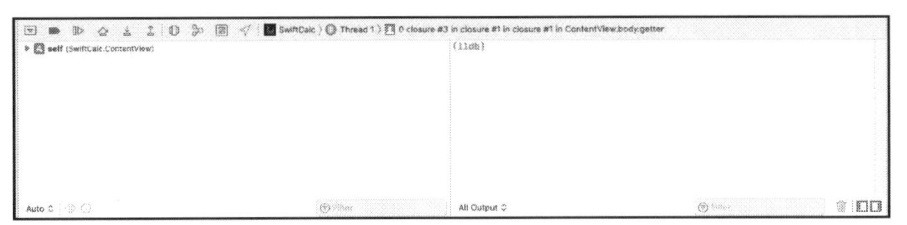

At the **(lldb)** prompt in the console, execute the following:

```
po self._memory._value
```

You'll see the result shows the contents of the `memory` state variable:

```
(lldb) po self._memory._value
0.0
```

Using breakpoints does more than halt code; it can also tell you whether or not the execution of the app actually reached this piece of code. If a breakpoint doesn't trigger, then you know something caused the app to skip the code.

The mixing of code and UI elements can be confusing, but breakpoints can help you make sense of what is executing and when. If you add a breakpoint and it never breaks, then you know that the execution never reached the declaration and the interface will not contain the element. If your breakpoint does get hit, you can investigate the state of the app at that point.

Exploring breakpoint control

When stopped at a breakpoint, you'll see a toolbar between the code editor and debug area. The first button in this toolbar toggles the visibility of the debug area. The second button disables all breakpoints but does not delete them. The third button continues the execution of the app. You can also select **Debug ▸ Continue** in the menu to continue app execution.

The next three buttons allow you to step through your code. Clicking the first executes the current line of code, including any method or function calls. The second button also executes the current line of code, but if there is a method call, it pauses at the first line of code inside that method or function. The final button executes code through to the end of the current method or function.

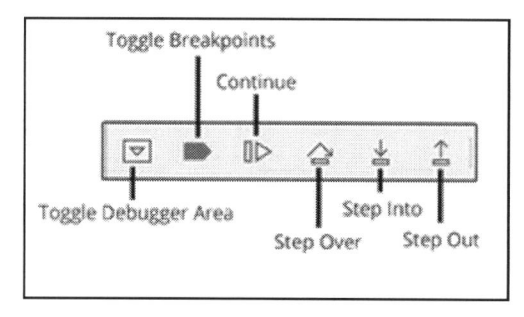

Continue execution of the app by using either the toolbar button or the menu. After another short pause, you'll see execution halt at the `Button` breakpoint again. **Continue** execution, and you'll see the app preview appear. Tap the **M+** button on the preview to see if your breakpoint triggers.

It does, and the code pauses at the breakpoint on the first line of the `Button`'s action block. As with the UI code, you can step through each line, check values using the debugger and do anything else that helps you understand and troubleshoot the app.

There's a bug in this code you'll notice when you **Continue**. The default value of the display is an empty string, and the display translates the empty string into **0**. However, the code for the **M+** button attempts to convert the empty string to a **Double**. When that conversion fails, the value **Error** appears to the user.

Even if you don't write a test for every case in your app, it's a beneficial practice to create tests when you find bugs. Creating a test ensures that you have, in fact, fixed the bug. It also provides early notice if this bug were to reappear in the future. In the next section, you're going to write a UI test for this bug.

> **Note**: Delete the Breakpoints you just created. You can do so by right-clicking on the breakpoint and choosing **Delete Breakpoint**.

Adding UI tests

In the starter project, go to **File ▸ New ▸ Target…**. Select **iOS** and scroll down to find **Test**. Click **UI Testing Bundle** and click **Next**.

Xcode suggests a name for the test bundle that combines the name of the project and the type of test. Accept the suggestion of **SwiftCalcUITests**. Select **SwiftCalc** as the **Project** and **Target to be Tested**. Finally, click **Finish**.

In the Project navigator, you'll see a new group named **SwiftCalcUITests**. This new target contains the framework where you build your UI tests; expand the group and open **SwiftCalcUITests.swift**.

You'll see the file starts by importing `XCTest`. The `XCTest` framework contains Apple's default testing libraries. You'll also see the test class inherits from `XCTestCase`, from which all test classes inherit their behavior.

You'll also see three default methods provided in the Xcode template. The first two methods are an important part of your test process. The test process calls `setUp()` before each test method in the class, and then calls `tearDown()` after each test method completes.

Remember: a test should verify that a known set of inputs results in an expected set of outputs. You use `setUp()` to ensure your app is in this known state before each test method begins. You use `tearDown()` to clean up after each test so that you're back to a known starting condition for the next test.

Note the following line in `setUp()`:

```
continueAfterFailure = false
```

This line stops testing if a failure occurs. Setting this value to `false` stops the test process after the first failure. Given the nature of UI testing, you will almost always end up in an unknown state when a test fails. Rather than continue what are often long-running tests for very little and potentially incorrect information, you should stop and fix the problem now.

In this chapter, you won't have any other setup or cleanup work to perform after your tests.

The third method in the template is `testExample()`, which contains a sample test. You'll also see the method has a small gray diamond next to its name; this means that Xcode recognizes it as a test, but the test hasn't been run yet. Once the test runs, the diamond will change to a green checkmark, if the test passes, or to a white **X** on a red background after completion, if the test fails.

Test names *must* begin with **test**. If not, the testing framework ignores the method and will not execute it when testing. For example, the framework ignores a method named `myCoolTest()`, but it will execute `testMyCoolCode()`.

```
func testExample() {
    // UI tests must launch the application that they test.
    let app = XCUIApplication()
    app.launch()

    // Use recording to get started writing UI tests.
    // Use XCTAssert and related functions to verify your tests produce the correct results.
}

func myCoolTest() {

}
```

You'll see a comment in the sample test suggesting you "Use recording to get started writing UI tests." Recording can save time when building UI tests, but the tooling doesn't yet work with SwiftUI. You'll be writing these tests from scratch.

Creating a UI Test

Proper test names should be precise and clear about what the test validates, as an app can end up with a large number of tests. Clear names make it easy to understand what failed. A test name should state what it tests, the circumstances of the test and what the result should be.

Rename `testExample()` to
`testPressMemoryPlusAtAppStartShowZeroInDisplay()`. Does that feel really
long? Test names are not the place or time for brevity; the name should clearly
provide all three elements at a glance.

A UI test begins with the app in the "just started" state, so you can write each test as
though the app has just started. Note that this doesn't mean the app state is reset
each run. You use the `setUp()` and `tearDown()` methods to ensure your app is in a
particular known state before each test and to clean up any changes made during the
test. If you expect settings, data, configuration, location or other information to be
present at the time the test is run, then you must set those up.

Clear the comments after the `app.launch()` command, and add a breakpoint at
`app.launch()` line in the test.

There are several ways to start UI tests. First, you can go to the Test navigator by
pressing **Command + 6** in Xcode. You'll see your test along with the default
`testLaunchPerformance()` test. If you hover the mouse over the name of a test,
you'll see a gray play button. Hover your mouse over the gray diamond to the left of
the function name, and you'll see a play button.

If you hover over the name of the class or the testing framework either in the Test
Navigator or the source code, a similar play button appears that will start a group of
tests to run in sequence.

This test isn't complete, as it doesn't test anything. This is a good time to run it and
learn a bit about how a test runs. For now, use either method to start your
`testPressMemoryPlusAtAppStartShowZeroInDisplay()` test.

Tests are Swift code, so you can debug tests just like you debug your app! You'll
sometimes need to determine why a test doesn't behave as expected. When the test
reaches the breakpoint, you'll see execution stop, just as your breakpoint would
behave in any other code.

The main element you'll want to explore is the app element where you placed the
breakpoint. Step over the command to launch the app using the toolbar button,
pressing **F6** or selecting **Debug ▸ Step Over** in the menu. In the simulator, you'll see
the app launch. Once you have the **(lldb)** prompt in the console, enter po app.

You'll see output similar to the following:

```
Element subtree:
 →Application, 0x60000249ee60, pid: 893, label: 'SwiftCalc'
    Window (Main), 0x60000249ebc0, {{0.0, 0.0}, {414.0, 896.0}}
      Other, 0x60000249eca0, {{0.0, 0.0}, {414.0, 896.0}}
        Other, 0x60000249dc00, {{0.0, 0.0}, {414.0, 896.0}}
          Other, 0x60000249dce0, {{0.0, 0.0}, {414.0, 896.0}}
            StaticText, 0x60000249e840, {{386.5, 44.0}, {17.5, 34.5}},
              label: '0'
            Button, 0x60000249ddc0, {{78.5, 102.5}, {45.0, 45.0}}, label:
              'MC'
            Button, 0x60000249e680, {{131.5, 102.5}, {45.0, 45.0}},
              label: 'MR'
            Button, 0x600002498540, {{184.5, 102.5}, {45.0, 45.0}},
              label: 'M+'
            Button, 0x600002498620, {{237.5, 102.5}, {45.0, 45.0}},
              label: 'C'
            Button, 0x600002498700, {{290.5, 102.5}, {45.0, 45.0}},
              label: 'AC'
            Button, 0x6000024987e0, {{78.5, 171.5}, {45.0, 45.0}}, label:
              '√'
            Button, 0x6000024988c0, {{131.5, 171.5}, {45.0, 45.0}},
              label: '7'
            Button, 0x6000024989a0, {{184.5, 171.5}, {45.0, 45.0}},
              label: '8'
            Button, 0x600002498a80, {{237.5, 171.5}, {45.0, 45.0}},
              label: '9'
            Button, 0x600002498b60, {{290.5, 171.5}, {45.0, 45.0}},
              label: '÷'
            Button, 0x600002498c40, {{78.5, 240.5}, {45.0, 45.0}}, label:
              'π'
            Button, 0x600002498d20, {{131.5, 240.5}, {45.0, 45.0}},
              label: '4'
```

The **po** command in the console lets you examine the state of an object; in this case, you're examining the app object, which you declared as an XCUIApplication, a subclass of XCUIElement. You'll be working with this object in all of your UI tests.

The app object contains a tree that begins with the application and continues through all of the UI elements in your app. Each of these elements is also of type XCUIElement. You'll access the UI elements in your app by running filter queries against the app object to select items in the tree that you see.

Next, you'll see how to run a query to find buttons in the app.

Accessing UI elements

Add the following code to the end of the test method:

```
let memoryButton = app.buttons["M+"]
memoryButton.tap()
```

XCUIApplication contains a set of elements for each type of user interface object. This query first filters for only .button elements in the app. It then filters to the element which has a label of **M+**.

SwiftUI apps render to the native elements of the platform; they're not new components. Even though SwiftUI provides a new way to define an interface, it still uses the existing elements of the platform. A SwiftUI Button becomes a UIButton on iOS and a NSButton on macOS. In this app, the filter matches the label you saw in the output from **po app**.

```
Button, 0x600002498540, {{184.5, 102.5}, {45.0, 45.0}}, label: 'M+'
```

Once you have the button object, you call the tap() method on the button. This method simulates someone tapping on the button. Rerun the test.

> **Note**: You can disable the Breakpoints by clicking on them. They should turn grey. Press them again whenever you want to reactivate them.

```
func testPressMemoryPlusAtAppStartShowZeroInDisplay() {
    // UI tests must launch the application that they test.
    let app = XCUIApplication()
    app.launch()

    let memoryButton = app.buttons["M+"]
    memoryButton.tap()
}
```

You'll see the app start and run in the simulator as the test runs. If you watch the simulator, you'll see the display of the calculator show **Error** just as it did when you ran it manually. Once the tests are done, the app will stop. You'll see the gray diamond changes into a green checkmark both next to the function and in the Test Navigator.

The green check signifies a passed test. In this case, the test didn't check anything. The framework treats a test that doesn't fail, as a passing test.

In a UI test, the known set of inputs to your test is the set of interactions with the app. Here you performed an interaction by tapping the **M+** button, so now you need to check the result. In the next section, you'll see how to get the value from a control.

Reading the user interface

You found the **M+** button by matching the label of the button. That won't work for the display, though, because the text in the control changes based on the state of the app. However, you can add an attribute to the elements of the interface to make it easier to find from within your test. Open **ContentView.swift**. In the view, look for the two comments `// Add display identifier` and replace both with the following line:

```
.accessibility(identifier: "display")
```

This method sets the `accessibilityIdentifer` for the resulting UI element. Despite the name, VoiceOver doesn't read the `accessibilityIdentifer` attribute; this simply provides a way to give a UI element a constant label for testing. If you don't provide this identifier for an element, it will generally be the same as the `label` for the control as it was with the **M+** button.

Go back to **SwiftCalcUITests.swift**. Add the following code at the end of `testPressMemoryPlusAtAppStartShowZeroInDisplay()`:

```
// 1
let display = app.staticTexts["display"]
// 2
let displayText = display.label
// 3
XCTAssert(displayText == "0")
```

You've written your first real test! Here's what each step does:

1. You use the `accessibility(identifier:)` you added to find the display element in your app.

2. The result of step 1 is an `XCUIElement`, as are most UI elements in a UI test. You want to investigate the `label` property of the element which contains the text of the label.

3. You use an assertion to verify the label matches the expected result. All testing assertions begin with the prefix `XCT` — a holdover from Objective-C naming conventions. In each test, you perform one or more assertions that determine if the test passes or fails.

In this case, you are checking that the text for display is the string "0". You already know the result will be a failing test, but still, run the completed test to see what happens. You'll get the expected failure and see a white **X** on red.

```
func testPressMemoryPlusAtAppStartShowZeroInDisplay() {
    // UI tests must launch the application that they test.
    let app = XCUIApplication()
    app.launch()

    let memoryButton = app.buttons["M+"]
    memoryButton.tap()
    // 1
    let display = app.staticTexts["display"]
    // 2
    let displayText = display.label
    // 3
    XCTAssert(displayText == "0")
}
```

Now that you have a test in place, you can fix the bug!

Fixing the bug

Open **ContentView.swift**, find the comment in the action for the **M+** button that reads `// Add Bug Fix Here`, and replace that with the following line:

```
self.display = ""
```

Rerun the test. You'll see that it passes.

```
func testPressMemoryPlusAtAppStartShowZeroInDisplay() {
    // UI tests must launch the application that they test.
    let app = XCUIApplication()
    app.launch()

    let memoryButton = app.buttons["M+"]
    memoryButton.tap()
    // 1
    let display = app.staticTexts["display"]
    // 2
    let displayText = display.label
    // 3
    XCTAssert(displayText == "0")
}
```

You may be wondering why you went through the extra effort: You changed one line of code to fix the bug, but you added another framework to your app and had to write five lines of code to create the test.

Although this may feel like a lot of work to prove that you've fixed a tiny issue, you'll find this pattern of writing a failing test, fixing the bug and then verifying that the test passes, to be a useful pattern. Taking an existing app without tests, and adding a test each time you fix a bug, quickly builds a useful set of tests for now, and more importantly, for the future.

Adding more complex tests

Ideally, you would be building out your UI tests at the same time as you built out your UI. This way, as your UI becomes more fleshed out, your test suite will expand along with it. However, with the realities of modern development, you'll usually be adding tests after the application already exists.

Add a more complex test that verifies adding two single-digit numbers gives the correct sum. Open **SwiftCalcUITests.swift** and add the following test at the end of the class:

```swift
func testAddingTwoDigits() {
  let app = XCUIApplication()
  app.launch()

  let threeButton = app.buttons["3"]
  threeButton.tap()

  let addButton = app.buttons["+"]
  addButton.tap()

  let fiveButton = app.buttons["5"]
  fiveButton.tap()

  let equalButton = app.buttons["="]
  equalButton.tap()

  let display = app.staticTexts["display"]
  let displayText = display.label
  XCTAssert(displayText == "8")
}
```

When you run the test, you might not expect it to fail. Three plus five does equal eight, right? Take a moment to see if you can figure out why before continuing.

Your test compares the label of the display to the string **8**. Place a breakpoint at XCTAssert statement and rerun the test. Wait until execution stops at the breakpoint. At the console prompt enter **po displayText**.

You'll see the text of the display reads **8.0**, not **8**. A UI test focuses on the user interface and not on the behind-the-scenes elements. A unit test, in contrast, would check that the code properly calculated **3 + 5 = 8**. The UI test should verify what the user sees when performing this calculation.

Change the final line of the test to:

```
XCTAssert(displayText == "8.0")
```

Rerun the test, and you'll see it passes now.

```
func testAddingTwoDigits() {
    let app = XCUIApplication()
    app.launch()

    let threeButton = app.buttons["3"]
    threeButton.tap()

    let addButton = app.buttons["+"]
    addButton.tap()

    let fiveButton = app.buttons["5"]
    fiveButton.tap()

    let equalButton = app.buttons["="]
    equalButton.tap()

    let display = app.staticTexts["display"]
    let displayText = display.label
    XCTAssert(displayText == "8.0")
}
```

Next, you'll make a change to the user interface, and, because you want to form good testing habits, you'll add a test to verify the change.

Simulating user interaction

You'll first add a gesture so that swiping the memory display to the left clears it. The effect of the gesture works the same as tapping the **MC** key by setting the value of `self.memory` to zero.

Open **ContentView.swift**. After the body definition, add a gesture:

```
let memorySwipe = DragGesture(minimumDistance: 20)
    .onEnded { _ in
```

```
    self.memory = 0.0
}
```

Now add `return` in front of the `GeometryReader` that previously began body to keep the compiler happy.

You can add this gesture to the memory display. Find the text `// Add gesture here` and replace it with:

```
.gesture(memorySwipe)
```

Like with display, you will also add an identifier to the display. Add the following line below `Text("\(self.memory)")`:

```
.accessibility(identifier: "memoryDisplay")
```

Build and run the app; type in a few digits and tap **M+** to store the value in memory. The memory display appears and shows the stored digits. Swipe the memory display to the left, and verify the display clears.

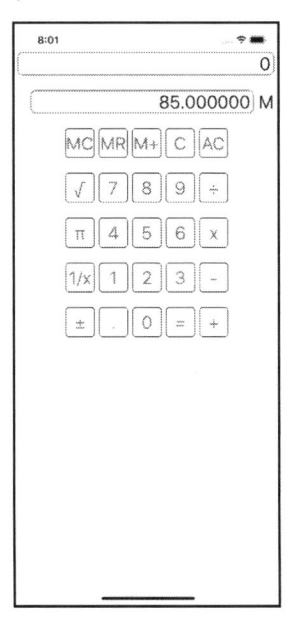

Now, because you're practicing good development and testing habits, you'll add a UI test to verify this behavior. The steps of the test replicate the actions you just performed manually.

Open **SwiftCalcUITests.swift** and add the following code after the existing tests:

```
func testSwipeToClearMemory() {
  let app = XCUIApplication()
  app.launch()

  let threeButton = app.buttons["3"]
  threeButton.tap()
  let fiveButton = app.buttons["5"]
  fiveButton.tap()

  let memoryButton = app.buttons["M+"]
  memoryButton.tap()

  let memoryDisplay = app.staticTexts["memoryDisplay"]
  // 1
  XCTAssert(memoryDisplay.exists)
  // 2
  memoryDisplay.swipeLeft()
  // 3
  XCTAssertFalse(memoryDisplay.exists)
}
```

You've seen most of this code before. Here's what the new code does:

1. The `exists` property on a `XCUIElement` is `true` when the element exists. If the memory display were not visible, then this assert would fail.

2. The `swipeLeft()` method produces a swipe action to the left on the calling element. There are additional methods for `swipeRight()`, `swipeUp()` and `swipeDown()`.

3. The `XCTAssertFalse()` test acts as an opposite for `XCTAssert`. It succeeds when the checked value is `false` instead of `true`. The swipe should set `memory` to zero after the gesture, and the action should hide the memory display, wiping it out of existence.

Run the test, and you'll see it confirms that your UI works as expected.

There are many testing elements beyond those discussed in this chapter. Some of the common attributes and methods that you haven't had a chance to use in this chapter are:

- **.isHittable**: An element is hittable if the element exists and the user can click, tap or press it at its current location. An offscreen element exists but is not hittable.

- **.typeText()**: This method acts as though the user types the text into the calling control.

- **.press(forDuration:)**: Allows you to perform a one-finger touch for a specified amount of time.

- **.press(forDuration:thenDragTo:)**: The `swipe` methods provide no guarantee of the velocity of the gesture. You can use this method to perform a more precise drag action.

- **.waitForExistence()**: Useful to pause when an element may not appear on the screen immediately.

You'll find a complete list of methods and properties in Apple's documentation at https://developer.apple.com/documentation/xctest/xcuielement

Testing multiple platforms

Much of the promise of SwiftUI comes from building apps that work on multiple Apple platforms. Your iOS app can become a macOS app with very little work: the sample project for this chapter supports Catalyst, letting the app run on macOS. However, there's always a few things that you'll have to take care of yourself, to ensure your apps, and their tests, work properly on all platforms.

In Xcode, change the target device for the app to **My Mac**. In the project settings, select the **SwiftCalc** target. Choose to **Signing and Capabilities** and change **Signing Certificate** to **Sign to Run Locally**. Now build and run the app to see it run for macOS.

You learned about using SwiftUI with different operating systems in Chapter 5, "**The Apple Ecosystem**". Since, as you expect, running on different platforms may require tweaks to the user interface, testing the UI on various operating systems will require different tests. Some UI actions translate directly; for instance, tapping a button on an iOS device works just clicking your mouse on a button would on macOS.

With the target device still set to **My Mac**, build and run your tests. You'll get a compilation error: "Value of type 'XCUIElement' has no member 'swipeLeft'". Aha — not all actions have direct equivalents on every operating system. The `.swipeLeft()` action produces an error, because Catalyst provides no swipe equivalent for macOS in the test framework.

The solution lies in Xcode's conditional compilation blocks. These blocks tell Xcode to only compile the wrapped code when one or more of the conditions are true at compile time. A block begins with `#if` followed by a test. You can optionally use `#elseif` and `#else` as with traditional `if` statements, and you end the block with

`#endif`.

You want to exclude the failing test when testing the app under Catalyst. Wrap the `testSwipeToClearMemory()` test inside a `targetEnvironment` check to exclude tests from Catalyst:

```
#if !targetEnvironment(macCatalyst)
    // Test to exclude
#endif
```

You can also specify the operating system as a condition. The operating system can be any one of `macOS`, `iOS`, `watchOS`, `tvOS` or `Linux`. For example, XCTest does not support watchOS yet. If you're building an app for watchOS, you'll need to wrap tests to prevent the code from running against watchOS. To exclude tests from watchOS, wrap the tests with a similar check that excludes watchOS:

```
#if !os(watchOS)
    // Your XCTest code
#endif
```

A best practice when designing UI tests for cross-platform apps is to keep tests for specific operating systems together in a single test class. Use conditional compilation wrappers to isolate the code to compile only under the target platform and operating system.

Key points

- Building and debugging tests requires a but more attention due to the combination of code and user interface elements in SwiftUI.
- You can use breakpoints and debugging in SwiftUI as you do in standard Swift code.
- Tests automate checking the behavior of your code. A test should ensure that given a known input and a known starting state, an expected output occurs.
- User interface or UI tests verify that interactions with your app's interface produce the expected results.
- Add an `accessibilityIdentifer` to elements that do not have static text for their label to improve location for testing.

- You find all user interface elements from the `XCUIApplication` element used to launch the app in the test.

- Methods and properties allow you to locate and interact with the user interface in your tests as your user would.

- Different platforms often need different user interface tests. Use conditional compilation to match tests to the platform and operating system.

Challenge

As noted earlier, the swipe gesture to clear the memory does not work under Catalyst. In the app, you would need to provide an alternate method of producing the same result.

For the Catalyst version of this app, add a double-tap gesture to the memory display to accomplish the same result as the swipe gesture. Update the `testSwipeToClearMemory()` test to check the functionality appropriately on each environment.

Challenge solution

You should begin by adding the new double-tap gesture. Change the current gesture definition to:

```
#if targetEnvironment(macCatalyst)
let doubleTap = TapGesture(count: 2)
  .onEnded { _ in
    self.memory = 0.0
}
#else
let memorySwipe = DragGesture(minimumDistance: 20)
  .onEnded { _ in
    self.memory = 0.0
}
#endif
```

This keeps the current swipe gesture on phones and tablets, but creates a tap gesture that expects two taps on Catalyst.

Now update the memory display to similarly use the correct gesture for each environment.

```
#if targetEnvironment(macCatalyst)
```

```
Text("\(self.memory)")
    .accessibility(identifier: "memoryDisplay")
    .padding(.horizontal, 5)
    .frame(width: geometry.size.width * 0.85,
alignment: .trailing)
    .overlay(RoundedRectangle(cornerRadius: 8).stroke(lineWidth:
2).foregroundColor(Color.gray))
    .gesture(doubleTap)
#else
Text("\(self.memory)")
    .accessibility(identifier: "memoryDisplay")
    .padding(.horizontal, 5)
    .frame(width: geometry.size.width * 0.85,
alignment: .trailing)
    .overlay(RoundedRectangle(cornerRadius: 8).stroke(lineWidth:
2).foregroundColor(Color.gray))
    .gesture(memorySwipe)
#endif
```

SwiftUI doesn't support putting a `targetEnvironment()` condition within the modifiers to a view. That means you have to place the view twice, changing the desired gesture in each.

Lastly, update your `testSwipeToClearMemory()` test and replace the code after the second step earlier with:

```
#if targetEnvironment(macCatalyst)
memoryDisplay.doubleTap()
#else
memoryDisplay.swipeLeft()
#endif
```

This will call the appropriate UI gesture on each environment. Run your test on both **My Mac** and the **iOS Simulator** to validate your changes.

Where to go from here?

This chapter provided an introduction to testing and debugging your SwiftUI projects. Your starting point to go more in-depth should be Apple's documentation on XCTest at https://developer.apple.com/documentation/xctest.

The book *iOS Test-Driven Development by Tutorials* provides a more in-depth look at testing iOS apps and test-driven development. You can find that book here:

- https://store.raywenderlich.com/products/ios-test-driven-development

You'll also find more about testing in the WWDC 2019 video **Testing in Xcode** at https://developer.apple.com/videos/play/wwdc2019/413/.

You'll find a lot more information about the Xcode debugger and using it in the deep-dive book *Advanced Apple Debugging & Reverse Engineering*, available here:

- https://store.raywenderlich.com/products/advanced-apple-debugging-and-reverse-engineering

Apple often releases new videos on the changes related to debugging each year at WWDC. For 2019, there's a video dedicated to Debugging in Xcode 11 at https://developer.apple.com/videos/play/wwdc2019/412/. Once you're ready to go deeper into debugging, you'll also want to watch **LLDB: Beyond "po"** at https://developer.apple.com/videos/play/wwdc2019/429/https://developer.apple.com/videos/play/wwdc2019/429/.

Chapter 12: Handling User Input

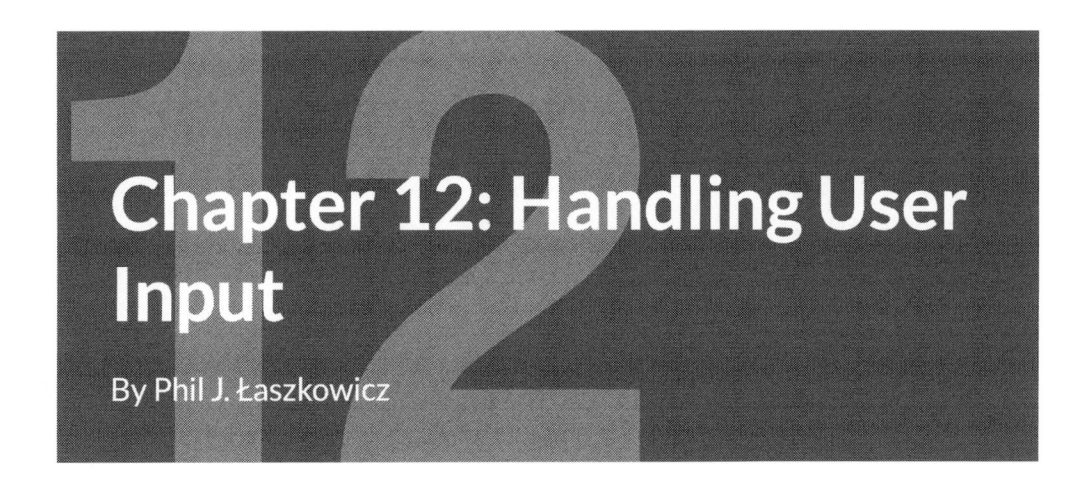

By Phil J. Łaszkowicz

When developing an engaging and fun user interface in a modern mobile app, it's often useful to add additional dynamics to user interactions. Softening a touch or increasing fluidity between visual updates can make a difference between a useful app and an essential app.

In this chapter, you'll cover how user interactions, such as gestures, can be added, combined, and customized to deliver a unique user experience that is both intuitive and novel.

You're going to go back to the Kuchi flash card app previously covered in this book; you'll add a new tab to the main tab bar for learning new words. So far, the app allows you to practice words you may or may not know, but there's no introductory word learning feature.

Let´s start by **opening the starter project**.

Adding the learn feature

To add a new tab to the tab bar you first need to create an empty view as your top-level view for the selected feature. As this new tab and view will be providing a new set of features for the app, you will place their files in a new group called *Learn*. This will sit at the same level as the existing *Practice* folder.

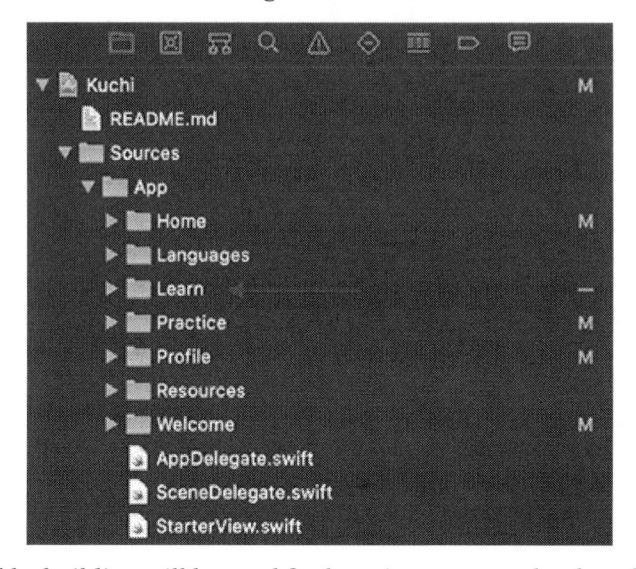

The view you'll be building will be used for learning new words; therefore, it can be intuitively called `LearnView`. So, go ahead and create a new SwiftUI view file named **LearnView.swift** inside the Learn group.

Once you've created the new view, you can leave it empty and go back to the view where you declared the tabs previously: **HomeView.swift**.

The user will probably want to learn words before practicing them, so you'll be placing the new learn tab before the practice tab. At the top of the `TabView` inside the body, add the following:

```
LearnView()
  .tabItem({
    VStack {
      Image(systemName: "bookmark")
      Text("Learn")
    }
  })
  .tag(0)
```

The tag order has been shifted to make the new `LearnView` the zero-indexed tag (`.tag(0)`). This means you must update the tag of `PracticeView`, `ProgressView`, and `ProfileView`. Their tag should be 1, 2, and 3 respectively.

Looking at the Canvas of `HomeView`, the new tab should be immediately visible. When developing new features in existing apps, it can be easy to dig deep into writing code before you've had a chance to think about the design and structure of the feature itself. By going at it this way, you take it one step at a time and can even see the result in the process.

Creating a flash card

With the tab in place, the first component of the Learn feature you'll be working on is the flash card. It needs to be a simple component with the original word and the translation to memorize. When talking about the card, there are two distinct understandings within the app that are useful to recognize: the visual card (a UI component) and the card data (the state). Both are integral to the card feature and the card itself is a composite of both elements. However, the visual card cannot exist without state; to start with, you need a data structure that can represent the state.

Create a new Swift file in your Learn folder named **FlashCard.swift**. It's going to be a simple struct. You'll need to reuse the data from the `Learning` library so start by adding the `import` statement to the top of the file:

```
import Learning
```

And follow that with the struct declaration:

```
struct FlashCard {

}
```

Within the struct, you'll need the data the user is trying to learn. In this case, it's the word, and this is where the existing `Languages` import comes in useful. Add a property of type `WordCard` with the name `card` to your struct:

```
var card: WordCard
```

This is the basic data structure for your flash card, but to make it useful for your SwiftUI views, you'll need a few more properties.

> **Note:** It may seem odd to be creating a whole new object to represent a card when you already have `WordCard` as part of your Languages library.
>
> However, in many projects you won't have access to modify the original data structures provided, whether you're using a SDK, a client library from a cloud platform vendor, or perhaps you're using a third-party library where changing the code is either impossible or impractical.
>
> For this exercise, the Languages and Learning libraries are being treated as third-party components, so the approaches taken will rely on working around established data structures for SwiftUI state objects.

First an `id` may be useful for iterating through multiple flash cards in a view. This is best achieved by making a structure comply with the `Identifiable` protocol, as the `ForEach` SwiftUI block will initially look for an `id` unless an explicit identifier has been specified.

As there are no `id` generators within the app you can simply rely on `Foundation`'s `UUID` constructor to provide a unique identifier each time a `FlashCard` is created. Add the following property to `FlashCard`:

```
let id = UUID()
```

As you can see, there's no explicit use of the `Identifiable` protocol yet. This will be covered shortly. The final step needed within your basic `FlashCard` state structure is to add a flag called `isActive`. Add the following property to the top of your structure:

```
var isActive = true
```

This is a simple property for filtering cards that are intended to be part of the learning session. The user may not want to go through a whole deck of cards that they already know each and every time so this allows you to selectively filter cards whether through user curation, or through internal logic.

To ensure compliance with the `Identifiable` protocol, create a new Swift file named **FlashCard+Identifiable.swift** in the same folder and add:

```
extension FlashCard: Identifiable {
}
```

You don't need to do anything extra to make `FlashCard` identifiable, but you will want to make sure it's `Equatable`. This will enable you to provide comparisons quickly and easily in code, to ensure the same card is not duplicated, or that one card matches another when relevant.

Add another code file and name it **FlashCard+Equatable.swift**. Within this file add the following static == operator:

```
extension FlashCard: Equatable {
    static func == (lhs: FlashCard, rhs: FlashCard) -> Bool {
      return lhs.card.word.original == rhs.card.word.original
        && lhs.card.word.translation == rhs.card.word.translation
    }
}
```

With this property, you'll be able to use the == operator to compare two flash cards.

There you go; that's your `FlashCard` state object defined and ready for use!

The user is not going to be learning one card at a time though, so you'll need to build on this object with the concept of a deck. There is a deck for the Practice feature of the app as a simple array of cards, but the Learn feature has different needs so you're going to be more explicit with how the deck works this time.

Building a flash deck

Although the deck is not a new concept, the *Learn* feature is going to be more explicit than *Practice* with the deck of cards by creating a whole new state structure for use in the UI. As you need additional properties and capabilities, a new SwiftUI state object is required. Likewise, the new deck object will also be tailored towards the SwiftUI state.

Start by creating a new Swift file called **FlashDeck.swift** inside the Learn group.

`FlashDeck` needs just a single property: an array of `FlashCard` objects.

```
import Learning

final internal class FlashDeck {
    var cards: [FlashCard]
}
```

What makes the `FlashDeck` a powerful SwiftUI state object comes from two modifications. The first will be from a constructor. Add the following:

```
init(from words: [WordCard]) {
  self.cards = words.map {
    FlashCard(card: $0)
  }
}
```

This constructor simply maps the words passed in into `FlashCards`.

The second power-up for the `FlashDeck` model comes from `Combine`. In order to make the UI responsive to changes in the deck, the `cards` property will be prefixed with the `@Published` attribute to allow subscribers of the model to receive notifications of updates.

Change the `cards` property from:

```
var cards: [FlashCard]
```

Into:

```
@Published var cards: [FlashCard]
```

And finally, you need to extend the class to be an `ObservableObject` (as per the *State and Data Flow* chapter).

To do so, create a new file named **FlashDeck+ObservableObject.swift** and add the following code:

```
import Combine

extension FlashDeck: ObservableObject {
}
```

You now have your `FlashCard` and `FlashDeck` built and ready to go. Although they're somewhat indirect state models with the data being being plain object models from the `Languages` and `Learning` libraries, this approach to wrapping external structures is something that is generally important to get to terms with. SwiftUI projects will often require `Combine` compatible wrappers around basic structures rather than new structures that can be tailored directly to the way SwiftUI works. This is especially true, if you are building on top of an app not yet using SwiftUI.

Final state

Your final state work for the Learn feature will be your top-level store, which will hold your deck (and cards) and provide the useful control to manage your deck and receive updates within your UI. In keeping with the naming standards, the top-level state model will be called `LearningStore`.

Create a new file name **LearningStore.swift**.

Next, populate the file with the following:

```swift
import Combine
import Languages
import Learning

final class LearningStore {
  // 1
  @Published var deck: FlashDeck

  // 2
  @Published var card: FlashCard

  // 3
  @Published var score = 0

  // 4
  init() {
    let deck = FlashDeck(from: DeckBuilder.learning.build())
    self.deck = deck
    self.card = FlashCard(
      card: WordCard(
        from: TranslatedWord(
          from: "",
          withPronunciation: "",
          andTranslation: "")))

    if let nextCard = self.getNextCard() {
      self.card = nextCard
    }
  }

  // 5
  func getNextCard() -> FlashCard? {
    if let nextCard = self.getLastCard() {
      self.card = nextCard
      self.deck.cards.removeLast()
    }

    return self.card
  }
```

```
    // 6
    func getLastCard() -> FlashCard? {
      if let lastCard = deck.cards.last {
        self.card = lastCard
        return self.card
      } else {
        return nil
      }
    }
  }
}
```

Going over this step-by-step:

1. Like in `FlashDeck`, you'll use `Combine` to provide `@Published` attributes to your properties. The store will maintain the complete deck (`deck`),
2. ...the current card (`card`),
3. ...and the current score (`score`).
4. You add an initializer that sets up the deck using a `Deckbuilder`.
5. You also add convenience methods called `getNextCard`, which will get the next card in the deck,
6. ...and `getLastCard` which will get the last card in the deck.

The final step of setting up this store is to make it conform to `ObservableObject`. To do this, create a new file named **LearningStore+ObservableObject.swift** and add the following:

```
extension LearningStore: ObservableObject {

}
```

Phew — that's a lot of setup without any UI code, right? But you've now made a nice foundation for building the view for the Learn feature.

And finally... building the UI

The UI for the Learn feature will be formed around a 3-tier view. The first is your currently empty `LearnView`. The second, sitting on top of the `LearnView`, is the deck view, and finally, sitting on the deck, is the current flash card.

You'll start by adding the missing views: `DeckView` and `CardView`.

First up, create a SwiftUI view file named **CardView.swift**, and replace the contents of body with:

```
ZStack {
  Rectangle()
    .fill(Color.red)
    .frame(width: 320, height: 210)
    .cornerRadius(12)
  VStack {
    Spacer()
    Text("Apple")
      .font(.largeTitle)
      .foregroundColor(.white)
    Text("Omena")
      .font(.caption)
      .foregroundColor(.white)
    Spacer()
  }
}
.shadow(radius: 8)
.frame(width: 320, height: 210)
.animation(.spring())
```

This creates a simple red card view with rounded corners and a couple of text labels centered on the card. You'll be expanding on this view later in the tutorial.

If you preview this in the Canvas you should see the following:

Next up, the deck view. Create a SwiftUI file named (you guessed it) **DeckView.swift** and replace the contents of body with:

```
ZStack {
  CardView()
  CardView()
}
```

This is a simple view containing two cards, but you'll flesh this view out shortly by using the state objects you created earlier to support the loading of dynamically generated cards into the learning flow.

As the cards are stacked on top of each other, previewing the deck view in the Canvas will give you the same result as before.

Next, you need to add `DeckView` to `LearnView`.

Go back to **LearnView.swift** and replace the contents of body with the following:

```
VStack {
  Spacer()
  Text("Swipe left if you remembered"
    + "\nSwipe right if you didn't")
    .font(.headline)
  DeckView()
  Spacer()
  Text("Remembered 0/0")
}
```

This is fairly simple: you have a `Text` label providing instructions, a score at the bottom, and the `DeckView` in the center of the screen.

Adding LearningStore to the views

Staying inside `LearnView`, you can add the store you previously created as a property to the view:

```
@ObservedObject private var learningStore = LearningStore()
```

As `LearningStore` is an `ObservableObject`, it can be used within the `LearnView` to ensure the view is rebuilt when any of the published properties change. With this setup, you can even update the score `Text` at the bottom of the view.

Replace:

```
Text("Remembered 0/0")
```

With:

```
Text("Remembered \(self.learningStore.score)"
  + "/\(self.learningStore.deck.cards.count)")
```

That's good for now. You'll come back to `LearnView` later, but now `DeckView` needs to be able to receive some of the data from within the `LearningStore` in order to pipe card data through to the individual `CardView` components.

To enable this, open up **DeckView.swift** and add the following at the top of the struct, before body:

```swift
@ObservedObject private var deck: FlashDeck

private let onMemorized: () -> Void

init(onMemorized: @escaping () -> Void, deck: FlashDeck) {
  self.onMemorized = onMemorized
  self.deck = deck
}
```

You're adding a `FlashDeck` property for getting the items the view will be subscribing to, as well as a callback `onMemorized`, for when the user memorizes a card. Both are passed in through a custom initializer.

For the preview to still work, you need to update `DeckView_Previews`'s previews to the following:

```swift
DeckView(onMemorized: {}, deck: LearningStore().deck)
```

And finally, inside **LearnView.swift** find `DeckView()` in the body and replace it with:

```swift
DeckView(onMemorized: { self.learningStore.score += 1 },
         deck: learningStore.deck)
```

Notice how you increase the score automatically when the user memorizes the card. There's not yet a way to trigger the `onMemorized`, but you'll be adding this later in the chapter.

Next up, getting the data from the learning store into the individual cards. To do so, open up **CardView.swift** and add the following to the top, before body:

```swift
private let flashCard: FlashCard

init(_ card: FlashCard) {
  self.flashCard = card
}
```

Here you add a `FlashCard` property to the view and pass it in through the initializer. The property isn't a state object because you're not planning on changing the value of the `FlashCard` at any time; the card data is fixed for the lifetime of the object.

With an actual card model, you can also update the body of the view to use it. Replace the contents of body with:

```
ZStack {
  Rectangle()
    .fill(Color.red)
    .frame(width: 320, height: 210)
    .cornerRadius(12)
  VStack {
    Spacer()
    Text(flashCard.card.word.original)
      .font(.largeTitle)
      .foregroundColor(.white)
    Text(flashCard.card.word.translation)
      .font(.caption)
      .foregroundColor(.white)
    Spacer()
  }
}
.shadow(radius: 8)
.frame(width: 320, height: 210)
.animation(.spring())
```

With the new initializer, you need to make an update to the places where `CardView` is used: in `CardView_Previews` and `DeckView`.

Inside **CardView.swift** first add the following import statements to the top:

```
import Learning
import Languages
```

Then, update `CardView_Previews`'s `previews` to:

```
let card = FlashCard(
  card: WordCard(
    from: TranslatedWord(
      from: "Apple",
      withPronunciation: "Apple",
      andTranslation: "Omena")))

return CardView(card)
```

Next, inside **DeckView.swift**, you'll need to modify the body to dynamically support multiple `CardView`s.

First, add the following helper methods at the bottom of the view:

```
private func getCardView(for card: FlashCard) -> CardView {
  let activeCards = deck.cards.filter { $0.isActive == true }
```

```
    if let lastCard = activeCards.last {
      if lastCard == card {
        return createCardView(for: card)
      }
    }

    let view = createCardView(for: card)

    return view
  }

  private func createCardView(for card: FlashCard) -> CardView {
    let view = CardView(card)

    return view
  }
```

These methods help with creating a `CardView` using a `FlashCard`.

Then, update the contents of body to the following:

```
ZStack {
  ForEach(deck.cards.filter { $0.isActive }) { card in
    self.getCardView(for: card)
  }
}
```

Here the `ForEach` takes all active cards from the deck and creates a `CardView` for each.

Looking at the Canvas for either `LearnView` or `DeckView`, you should now see the following card:

Your first gesture

Gestures in SwiftUI are not that dissimilar from their cousins in AppKit and UIKit, but they are simpler and somewhat more elegant, giving a perception amongst some developers of being more powerful.

Although they're not any better than their predecessors in terms of capability, their SwiftUI approach makes for easier and more compelling uses for gestures where before they were often nice-to-haves.

Starting with a basic gesture, it's time to revisit `CardView`. Previously, you added both the original word and the translated word to `CardView`, which is somewhat useful. But what if the user wanted to test their knowledge without being given the answer immediately?

It would be nice if the card had the original word, and then the translated word could be displayed if needed.

To achieve this, you can add a simple tap gesture (literally a `TapGesture`) for this interaction to happen. Taps are ubiquitous and necessary, so it's a great place to start with gestures.

Start by opening **CardView.swift**, then add the following property stating whether the answer has been revealed or not to the top of the view:

```
@State private var revealed = false
```

Next, in the body add the following `.gesture` modifer at the bottom, after `.animation(.spring())`:

```
.gesture(TapGesture()
  .onEnded {
    withAnimation(.easeIn, {
      self.revealed = !self.revealed
    })
})
```

Here you're using a pre-built gesture from Apple that adds a lot of convenience by dealing with human tap gestures consistently across all apps. The `onEnded` block enables you to provide additional code for what happens once the tap gesture has ended. In this case you've provided an animation that eases in (`.easeIn`) with the `revealed` property being inverted.

Currently, inverting `revealed` does nothing, but what you want to do is have the `Text` displaying the translation render only when `relevated` is `true`.

To achieve this, inside body, replace the following:

```
Text(flashCard.card.word.translation)
    .font(.caption)
    .foregroundColor(.white)
```

With:

```
if self.revealed {
  Text(flashCard.card.word.translation)
    .font(.caption)
    .foregroundColor(.white)
}
```

Try previewing the app in the Canvas with Live Preview and tapping the card. You should see a rather fluid and pleasant ease-in animation for the translated word. This is as simple as gestures get, and with the animation blocks, it provides a level of fluidity and sophistication users will appreciate.

Easy, right?

Custom gestures

Although the tap gesture, and other simple gestures, provide a lot of mileage for interactions, there are often cases when more sophisticated gestures are worthwhile additions, providing a greater sense of sophistication amongst the deluge of apps available in the App Store.

For this app, you still need to provide an interaction for the user to declare whether they've memorized a card or not. You can do this by adding a custom drag gesture and evaluating the result based on the direction of the drag. That's much more complicated than a simple tap gesture but, thanks to the elegance of SwiftUI, it's still quite painless compared to previous methods of achieving the same thing.

The first step is adding an enum that denotes the direction a card is discarded in. Create a Swift file named **DiscardedDirection.swift** inside the Learn group and add the following code:

```
internal enum DiscardedDirection {
  case left
  case right
}
```

You could identify more complicated metrics for this interaction (up, down, ...) but this view only needs to understand two potential options.

Next, time to make cards draggable! In **CardView.swift** add a new typealias and property to the top of the file, just below the revealed variable definition:

```
typealias CardDrag = (_ card: FlashCard,
                      _ direction: DiscardedDirection) -> Void

private let dragged: CardDrag
```

Called `dragged`, this property accepts the card to be dragged and the enum result for which direction the card was dragged in.

Next, update `init` to accept the dragged closure as a parameter:

```
init(_ card: FlashCard,
     onDrag dragged: @escaping CardDrag = {_,_ in }) {
  self.flashCard = card
  self.dragged = dragged
}
```

Next up, you need to modify `DeckView` so it supports the new card functionality. Open up **DeckView.swift** and replace the implementation `createCardView(for:)` with the following:

```
func createCardView(for card: FlashCard) -> CardView {
  let view = CardView(card, onDrag: { card, direction in
    if direction == .left {
      self.onMemorized()
    }
  })

  return view
}
```

Here you add the onDrag callback to the CardView instance. If the drag direction is .left, you trigger onMemorized(), and the counter in LearningStore will be incremented by one.

The final step is to add the actual drag gesture. Go back to **CardView.swift**, then add the following property to the top again:

```
@State var offset: CGSize = .zero
```

To move the card around, the offset needs to be updated.

Next up, creating the drag gesture. At the top of the body change the line:

```
ZStack {
```

into:

```
return ZStack {
```

You need to return the ZStack as you'll be adding the drag gesture setup above it. Right above this code line, and inside the body, add the following:

```
let drag = DragGesture()
  .onChanged { self.offset = $0.translation }
  .onEnded {
    if $0.translation.width < -100 {
      self.offset = .init(width: -1000, height: 0)
      self.dragged(self.flashCard, .left)
    } else if $0.translation.width > 100 {
      self.offset = .init(width: 1000, height: 0)
      self.dragged(self.flashCard, .right)
    } else {
      self.offset = .zero
    }
  }
```

This DragGesture does most of the work for you, but there are a few things worth noting. Firstly, with each movement recorded during the drag, the onChanged event will occur. You're modifying the offset property (which is an x and y coordinate object) to match the drag motion of the user. For example, if the user started dragging at (0, 0) in the coordinate space, and the onChanged triggered when the user was still dragged at (200, -100) then the offset x-axis would be increased by 200 and the offset y-axis would be decreased by 100. Essentially this means the component would move right and up on the screen to match the motion of the users finger.

The onEnded event occurs when the user stops dragging, typically when their finger is removed from the screen. At this point you want to determine which direction the user dragged the card and whether they dragged it far enough to be considered a decision (at which point you record the decision and discard the card) or whether you consider it still undecided (at which point you reset the card to the original coordinates).

You're using -1000 and 1000 as the decision markers for whether the user selected left or right during the drag, and that decision is being passed into the `dragged` closure.

That's all you need for the drag gesture. Now you simply need to add it to the body as a modifer along with the previously defined `offset`. Right above `.gesture(TapGesture()`, add:

```
.offset(self.offset)
.gesture(drag)
```

There's a spring animation also included to make the card spring back to position smoothly. The drag gesture can be passed into the gesture method as a parameter, and you should see that the tap gesture is simply another gesture added to the object: there is no conflict with including multiple gestures and stacking them up in an object if needed. **Build and run** to check your progress.

But, what if you want to *combine* gestures though?

Combining gestures for more complex interactions

Perhaps you want to provide an elegant visual indicator to the user if they select the card long enough so that they understand there's further interaction available. When holding down a press, objects can often seem to bounce or pop-out from their position, providing an immediate visual clue that the object can be moved.

SwiftUI provides the ability to add such a change by combining two gestures together. When combining gestures SwiftUI provides sequenced, simultaneous, and exclusive gestures. A sequenced gesture means a gesture that follows another gesture. Simultaneous gestures mean gestures that are both active at the same time. Exclusive gestures are gestures that may both be possible, but only one can be active at a time.

You're going to add a simultaneous gesture in this case because you want to provide a simple clue to the potential of the drag gesture possible, without preventing the drag gesture being invoked at the same time.

This may sound complicated, but it's incredibly simple, as you'll see.

First, add a new property to store the state of the drag gesture in your **CardView.swift** file:

```
@GestureState var isLongPressed = false
```

You'll notice a new state attribute called `@GestureState`. This attribute enables the state of a gesture to be stored and read during a gesture in order to influence the effects that gesture may have on the drawing of the view. This property will be used to record whether the card has been pressed for a long time or not, and will be reset when the gesture is completed, unlike `@State` property wrappers which will not be reset when a gesture has ended.

Next, at the top of the body, right below the setup of `drag`, add a new gesture for the long press:

```
let longPress = LongPressGesture()
  .updating($isLongPressed) { value, state, transition in
    state = value
  }.simultaneously(with: drag)
```

This gesture is a `LongPressGesture`: another consistent gesture provided by Apple. In it, you're using the `updating` body to bind a value to the state, and then adding the previous drag gesture as a potential simultaneous gesture.

To see it in action, at the bottom of body replace the previously created drag gesture:

```
.gesture(drag)
```

with:

```
.gesture(longPress)
.scaleEffect(isLongPressed ? 1.1 : 1)
```

Note that you've also added a `scaleEffect` modifer to increase the scale of the view 10% if the `isLongPressed` property is `true`.

Try it out; you should now be able to press the card and see it scale, whilst still being able to drag it left or right. This is a simple, but effective simultaneous combined gesture written with just a handful of code and a simple gesture modifier. Great job!

Key points

And that's it: gestures are a wonderful way of turning a basic app into a pleasure and intuitive user experience, and SwiftUI has added powerful modifiers to make it simple and effective in any and every app you write. In this chapter you've learned:

- How to create simple gestures from Apple's built-in library. Simply use the gesture modifier along with the gesture to use.

- How to create custom gestures for more unique interactions.

- How to combine animations and gestures for more fluid experiences.

Where to go from here?

You've done a lot with gestures but there's a lot more that's possible. Check out of the following resources for more information on where to go from here:

- SwiftUI gesture documentation: https://developer.apple.com/documentation/swiftui/gestures

Chapter 13: Drawing & Custom Graphics

By Bill Morefield

As you begin to develop more complex apps, you'll find that you need more flexibility or flash than the built-in controls of SwiftUI offer. Fortunately, SwiftUI provides a rich library to assist in the creation of graphics within you app.

Graphics convey information to the user in an efficient and understandable manner; for instance, you can augment text that takes time to read with a graphics that summarizes the same information.

In this chapter, you'll explore the use of graphics in SwiftUI by creating several award graphics for a simple airport app. In later chapters, you'll expand on this app to enrich it and help it stand out.

Creating shapes

Open the starter project for this chapter; build and run the project in Xcode and you'll see an early, in-progress app for a small airport, showing flight boards for arrivals and departures. These function as the in-app equivalent to the large-screen displays that show flights arriving and leaving from the airport.

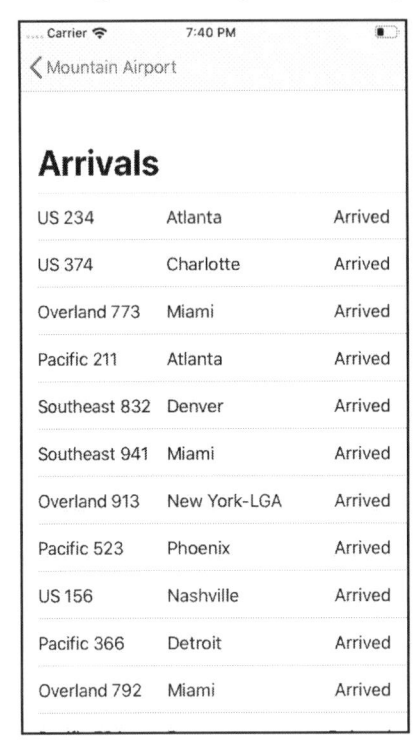

You'll also see a page to display a user's award badges. In this chapter, you'll create four initial awards. The first badge you'll create is awarded the first time someone comes to the airport, and will look like this when you're done:

First up, create a new **SwiftUI View** named **FirstVisitAward.swift**. Then, open the new file and, if the preview doesn't show, select **Editor ▸ Editor and Canvas** to show it. The preview view will make the iterative process of creating drawings and animations much easier.

One of the basic drawing structures in SwiftUI is the Shape, which is a set of simple primitives you use to build up more complex drawings.

First, you'll need to add a rectangle shape to the SwiftUI view. To do this, replace the default Text from the view template's body with the following code:

```
Rectangle()
```

The preview is a little underwhelming, since all you have is a black rectangle that fills the screen. By default, a shape in SwiftUI fills the entirety of its container, but you can specify a smaller container for the preview.

Add the following line below the Rectangle() method in the view to set the size:

```
.frame(width: 200, height: 200)
```

You will now see a black square, 200 points on each side. in the middle of the view.

This view demonstrates a few defaults that apply when drawing in SwiftUI. If you don't make an explicit fill or stroke call, the shape will fill with the current foreground color, which is Color.primary. You'll get one color for Color.primary when your app runs in light mode, and a different color for that same variable when running in dark mode.

Below the frame method in the preview, add the following line:

```
.environment(\.colorScheme, .dark)
```

In dark mode, `Color.primary` is white, so now you should see a white square against the black background. But although that looks good in light mode, it's a good idea to always consider how your drawings will appear under dark mode. To see how it looks in dark mode, you can change the code for the preview so you can preview both light and dark mode. Change the preview as follows:

```
struct FirstVisitAward_Previews: PreviewProvider {
  static var previews: some View {
    Group {
      FirstVisitAward()
        .environment(\.colorScheme, .light)

      FirstVisitAward()
        .environment(\.colorScheme, .dark)
    }
  }
}
```

It's easy to change the color of the fill. Back in your view, add the following between the `Rectangle()` and `frame(width:height:)` lines:

```
.fill(Color.blue)
```

Providing a color overrides the default: The square fills with blue in both light and dark modes. Note that order matters here, as you must call `fill` before the `frame`. You could also use the `border(_:width:)` to outline the shape instead of filling it.

Using gradients

A solid color fill works well for many cases, but for this badge, you'll use a gradient fill instead to provide a smooth transition between two or more colors.

Replace the current solid color `fill(_)` with:

```
.fill(
  LinearGradient(gradient: .init(colors: [Color.green,
Color.blue]),
               startPoint: .init(x: 0, y: 1),
               endPoint: .init(x: 1, y: 0)
))
```

A linear gradient provides a smooth transition between colors along a straight line through the object. The values for `startPoint` and `endPoint` use a `UnitPoint` struct. This struct scales a range of values into a zero to one range, which makes it easier to define a range without needing to worry about the exact values.

`UnitPoint`s origin coordinate is at (0, 0) in the top-left corner and increases to the right and downward. You define the start point of the transition to be the bottom left corner, and the end point of the transition to be at the top right corner.

A linear gradient does not limit you to a zero to one range, nor do you have to set the endpoints of a gradient to zero or one. You can define the start and endpoints anywhere you wish, even outside of the view, and the gradient will adjust. Note that these points signify not the end of the *color*, but instead the end of the *transition* between the colors. The colors continue past these points, carrying on with the corresponding end color.

For this badge, you'll also need to apply a rotation. If you look at the original shape, you'll see the background consists of three squares, each rotated 60 degrees counterclockwise from the preceding one.

Rotating shapes

You could repeat the code to draw the square three times, and rotate two of the shapes. However, SwiftUI provides a more general way to do this — the `ForEach()` method.

Replace the body of the view with:

```
// 1
ZStack {
  // 2
  ForEach(0..<3) { i in
    Rectangle()
      .fill(
        LinearGradient(gradient: .init(colors: [Color.green,
                                                Color.blue]),
                       startPoint: .init(x: 0, y: 1),
                       endPoint: .init(x: 1, y: 0))
      )
      .frame(width: 200, height: 200)
      // 3
      .rotationEffect(.degrees(Double(i) * 60.0))
  }
}
```

Here's what the new code does:

1. You first create a `ZStack` to hold the three squares. A `ZStack` overlays its contents and aligns them on both axes. Here, it will make the squares appear stacked.

2. You use `ForEach` to loop through a set. The set consists of the numbers zero, one and two. Each time through the loop, the variable `i` gets the current loop value.

3. The rectangle code doesn't change; you simply apply a rotation effect to the shape using the `.degrees` specifier for the angle. Each time through the loop, the rotation increases by 60 degrees. Note that the effects to the rectangle — a fill, a frame and a rotation — will be applied in the order specified.

The next step is to add the airplane.

Adding images

Mixing prebuilt images with your drawings can save a lot of time and work. The airplane image for this award is from the new set of SF Symbols in iOS 13. Add the following code after the `ForEach` loop:

```
Image(systemName: "airplane")
```

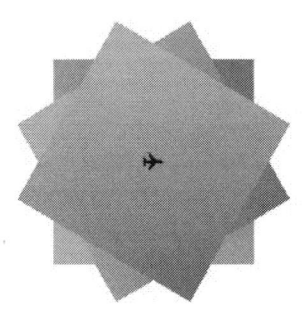

There's a few things to fix here. First, you applied the frame to only the rectangle, so it doesn't affect the image. Instead, the image shows at its default size.

Creating the rectangle with a specified size makes it more difficult to work with your image. A better option would be to adapt the view for any size by filling the frame it's displayed in. This means you can use the view anywhere in your app and it will stay responsive.

Remove the `frame()` from the rectangle. The, move the frame down to the preview and it will place a frame on the preview. Change your preview code to:

```
Group {
  FirstVisitAward()
    .environment(\.colorScheme, .light)
    .frame(width: 200, height: 200)

  FirstVisitAward()
    .environment(\.colorScheme, .dark)
    .frame(width: 200, height: 200)
}
```

The rectangle still looks good, but you still need to fix the airplane image. Add the following code at the end of the image:

```
.resizable()
```

This call tells SwiftUI to resize the image to fill the frame. Add the following code to the image to match the award design:

```
.rotationEffect(.degrees(-90))
.opacity(0.5)
```

This rotates the airplane to point upward and fades it out so that some of the background shows through.

Scaling drawings in views

The badge looks pretty good right now, but there's a subtle bug you might not have noticed. To see it, you'll need to add the award to a view. Open **AirportAwards.swift** and replace the view code with the following:

```
VStack {
  ScrollView {
    FirstVisitAward()
      .frame(width: 250, height: 250)
    Text("First Visit")
  }
}.navigationBarTitle("Your Awards")
```

When you preview your image, you'll see the problem. The rotated squares bleed outside of the frame and into the title above and text below. The rotation you applied doesn't scale to remain inside the frame; instead, the view part of the award clips and a part of the view bleeds into the text. To fix this, you need to size the squares in the award so the rotated shapes fit inside the frame.

Go back to **FirstVisitAward.swift**. Replace the contents of the view with:

```
// 1
GeometryReader { geometry in
  ZStack {
    ForEach(0..<3) { i in
      Rectangle()
        .fill(
          LinearGradient(
            gradient: .init(colors: [Color.green, Color.blue]),
            startPoint: .init(x: 0, y: 1),
            endPoint: .init(x: 1, y: 0)
          )
        )
        // 2
        .frame(width: geometry.size.width * 0.7,
               height: geometry.size.width * 0.7)
        .rotationEffect(.degrees(Double(i) * 60.0))
    }
    Image(systemName: "airplane")
      .resizable().rotationEffect(.degrees(-90))
      .opacity(0.5)
      // 3
      .scaleEffect(0.7)
  }
}
```

The changes are spelled out below:

1. The `GeometryReader` container provides a way to get the size and shape of a view from within it. This lets you write code without relying on constants.

2. You use the size property of the `geometry` instance to get the width and height of the view. You multiply both by 0.7 to scale down the squares so they will fit inside the frame after they're rotated. You could calculate this scaling factor with trigonometry, or you can also simply try values until you get the look you're going for. The beauty of SwiftUI preview is that you can make changes and see the results immediately without the compile–run loop. This makes it easy to tweak the value until you get the desired result.

3. You also need to scale the image the same amount that you scaled the squares. You do this with the `.scaleEffect()` call on the image.

View the award on the Airport Awards view and you will see that the award now fits into the view. Smart, right?

Other shapes

You only used one shape for this first award, but SwiftUI provides several more shapes:

- **Circle**: The circle's radius will be half the length of the framing rectangle's smallest edge.

- **Ellipse**: The ellipse will align inside the frame of the view containing it.

- **Rounded Rectangle**: A rectangle, but with rounded corners instead of sharp corners. It draws within the containing frame.

- **Capsule**: A capsule shape is a rounded rectangle where the corner radius is half the length of the rectangle's smallest edge.

All scale and other effects work within the framing view just as the rectangle does. You'll find that combining these shapes can often produce complex results. For more complex drawing, you can use **Paths**.

> **Exercise:** Try replacing the rectangle in the award with another shape and notice the results. Make sure to change it back before continuing.

Drawing lines with paths

Sometimes you want to define your own shape, and not use the built-in ones. For this, you use **Paths**, which allow you to define a shape by combining individual segments. These segments make up the outline of a two-dimensional shape. You'll create your next award using paths.

First up, create a new SwiftUI View named **OverNightParkAward.swift** inside the **MountainAirport** group.

The simplest element that you can add to a path is the line. This award uses lines to draw a road.

First up, update the new view's body to:

```
Path { path in
  path.move(to: CGPoint(x: 120, y: 20))
  path.addLine(to: .init(x: 180, y: 180))
  path.addLine(to: .init(x: 20, y: 180))
  path.addLine(to: .init(x: 80, y: 20))
}
```

Path creates an enclosure you use to build the path. The initial move(to:) call sets the starting location for the path; a move(to:) call moves the current position, but doesn't add anything to the path. You next add three lines to create a polygon that is narrow at the top and widens toward the bottom. This give a pseudo-3D effect of a road going off into the distance. Notice that you don't have to close the path by adding a line back to the initial point — this is handled for you automatically.

> **Note**: Using constant values limits the flexibility of your view. When you can, design drawings to adapt to the size of the frame instead of hard-coding values.

First up, add the following code to the preview:

```
.frame(width: 200, height: 200)
```

Then, add a `GeometryReader` replacing the body so it looks like the following:

```
GeometryReader { geometry in
  Path { path in
    let size = min(geometry.size.width, geometry.size.height)
    let nearLine = size * 0.1
    let farLine = size * 0.9

    path.move(to: CGPoint(x: size/2 + nearLine, y: nearLine))
    path.addLine(to: .init(x: farLine, y: farLine))
    path.addLine(to: .init(x: nearLine, y: farLine))
    path.addLine(to: .init(x: size/2 - nearLine, y: nearLine))
  }
}
```

Inside of a path, you have more flexibility with adding calculated values than in most view code. These calculations let you produce more frame-independent code; wrapping the `Path` inside a `GeometryReader` lets you adapt the path to the frame.

The first three lines determine a `size` as the smaller dimension between the width and height. You then define a near and far value based on the `size`. Again, instead of using constant numbers, you can define the path using these relative values. If you had 200 as the `size`, you would end up with the original constant numbers. You'll see that the result didn't change.

If the frame changes, the size of the drawing will adapt.

Add the following code after the path to change the color to a dark gray, which makes your image look more like a a road. Here, you use the `Color.init(_:red:green:blue:opacity:)` method to define the custom color.

```
.fill(Color.init(red: 0.4, green: 0.4, blue: 0.4))
```

Drawing dashed lines

Next, you'll add a dashed white line down the middle of the road. First, wrap the current Path inside a ZStack. Then, add a new Path after the first Path, like so:

```
GeometryReader { geometry in
  ZStack {
    // First road path
    // ...

    // Second dashed line path
    Path { path in
      let size = min(geometry.size.width, geometry.size.height)
      let nearLine = size * 0.1
      let farLine = size * 0.9
      let middle = size / 2

      path.move(to: .init(x: middle, y: farLine))
      path.addLine(to: .init(x: middle, y: nearLine))
    }
    .stroke(Color.white,
            style: .init(lineWidth: 3.0,
                dash: [geometry.size.height / 20,
                       geometry.size.height / 30],
                dashPhase: 0))
  }
}
```

Much of the code here is the same as before. You once again define a variable with the coordinate of the middle of the view. Instead of using a fill, you tell SwiftUI to stroke the path as opposed to filling the path.

You set the color of the line to white, and you also define a custom line style to replace the default line that is solid, black, and one point wide. To make the dashed center line stand out, you set its width to three points, and you calculate the length of each dash as ratio of the height of the view.

Note that the variables defined inside the path are no longer available as they are no longer in scope.

One more touch: adding the car. Add the following code below the two Paths:

```
Image(systemName: "car.fill")
  .resizable()
  .foregroundColor(Color.blue)
  .scaleEffect(0.20)
  .offset(x: -geometry.size.width / 7.25)
```

You use a SF Symbol image for the car and scale it to fit a lane of the road. An offset shifts the image from the center. Again, you define the amount in proportion to the size of the frame so the car appears centered in the right lane.

To finish, add this new view to the awards view. Open **AirportAwards.swift** and add the following code below the first award:

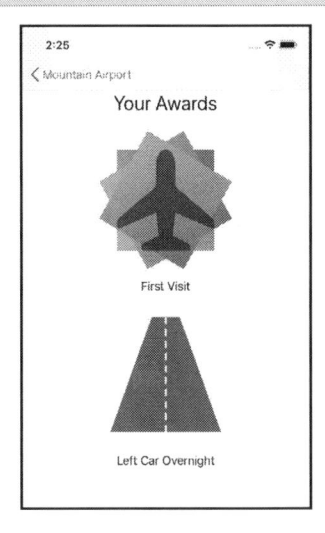

```
OverNightParkAward()
  .frame(width: 250, height: 250)
Text("Left Car Overnight")
```

Drawing arcs and curves

Paths offer more flexibility than drawing lines. You'll find a wide range of options, including shapes that are better suited for drawing curved objects. You'll create the next award using arcs and quadratic curves.

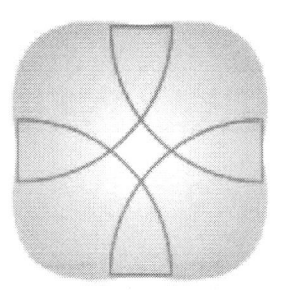

As with the previous awards, start out by creating a new **SwiftUI View** and name it **AirportMealAward.swift**.

Then add a frame to the preview:

```
.frame(width: 200, height: 200)
```

And replace the body of the view with some familiar code:

```
GeometryReader { geometry in
  ZStack {
    Path { path in
      let size = min(geometry.size.width, geometry.size.height)
      let nearLine = size * 0.1
      let farLine = size * 0.9
      let mid = size / 2
    }
  }
}
```

This creates a `GeometryReader`, a `ZStack` and a `Path`. You again calculate the locations you'll use to draw the path independent of the size of the frame. You also calculate the middle of the view for later use.

Drawing quadratic curves

The name of a quadratic curve comes from its definition by following the line plot of a quadratic math equation. SwiftUI handles the math part (phew!) so you can simply think of a quadratic curve as a elastic line pulled toward a third point, known as the **control point**. At each end, the curve starts parallel to a line drawn to the control point and curves smoothly between all points.

You will define these curves between the middle of each side and the middle of the adjacent side. You'll place the control point in the corner between the midpoints to bend the curve outward toward the corner.

Add the following code below the `mid` variable in the path:

```
path.move(to: .init(x: mid, y: nearLine))
path.addQuadCurve(
  to: .init(x: farLine, y: mid),
  control: .init(x: size, y: 0))
path.addQuadCurve(
  to: .init(x: mid, y: farLine),
  control: .init(x: size, y: size))
path.addQuadCurve(
  to: .init(x: nearLine, y: mid),
  control: .init(x: 0, y: size))
path.addQuadCurve(
  to: .init(x: mid, y: nearLine),
  control: .init(x: 0, y: 0))
```

You will now change the path to use a radial gradient, which starts at a central point and transitions outward from that point. You define the central point of the gradient, as well as the distances at which the transition begins and ends.

Add the following to the end of the path:

```
.fill(
  RadialGradient(
    gradient: .init(colors: [Color.white, Color.yellow]),
    center: .init(x: 0.5, y: 0.5),
    startRadius: geometry.size.width * 0.05,
    endRadius: geometry.size.width * 0.6)
)
```

You'll now see a transition start near the center and extend just past halfway toward the edge of the edge of the shape, fading from white to yellow. Again, you're using UnitCoordinate to specify the center point. A value of 0.5 puts the center point of the gradient at the center of the *view*, not the *path*. In this case, the path and view are the same, but that's not always the case. The start and end radius of the transition are not UnitCoordinates, since you don't have access to the calculations inside the path.

For the next part of your award, you'll add arcs that resemble the functional and decorative scores on a loaf of fancy bread. Add the following code *after* the existing path:

```
Path { path in
  let size = min(geometry.size.width, geometry.size.height)
  let nearLine = size * 0.1
  let farLine = size * 0.9
```

```
        path.addArc(center: .init(x: nearLine, y: nearLine),
                radius: size / 2,
                startAngle: .degrees(90),
                endAngle: .degrees(0),
                clockwise: true)
        path.addArc(center: .init(x: farLine, y: nearLine),
                radius: size / 2,
                startAngle: .degrees(180),
                endAngle: .degrees(90),
                clockwise: true)
        path.addArc(center: .init(x: farLine, y: farLine),
                radius: size / 2,
                startAngle: .degrees(270),
                endAngle: .degrees(180),
                clockwise: true)
        path.addArc(center: .init(x: nearLine, y: farLine),
                radius: size / 2,
                startAngle: .degrees(0),
                endAngle: .degrees(270),
                clockwise: true)
      path.closeSubpath()
    }
    .stroke(Color.orange, lineWidth: 2)
```

The `addArc` method adds a partial circle to a path; you specify the center of a circle and its radius. A full circle makes a complete sweep through 360 degrees. Since an arc is a partial circle, you specify what part of the full arc that SwiftUI should draw. In this code, you draw a 90 degree sweep of each circle. You also specify the direction the arc should draw, between the starting and ending angles.

Beautiful!

Now, open **AirportAwards.swift** and add the following to the end of the view to add it to the collection of awards:

```
AirportMealAward()
   .frame(width: 250, height: 250)
Text("Ate Meal at Airport")
```

Key points

- Shapes provide a quick way to draw simple controls. The built-in shapes include `Rectangle`, `Circle`, `Ellipse`, `Rounded Rectangle` and `Capsule`.
- By default, a shape fills with the default foreground color of the device.
- Shapes can be filled with solid colors or with a defined gradient.
- Gradients can transition in a linear, radial, or angular manner.
- `rotationEffect` will rotate a shape around its axis.
- `ZStack` will let you combine graphics so they share a common axis. You can mix drawn graphics and images.
- `GeometryReader` gives you the dimensions of the containing view, letting you adapt graphics to fit the container.
- `Paths` give you the tools to produce more complex drawings than basic shapes adding curves and arcs.
- You can modify the shapes and fill on paths as you do with shapes.

Where to go from here?

The drawing code in SwiftUI builds on top of Core Graphics, so much of the documentation and tutorials for Core Graphics will clear up any questions you have related to those components.

The SwiftUI Drawing and Animation documentation at https://developer.apple.com/documentation/swiftui/drawing_and_animation documents changes in SwiftUI compared to Apple's graphics libraries.

The WWDC 2019 session *Building Custom Views with SwiftUI* at https://developer.apple.com/videos/play/wwdc2019/237/ provides more examples of layout and graphics.

The classic text *Computer Graphics: Principles and Practice by John F. Hughes, et al.* provides a very nice overview of most graphics topics when you need to build graphics beyond the frameworks that Apple provides.

The following two chapters will continue to build on this project, by adding animations and showing you more ways to build views designed for reuse. See you there!

Chapter 14: Animations

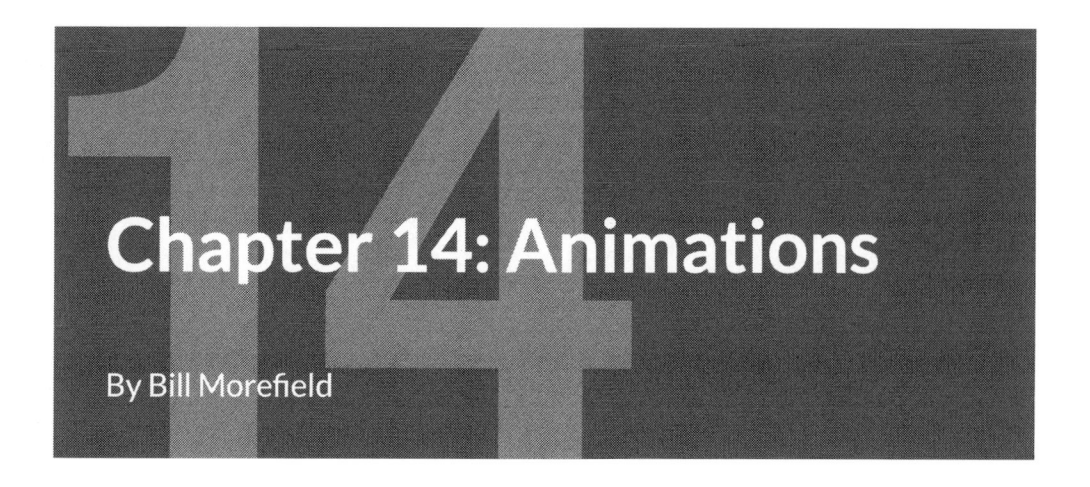

By Bill Morefield

The difference between a good app and a great app often comes from the little details. Using the right animations at the right places can delight users and make your app stand out in the crowded App Store.

Animations can make your app more fun to use, and they can play a powerful role in drawing the user's attention in certain areas. Good animations make your app more appealing and easier to use.

Animation in SwiftUI is much simpler than animation in AppKit or UIKit. SwiftUI animations are higher-level abstractions that handle all the tedious work for you. If you have experience with animations in Apple platforms, a lot of this chapter will seem familiar. You'll find it a lot less effort to produce animations in your app. You can combine or overlap animations and interrupt them without care. Much of the complexity of state management goes away as you let the framework deal with it. This frees you up to make great animations instead of handling edge cases and complexity.

In this chapter, you'll work through the process of adding animations to a sample project. Time to get the screen shaking!

Animating state changes

First, open the starter project for this chapter. Build and run the project in XCode 11, and you'll see an app that shows flight information for an airport. The lists provide flyers with the time and the gate where the flight will leave or arrive.

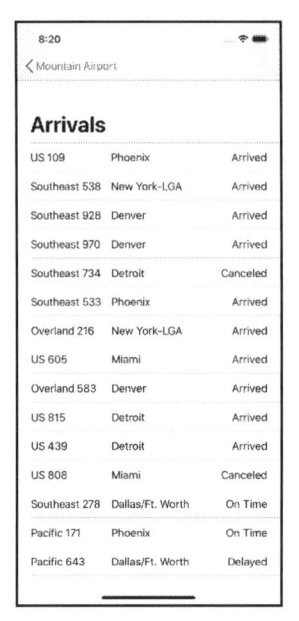

> **Note**: Unfortunately, it's difficult to show animations on a printed page. You'll need to work through this chapter using preview, the simulator or on a device.

Tap on the **Arrivals** button, and you'll see a list of the day's flights. The flights are randomly generated when you start the app so don't worry if you see a different list.

Open **FlightBoard.swift**. If you do not see the preview canvas, select **Editor ▸ Editor and Canvas** to show it. Click **Resume** on the canvas to display the preview. Click the **Play** button in the preview so you can interact with the view.

Tap any of the flights listed to bring up the details view for the flight. This view shows more information for a flight at the airport. By default, the app hides part of the information. A button allows the user to display this extra information. This additional info shows details about the gate, times and a map of the terminal. There also is a chevron with an arrow as a visual indicator of what tapping the button does.

Already, SwiftUI handles a lot of the work for you. When you tap the button, SwiftUI smoothly adds or removes the flight detail view. The default animation chains fading out the old view and then fading in the new view. That's a lot of help with no work on your part.

Adding animation

To start, open **FlightBoardInformation.swift** and look for the following code:

```
Button(action: {
  self.showDetails.toggle()
}) {
   HStack {
  if showDetails {
      Text("Hide Details")
      Spacer()
      Image(systemName: "chevron.up.square")
    } else {
      Text("Show Details")
      Spacer()
      Image(systemName: "chevron.down.square")
    }
  }
}
```

This code changes the text and image depending on whether it shows the flight details. That works, but it would look smoother if you applied an animation to the chevron. Replace this code with:

```
Button(action: {
  self.showDetails.toggle()
}) {
  HStack {
    Text(showDetails ? "Hide Details" : "Show Details")
    Spacer()
    Image(systemName: "chevron.up.square")
      .rotationEffect(.degrees(showDetails ? 0 : 180))
  }
}
```

Again, press **Play** to interact with the view, and you'll see that it functions the same as before. However, instead of the default fade animation, you're now using a custom `rotationEffect` animation.

An animation occurs over the period of change from a starting state to an ending state. You tell SwiftUI the type of animation, and it handles the interpolation for you. Change the Image view to read:

```
Image(systemName: "chevron.up.square")
  .rotationEffect(.degrees(showDetails ? 0 : 180))
  .animation(.default)
```

Preview the updated view and tap the button to show flight details. You will see the chevron now rotates between the up and down positions. The rotation from zero to 180 degrees acts as a state change, and you've told SwiftUI to animate this state change. The animation only applies to the rotation on the **Image** element and no other elements on the page.

The angles in the change matter when you create an animation. You could specify the second angle as -180 degrees since both provide a half rotation. Change the angle of the rotation from 180 to –180. Now preview and tap the button.

You will see chevron rotates in the opposite direction. Positive angles rotate clockwise and negative angles rotate counterclockwise. Before, the chevron rotated *clockwise* from pointing upward to pointing downward. Now it rotates *counterclockwise* from zero to -180 degrees.

You're not limited to the angle of rotations of the 0 - 360 degrees range of a single rotation. Change the –180 to 540. Try the app now, and you'll see that it rotates a full time and half before stopping.

> **Exercise**: Try other angles for both the starting and ending angle to observe how different angles affect the animation and positions.

Before continuing, change the rotation back to:

```
.rotationEffect(.degrees(showDetails ? 0 : 180))
```

Animation types

So far, you've worked with a single type of animation: the default animation. SwiftUI provides more animation types. The differences can be subtle and hard to see on the small chevron. To make the changes easier to notice, you'll add another animation to this view.

Animating the Details view

Stay in **FlightBoardInformation.swift**. The code to show the details for the flight looks like:

```
if showDetails {
  FlightDetails(flight: flight)
}
```

If showDetails is true, then the view with details on the flight appears. If not, the view isn't added. You can animate the transition of adding and removing views and will do so later in this chapter. For now, you can animate the appearance of the view by shifting the view from off the screen. Change this code to:

```
FlightDetails(flight: flight)
  .offset(x: showDetails ? 0 : -UIScreen.main.bounds.width)
```

This replaces the condition with an offset on the FlightDetails view. You'll learn more about offsets in the next chapter. For now, know that this code shifts the **x** or horizontal coordinate of the view. When showDetails is true, no shift occurs. When the details should not hidden, then the view shifts UIScreen.main.bounds.width — the width of the current screen — to the left, ensuring it is not visible.

Preview the view, and you'll see little difference.

Default animation

Now, you'll change the code to add an animation. After the offset, add:

```
.animation(.default)
```

Now in the preview, you'll notice the flight details view slides in from the left side of your app. When hidden, it slides back off the left side.

The **default** animation is the simplest animation type. It provides a linear change at a constant rate from the original state to the final state. If you graphed the change vertically against time horizontally, the transition would look like:

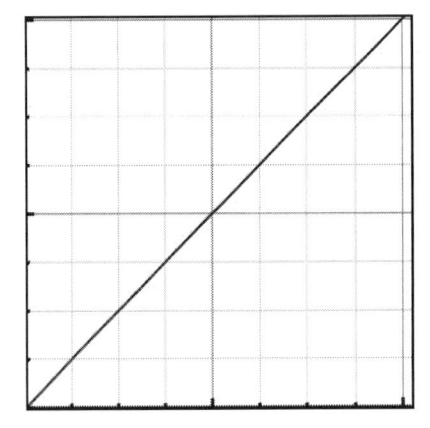

Eased animations

Eased animations might be the most common in apps. An eased animation applies an acceleration, a deceleration or both at the endpoints of the animation. They generally look more natural since it's impossible for something to instantaneously change the speed in the real world. The animation reflects the acceleration or deceleration of real-world movement.

First, change the animation for the details view to:

```
.animation(.easeOut)
```

Preview the view and when you show the flight details, you'll see the view slides in quickly and slows down shortly before coming to a stop.

Graphing the movement in this animation against time would look like:

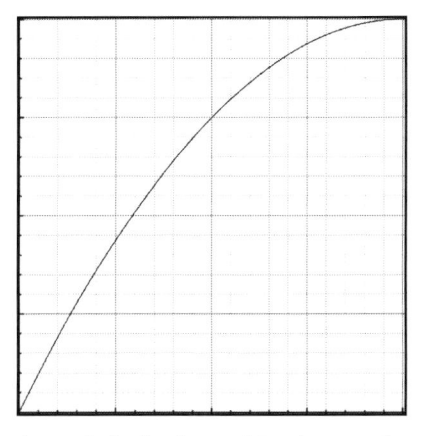

Eased animations have a short default time of 0.35 seconds. You can specify a different length with the `duration:` parameter. To do so, change the animation to:

```
.animation(.easeOut(duration: 2))
```

You will see the same animation, but it will now take two seconds to complete. You can specify a duration for any eased animation.

In addition to `easeOut`, you also can specify `easeIn` which starts slow and accelerates at the start of the animation.

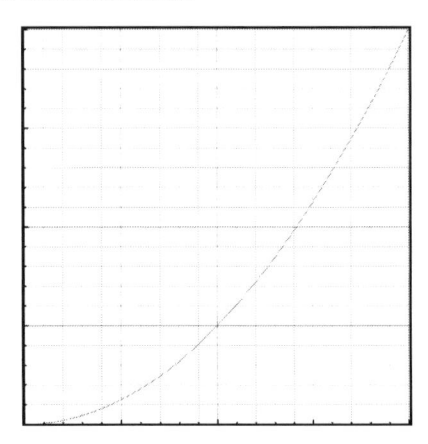

You can combine the two using the `easeInOut` type. This applies acceleration at the beginning and the deceleration at the end of the animation.

Graphed, it looks like this:

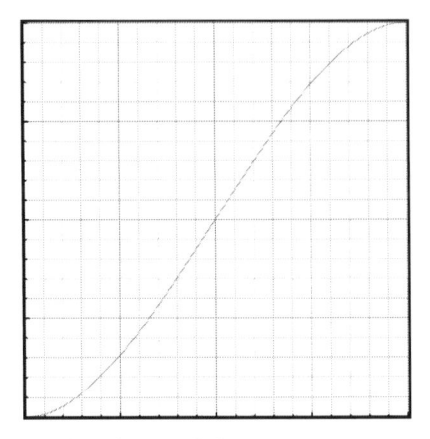

If you need fine control over the shape of the curve, you can use the `timingCurve(_:_:_:_)` type method. SwiftUI uses a bézier curve for easing animations. This method will let you define the control points for that curve in a range of 0...1. The shape of the curve will reflect the specified control points.

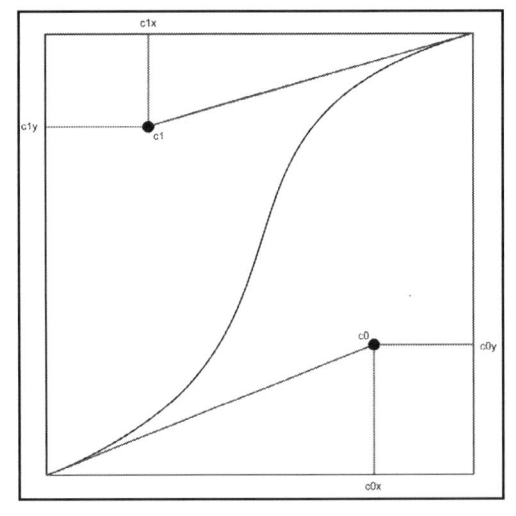

timingCurve(cx0, cy0, cx1, cy1)

> **Exercise**: Try the various eased animations and observe the results. In particular see what different control points do in the `timingCurve(_:_:_:_)` animation type.

Spring animations

Eased animations always transition between the start and end states in a single direction. They also never pass either end state. The final category of SwiftUI animations is spring animations. These let you add a bit of bounce at the end of the state change. Change the animation line to:

```
.animation(.interpolatingSpring(mass: 1.0,
                                stiffness: 100.0,
                                damping: 10,
                                initialVelocity: 0))
```

Preview the view and tap the details button. You'll see the view slide in, move a bit past the destination, slide back and then bounce around the final position before stopping. The physical model for this type of animation gives it the name: a spring.

Why a spring makes a useful animation

Springs resist stretching and compression. The greater the stretch or compression of the spring, the more resistance the spring presents. Imagine you take a weight and attach it to one end of a spring. Then you attach the other end of the spring to a fixed point and let the spring drop vertically with the weight at the bottom.

The weight of the object will stretch the spring to an equilibrium point where the pull of gravity exactly cancels out the resistance of the stretched spring.

If you now pull the weight down and then let it go, the spring's stretch resistance is greater than the gravity on the weight. The spring will pull the weight upward. After some time the weight will be above that initial equilibrium point. Now gravity begins to exert more pull on the weight than the spring's resistance causing it to slow then stop.

The weight will then begin to move downward under the greater pull of gravity. The weight will now continue to and pass the equilibrium point. Now the spring will again begin to exert more force than gravity slowing the weight down until it stops where originally released.

This cycle defines **simple harmonic motion**. In a frictionless world, an **undamped** system, this cycle would repeat forever.

If you were to graph the location of the weight against the time, you'd end up with this:

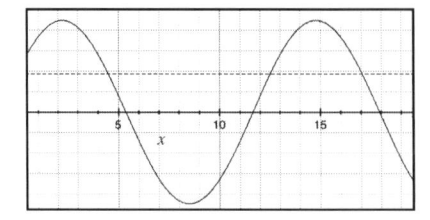

In the real world, friction and other outside forces ensure that the system loses energy each time through the cycle. This makes the system **damped**. These accumulated losses add up and eventually, the weight will return motionless to the equilibrium point. The graph of this movement looks more like this:

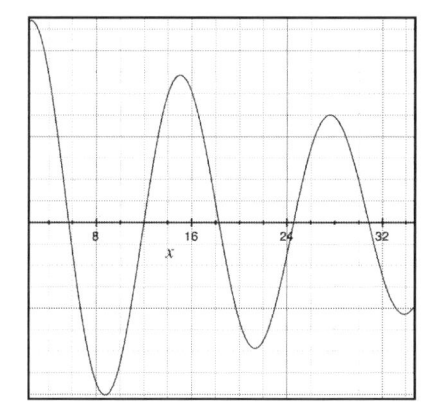

I'll spare you the math, but four elements affect the shape of this graph:

1. **Mass**: The mass of the weight. A larger weight will bounce for longer since gravity exerts more force on it than a smaller weight.

2. **Spring Resistance**: How stiff the spring is and thus how much it resists when stretched or compressed

3. **Damping**: How much friction and other forces affect the system. More damping means the weight slows down faster.

4. **Initial Velocity**: In the example, you started the system by pulling the spring downward and letting go. If the weight isn't motionless, then that velocity affects the system.

You might be asking, "So what?" Spring animations in SwiftUI simulate this **damped simple harmonic motion** from the real world. It turns out that these are the same four parameters that you traditionally specify when creating a spring animation.

Changes to these parameters change the animation the same way changing the values would affect the real world motion of the weight.

Creating spring animations

Now that you have a bit more understanding of how a spring animation works, you'll see how these parameters affect your animation. The traditional spring animation you create with the `interpolatingSpring(mass:stiffness:damping:initialVelocity:)` method uses these parameters.

Change the animation to:

```
animation(.interpolatingSpring(mass: 1, stiffness: 100,
                               damping: 10, initialVelocity: 0))
```

The parameters affect the animation by:

- `mass`: Controls how long the system "bounces".
- `stiffness`: Controls the speed of the initial movement.
- `damping`: Controls how fast the system slows down and stops.
- `initialVelocity`: Gives an extra initial motion.

> **Exercise**: Before continuing see if you can determine how changes to the parameters affect the animation.
>
> **Hint**: Experiment with one element at a time. First, double a value and then halve it from the original value. You might want to temporarily add a second view so you can compare two animations with slightly different parameters.

Increasing the mass causes the animation to last longer and bounce further on each side of the endpoint. A smaller mass stops faster and moves less past the endpoints on each bounce. Increasing the stiffness causes each bounce to move further past the endpoints, but has less effect on the length of the animation. Increasing the damping causes the animation to smooth and end faster. Increasing the initial velocity causes the animation to bounce further. A negative initial velocity causes a small lag in the system as (out of view) the movement has to overcome the initial velocity in the other direction.

The physical model of the animation doesn't intuitively map to the results. SwiftUI introduces a more intuitive way to define a spring animation. The underlying model doesn't change, but you can specify parameters to the model better related to how you want the animation to appear in your app. Change your animation to:

```
.animation(.spring(response: 0.55, dampingFraction: 0.45,
            blendDuration: 0))
```

The `dampingFraction` controls how fast the "springiness" stops. A value of zero will never stop. This corresponds to an undamped spring. A value of one or greater will cause the system to stop without oscillation. This **overdamped** state will look much like the eased animations of the previous section.

You will normally use a value between zero and one, which will result in some oscillation before the animation ends. Greater values slow down faster.

The `response` parameter defines the time it takes the system to complete a single oscillation if the `dampingFraction` is set to zero. It allows you to tune the length of time before the animation ends.

Again, try varying these parameters and compare the animations produced. Before moving to the next section, delete any extra views your created during the exercises.

Removing and combining animations

There are times that you may apply modifications to a view, but you only want to animate some of them. You do this by passing a `nil` to the `animation()` method.

Add another change to the chevron. Still in **FlightBoardInformation.swift** replace the code for the button, so it reads:

```
Button(action: {
  self.showDetails.toggle()
}) {
  HStack {
    Text(showDetails ? "Hide Details" : "Show Details")
    Spacer()
    Image(systemName: "chevron.up.square")
      .scaleEffect(showDetails ? 2 : 1)
      .rotationEffect(.degrees(showDetails ? 0 : 180))
      .animation(.easeInOut)
  }
}
```

This adds a scaling to double the size of the image when showing the details view. If you view the animation you will see that the button grows in sync with the rotation. An animation affects all state changes that occur on the element where you apply the animation. Add `.animation(nil)` between the `scaleEffect()` and `rotationEffect()` method and preview the animation again. You should now see the scale change take effect immediately with the fade-out/fade-in effect seen before you added any animation to the view.

You can combine different animations by using `.animation()` multiple times. Change the button class so instead of `nil` you pass a `.spring()` animation like below:

```
Button(action: {
  self.showDetails.toggle()
}) {
  HStack {
    Text(showDetails ? "Hide Details" : "Show Details")
    Spacer()
    Image(systemName: "chevron.up.square")
      .scaleEffect(showDetails ? 2 : 1)
      .animation(.spring())
      .rotationEffect(.degrees(showDetails ? 0 : 180))
      .animation(.easeInOut)
  }
}
```

Preview the view and you will see the rotation and scaling has the easing animation as before. The scaling animation now also has that little bounce from the spring animation.

Animating from state changes

You've applied animations to state changes at the state change. You can apply the animation at the point of the state change. When doing so, the animation applies to all changes that occur because of the state change. Modify the code for the `Button` and details view to:

```
Button(action: {
    withAnimation(.default) {
  self.showDetails.toggle()
    }
}) {
  HStack {
    Text(showDetails ? "Hide Details" : "Show Details")
    Spacer()
```

```
      Image(systemName: "chevron.up.square")
        .scaleEffect(showDetails ? 2 : 1)
        .rotationEffect(.degrees(showDetails ? 0 : 180))
    }
  }
  FlightDetails(flight: flight)
    .offset(x: showDetails ? 0 : -UIScreen.main.bounds.width)
```

You removed the individual .animation(_:) modifiers. In their place, you have a new withAnimation() function inside the Button's action: that wraps the state change to showDetails. This call uses the default animation, but you can pass any animation to this function.

If you preview the view and click the details button, you will see that all the elements the state change affects—the button text label, the chevron, and the details view—use the same animation. This gives a connivent way to apply animation for the same change to many places at the same time. If you apply an animation directly on the state change as you'd done previously in this chapter, it will override the animation at the state level.

Add a .spring() animation back to the flight details offset and notice that while the chevron animations remain the same, the view now slides in with the spring effect. Make sure to leave the spring animation in place for the next section.

Adjusting animations

There are a few instance methods common to all animations. These methods let you delay an animation, change the speed of the animation and repeat the animation.

Delay

The delay() method allows you to specify a time in seconds before the animation occurs. Change the spring animation added in the previous section so that the flight details view reads:

```
FlightDetails(flight: flight)
  .offset(x: showDetails ? 5 : -UIScreen.main.bounds.width)
  .animation(Animation.spring().delay(1))
```

Preview the flight details view and click the details button. You'll notice the chevron animates immediately, but the details for the flight do not appear until one second later.

When you click the button again, the chevron again moves immediately, but the details for the flight do not slide away until one second passes.

A delay before an animation begins makes a great way to give animations a chained appearance.

Speed

You use the `.speed()` method to change the speed of the animation. If you have an animation that takes two seconds and apply `.speed(0.5)`, it will be at 50% of the normal speed leading the animation to last one second. This can be useful to adjust the time an animation lacking a direct time element such as default and spring animations. It also works well to match the times of concurrent animations.

Change the animation line on the offset to replace the `delay()` with a `speed(_:)` method call so it reads:

```
.animation(Animation.spring().speed(2))
```

Preview the view and you should see the spring animation is twice as fast. Speed changes also help you during development to slow down an animation to see fine details.

Repeating animations

To repeat an animation you call `.repeatCount(repeatCount:,autoreverses:)` with the number of times, the animation will repeat. You can also control if the animation reverses before repeating. Without reversing, the animation will return to the initial state instantaneously. With reversing, the animation goes back to the initial state before repeating. The `repeatForever(autoreverses:)` loops the animation forever, but you still specify if the animation should reverse before repeating.

Change the previous `speed()` method to use the `repeatCount(repeatCount:,autoreverses:)` method so it reads:

```
.animation(Animation.spring().repeatCount(2, autoreverses: false))
```

Preview the view and tap the show details button. You should see the view appear, then disappear and appear again. This is the animation repeating twice. Since you told it not to reverse, the animation the view moved back offscreen without animation.

Change the `false` to `true` in the animation and preview again. notice the difference.

Remove these methods before continuing to the next section so it again looks like:

```
.animation(.spring())
```

Extracting animations from the view

To this point, you've defined animations directly within the view. For exploring and learning that works well. In real apps, it's easier to maintain code when you keep different elements of your code separate. Animation can be defined outside the view where you can also reuse them. In **FlightBoardInformation.swift**, add the following code above the body structure:

```
var flightDetailAnimation : Animation {
    Animation.easeInOut
}
```

This defines a custom animation property. Now replace the `withAnimation()` in the button with:

```
withAnimation(self.flightDetailAnimation) {
```

Preview the view and confirm the animation did not change. You can make modifications to the animation on this property instead of adding clutter to your view code. For more complex animations, this will improve the readability of your code.

Animating view transitions

You've applied animations on elements in a view and on a view. Transitions are specific animations for showing and hiding views. By default, views transition on and off the screen by fading in and out. You've likely noticed this in the initial view of the starter app and with the text of the button to toggle the details.

Much of what you've already learned about animations work with transitions. As with animation, the default transition is only a single possible animation.

Delete the offset and animation code for the `FlightDetails` view to read:

```
if showDetails {
  FlightDetails(flight: flight)
    .transition(.slide)
}
```

In the button code change it to read:

```
Button(action: {
  withAnimation {
    self.showDetails.toggle()
  }
}) {
```

Since transitions are a type of animation, you must specify the `withAnimation()` function around the state change. or SwiftUI will not show the transition.

Preview the **FlightBoardInformation** view and tap the button to bring up the flight details. You'll see that the view now slides in from the left. You'd done that before by modifying the offset, but now you didn't need to specify anything related to positioning. SwiftUI took care of that for you. When you tap the button again, you'll see the view slide off the trailing edge. These transitions handle cases where the text reading reads right-to-left for you.

Before the flight details view always existed, but you positioned it off-screen. It still needed resources. Now the animation occurs when SwiftUI adds the view. The framework slides the view in from the leading edge. It also animates the view off the trailing edge and then removes it so that it's no longer takes up resources.

You could do all these things with animations, but you would need to handle these extra steps yourself. The built-in transitions make it much easier to deal with view animations.

You can still use the animations you used earlier in this chapter on state changes. Add the following code after the `.rotationEffect(_)` call on the chevron:

```
.animation(flightDetailAnimation)
```

Preview the and you'll see the chevron animation in addition to the view transition when you tap to show the flight details.

View transition types

You used a slide transition above. The slide transition slides a view from the leading edge and leaves by sliding off the trailing edge. There are several other transition animations you can use.

The default transition type changes the opacity of the view when adding or removing it. The view goes from transparent to opaque on insertion, and from opaque to transparent on removal. You can specify the transition using the `.opacity` transition.

The `.move(edge:)` transition moves the view from or to a specified edge when added or removed. To see the view move to and from the bottom, change the transition to:

```
.transition(.move(edge: .bottom))
```

The other edges are `.top`, `.leading` and `.training`.

Beyond moving, transitions can also animate views to appear on the screen. The `.scale()` transition causes the view to expand when inserted from a single point of collapse when removed to a single point at the center. You can optionally specify a scale factor parameter for the transition. The scale factor defines the ratio of the size of the initial view. A scale of zero provides the default transition to a single point. A value less than one causes the view to expand from that scaled size when inserted or collapse to it when removed. Values greater than one work the same except the opposite end of the transition is large then the final view.

You can also specify an `anchor` parameter for the location the point on the view where the animation centers. An enumeration provides constants for the corners, sides, and center of the view. You can also specify a custom offset.

The final transition type allows you to specify an offset either as a **CGSize** or a pair of **Length** values. The view moves from that offset when inserted and toward it when removed. The result looks much like the animation you did with the view earlier in this chapter.

> **Exercise**: As with animations, the best way to see how transitions work is to try them. Take each transition and use it in place of `.slide` in the transition on `FlightDetails`. Toggle the view on and off and notice how the animation works when the view comes in and out.

Extracting transitions from the view

You can extract your transitions from the view as you did with animations. You do not add this at the **struct** level as with an animation but at the file scope. At the top of **FlightBoardInformation.swift** add the following:

```swift
extension AnyTransition {
  static var flightDetailsTransition: AnyTransition {
    AnyTransition.slide
  }
}
```

This declares your transition as a static property of **AnyTransition**. Now update the transition on `FlightDetails()` call to use it:

```swift
if showDetails {
  FlightDetails(flight: flight)
    .transition(.flightDetailsTransition)
}
```

Preview the **FlightDetails** view and tap the button to watch the animation and you'll see it works as did the first transition example.

Async transitions

SwiftUI lets you specify separate transitions when adding and removing a view. Change the static property to:

```swift
extension AnyTransition {
  static var flightDetailsTransition: AnyTransition {
    let insertion = AnyTransition.move(edge: .trailing)
      .combined(with: .opacity)
    let removal = AnyTransition.scale(scale: 1.0)
      .combined(with: .opacity)
    return .asymmetric(insertion: insertion, removal: removal)
  }
}
```

Preview this new transition. You will see the view will move in from the trailing edge and fade in when added. When SwiftUI removes the view, it will scale down to a point while fading out.

Challenge

Challenge: Changing the flight details view

Change the final project for this chapter so that the flight details view slides in from the leading edge. When you hide it, make the view slide to the bottom and fades away. Also, change the button text to transition. When added the button text view should move from the leading edge. When removed to button text view should vanish using a scale transition.

Hint, you will need to think about how SwiftUI applies transitions and animations and make a small change to how the button text view shows.

Key points

- Don't use animations simply for the sake of doing so. Have a purpose for each animation.
- Keep animations between 0.25 and 1.0 second in length. Shorter animations are often not noticeable. Longer animations risk annoying your user wanting to get something done.
- Keep animations consistent within an app and with platform usage.
- Animations should be optional. Respect accessibility settings to reduce or eliminate application animations.
- Make sure animations are smooth and flow from one state to another.
- Animations can make a huge difference in an app if used wisely.

Where to go from here?

This chapter focused on how to create animations and transitions, but not why and when to use them. A good starting point for UI related questions on Apple platforms is the Human Interface Guidelines here: https://developer.apple.com/design/human-interface-guidelines/. The WWDC 2018 session Designing Fluid Interfaces also goes into detail on gestures and motion in apps, which you can see, here: https://developer.apple.com/videos/play/wwdc2018/803.

Section III: Advanced SwiftUI

Level up your SwiftUI skills with this final chapter:

Chapter 15: Complex Interfaces: In this chapter, you will learn how to develop more complex interfaces. Get out of your comfort zone and dive into more advanced concepts that will allow you to generate almost any UI you can image. You'll learn the limitations you may find while developing advanced SwiftUI interfaces.

Chapter 15: Complex Interfaces

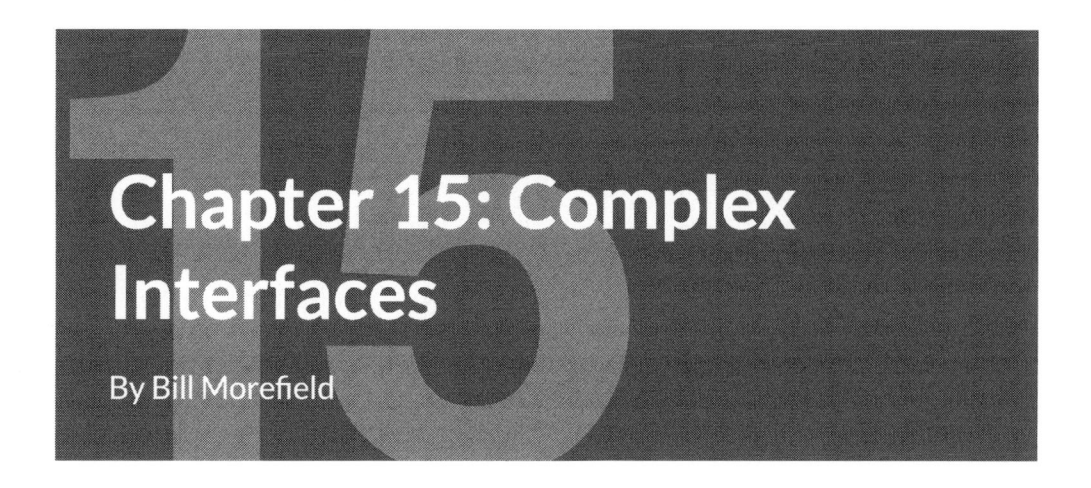

By Bill Morefield

SwiftUI represents an exciting new paradigm for UI design. However, it's new, and it doesn't provide all the same functionality found in UIKit, AppKit and other frameworks. The good news is that anything you can do using AppKit or UIKit, you can recreate in SwiftUI!

If you were building apps before SwiftUI came along, you likely have custom controls that you've already written yourself, or existing ones that you've integrated into your apps. SwiftUI can work with UIKit or AppKit to reuse both native and existing views and view controllers.

SwiftUI does, though, provide the ability to build upon an existing framework and extend it to add missing features. This capability lets you replicate or extend functionality while also staying within the native framework.

In this chapter, you'll first add an open-source custom control within a UIKit view in a SwiftUI app. You'll also work through building a reusable view that can display other views in a grid.

Integrating with other frameworks

You'll likely need to integrate with pre-SwiftUI frameworks in any moderately complex app. That's because many of the built-in frameworks, such as MapKit, do not have a corresponding component in SwiftUI. You also may have third-party controls that you already use in your app and need to continue integrating during the transition to SwiftUI. In this section, you'll take a simple open-source timeline view built for a UITableView and integrate it into a SwiftUI app.

You'll use Zheng-Xiang Ke's `TimelineTableViewCell` control to display a timeline of all the day's flights. This control is open source and available at the following link:

- https://github.com/kf99916/TimelineTableViewCell.

You can't add it as a Swift Package, so the starter project for this chapter includes the necessary files for the control as the **TimelineTableViewCell** group.

To work with UIViews and UIViewControllers in SwiftUI, you must create types that conform to the `UIViewRepresentable` and `UIViewControllerRepresentable` protocols. SwiftUI will manage the life cycle of these views, so you only to create and configure the views and the underlying frameworks will take care of the rest. Open the starter project and create a new Swift file — *not* SwiftUI view — named **FlightTimeline.swift** in the **MountainAirport** group.

Replace the contents of **FlightTimeline.swift** with:

```
import SwiftUI

struct FlightTimeline: UIViewControllerRepresentable {
  var flights: [FlightInformation]
}
```

This code creates the type that will wrap the UITableViewController. SwiftUI includes several protocols that allow integration to views, view controllers and other app framework components. You will pass in an array of `FlightInformation` values as would to a SwiftUI view. There are two methods in the `UIViewControllerRepresentable` protocol you will need to implement: `makeUIViewController(context:)`, and `updateUIViewController(_:context:)`. You'll create those now.

Add the following code to the struct below the `flights` parameter:

```
func makeUIViewController(context: Context) ->
                    UITableViewController {
```

```
    UITableViewController()
}
```

SwiftUI will call `makeUIViewController(context:)` once when it is ready to display the view. Here, you create a `UITableViewController` programmatically and return it. Any UIKit ViewController would work here; there are similar protocols for AppKit, WatchKit and other views and view controllers on the appropriate platform.

Now add this code to the end of the struct to implement the second method:

```
func updateUIViewController(_ viewController:
      UITableViewController, context: Context) {
  let timelineTableViewCellNib =
    UINib(nibName: "TimelineTableViewCell", bundle: Bundle.main)
  viewController.tableView.register(timelineTableViewCellNib,
          forCellReuseIdentifier: "TimelineTableViewCell")
}
```

SwiftUI calls `updateUIViewController(_:context:)` when it wants you to update the configuration for the presented view controller. Much of the setup you would typically do in `viewDidLoad()` in a UIKit view will go into this method. For the moment, you load the nib for the timeline cell and register it in the UITableView using the `viewController` passed into this method.

Connecting delegates, data sources and more

If you're familiar with UITableView in iOS, you might wonder how you provide the data source and delegates to this UITableViewController. You have the required data inside the struct, but if you try accessing that data directly from UIKit, your app will crash. Instead, you have to create a `Coordinator` object as a `NSObject` derived class.

This class acts as a transition or bridge between the data inside SwiftUI and the external framework. You can see `content` passed in as the second parameter in the `updateUIViewController(_:context:)` method. Add the following code for the new class at the top of `FlightTimeline`, *outside* the struct:

```
class Coordinator: NSObject {
  var flightData: [FlightInformation]

  init(flights: [FlightInformation]) {
    self.flightData = flights
  }
}
```

You're creating the class along with a custom initializer to pass in the flight information to the class. This `Coordinator` will allow you to connect the delegate and data source for the UITableView. You could also use it to deal with user events.

You need to tell SwiftUI about the `Coordinator` class. Add the following code to the top of the `FlightTimeline` struct:

```
func makeCoordinator() -> Coordinator {
  Coordinator(flights: flights)
}
```

This creates the coordinator and returns it to the SwiftUI framework to pass in where necessary. SwiftUI will call `makeCoordinator()` before `makeUIViewController(context:)` so it's available during the creation and configuration of your non-SwiftUI components.

You can now implement `UITableViewDelegate` and `UITableViewDataSource` in the `Controller` class for your UITableView. You won't use `UITableViewDelegate` for this UITableView, but you will implement `UITableViewDataSource`. Add the following class extension after the current `Coordinator` class definition:

```
extension Coordinator: UITableViewDataSource {
  func tableView(_ tableView: UITableView,
                 numberOfRowsInSection section: Int)
    -> Int {
    flightData.count
  }

  func tableView(_ tableView: UITableView,
                 cellForRowAt indexPath: IndexPath)
    -> UITableViewCell {
    let timeFormatter = DateFormatter()
    timeFormatter.timeStyle = .short
    timeFormatter.dateStyle = .none

    let flight = self.flightData[indexPath.row]
    let scheduledString =
      timeFormatter.string(from: flight.scheduledTime)
    let currentString =
      timeFormatter.string(from: flight.currentTime ??
                                  flight.scheduledTime)

    let cell = tableView.dequeueReusableCell(
      withIdentifier: "TimelineTableViewCell",
      for: indexPath) as! TimelineTableViewCell

    var flightInfo = "\(flight.airline) \(flight.number) "
    flightInfo = flightInfo +
      "\(flight.direction == .departure ? "to" : "from")"
```

```
        flightInfo = flightInfo + " \(flight.otherAirport)"
        flightInfo = flightInfo + " - \(flight.flightStatus)"
        cell.descriptionLabel.text = flightInfo

        if flight.status == .cancelled {
          cell.titleLabel.text = "Cancelled"
        } else if flight.timeDifference != 0 {
          if flight.status == .cancelled {
            cell.titleLabel.text = "Cancelled"
          } else if flight.timeDifference != 0 {
            var title = "\(scheduledString)"
            title = title + " Now: \(currentString)"
            cell.titleLabel.text = title
          } else {
            cell.titleLabel.text =
              "On Time for \(scheduledString)"
          }         } else {
          cell.titleLabel.text =
            "On Time for \(scheduledString)"
        }

        cell.titleLabel.textColor = UIColor.black
        cell.bubbleColor = flight.timelineColor
        return cell
  }
}
```

These two methods provide data for the UITableView. tableView(_, numberOfRowsInSection) returns the number of items in the array as the number of items in the table. In tableView(_:, indexPath), you use the TimelineTableViewCell registered in the updateUIViewController(_:context:) method to create a timeline cell for that flight and return it. Note that this class and control know nothing about SwiftUI. The code you've used here works as it does in UIKit.

Now that you've implemented a UITableViewDataSource you can set it for the UITableView. Add the following line to the top of updateUIViewController(_:context:):

```
        viewController.tableView.dataSource = context.coordinator
```

Now you can add the new view to the app. Open **ContentView.swift** and add the following code before the NavigationLink to the Awards view:

```
NavigationLink(destination:
  FlightTimeline(flights: self.flightInfo)) {
    Text("Flight Timeline")
}
```

Build and run the app. Tap on the **Flight Timeline** button, and you'll see the new timeline in action:

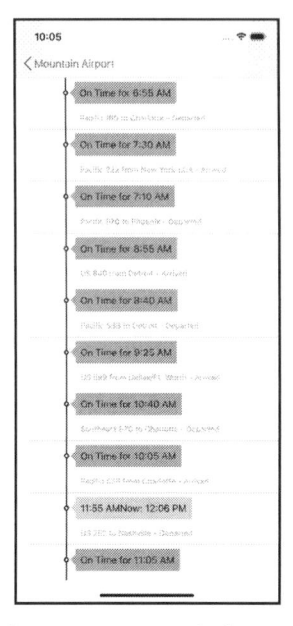

It doesn't take a lot of work to integrate pre-existing Apple frameworks into your SwiftUI app. Over time, you'll likely move more of your app's functionality to SwiftUI when possible. The ability to integrate SwiftUI in your legacy apps gives you a tidy way to begin using SwiftUI, without having to start from scratch.

In the next section, you'll build a more complex SwiftUI view that will reflect more of the work you'll be doing as part of that transition.

Building reusable views

SwiftUI builds upon the idea of composing views smaller views. Because of this, you can often end up with huge blocks of views within views within views, as well as SwiftUI views that span screens of code.

Splitting components into separate views makes your code cleaner. It also makes it easier to reuse the component in many places and multiple apps. In this chapter, you're going to rework the Awards view from Chapter 12, "Drawing", from its current iteration as a single, vertical list, into a grid. Don't worry if you haven't worked through that chapter, as the starter app for this chapter contains everything you need.

Open the project, and build and run the app. Tap on the **Awards** button to bring up the award view, and you'll see a single scrolling list of the awards. As you might guess, it's built from a SwiftUI List(). It would be nice to have the awards display in a grid, instead of a list, to save the user from excess scrolling.

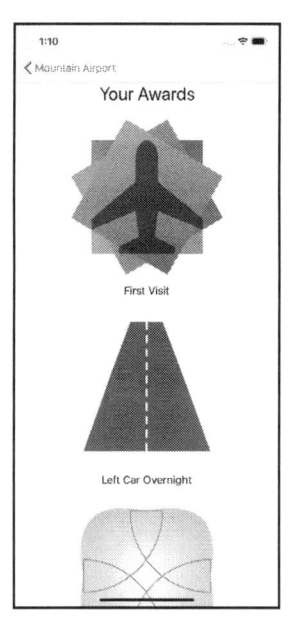

In a UIKit app, you'd likely use a **UICollectionView** to create the grid. Unfortunately, the current version of SwiftUI doesn't have an equivalent to this popular view. So you're going to create your own grid in SwiftUI in place of the **UICollectionView**.

You'll first need to create an array holding information on all the current awards. The first three awards are those you built in Chapter 12, "Drawing". The remaining bits draw a curve from passed parameters. You also provide a title and description for each award and for testing you set all awards awarded. The second property filters the full array to only the awarded items to show in the view.

Now you can update the view to use this list.

You're not going to build a full replacement for UICollectionView, but instead you'll create a grid view similar to a UICollectionView grid.

Create a new **SwiftUI View** in the **MountainAirport** group. Name the file **GridView.swift**.

It's useful to keep a new solution simple in development instead of trying to do everything at once. The initial grid will only store and display integers. That doesn't seem too exciting, but you'll expand it to be more flexible later in the chapter.

In **GridView.swift**, add a property to hold the array of integers to the top of the struct:

```
var items: [Int]
```

Now change the body view to:

```
ScrollView {
  VStack {
    ForEach(0..<items.count) { index in
      Text("\(self.items[index])")
    }
  }
}
```

Make sure the preview is available. Update the preview to pass an array of integers for the preview:

```
GridView(items: [11, 3, 7, 17, 5, 2])
```

Next, you'll change this list into a grid.

Displaying a grid

There are several ways to organize a grid, but the most common one is to create a set of rows that consist of several columns. The items in the grid begin at the first row and first column and continue horizontally across the first row. Then, the next row picks up where the first row stops. This repeats until you reach the end of the items to display.

If there are fewer items than needed to fill the final row, the grid leaves them empty. In SwiftUI terms, you can build a grid as a `VStack` consisting of `HStack` views for each row. The contents of the `HStack` correspond to the columns of the grid.

Add a new parameter to set the number of columns before the `items` property:

```
var columns: Int
```

The original loop inside the `VStack` goes through each element of the array. You'll change the loop to go through rows instead as the `VStack` will now wrap each row of the grid.

Add the following property after `items` to calculate the number of rows:

```
var numberRows: Int {
   (items.count - 1) / columns
}
```

This code gives the zero-based number of rows needed to include all items in the array. It simplifies the math for the loop to start rows at zero.

> **Note**: A common point of confusion when working with arrays is that while you usually think of numbers as starting at one, arrays start counting at zero. An array of three items indexes those items as zero, one and two.

Change the `ForEach` loop to:

```
// 1
ForEach(0...numberRows) { row in
   HStack {
      // 2
      ForEach(0..<self.columns) { column in
         // 3
         Text("\(self.items[row * self.columns + column])")
      }
   }
}
```

Here are the changes:

1. As noted, you're now looping through rows inside the `VStack`. The loop includes the zero row through the maximum row.

2. You know the number of columns, so you loop through each column again starting at zero and ending at the number one less than the number of columns because of the zero index.

3. To display the element of the array, you calculate the index that corresponds to the row and column. This calculation is more straightforward when you start counting rows at zero. For the start of each row, you multiply the row number by the number of columns in each row. The first row of any grid starts with zero. You then add the number of the column, so the first column of that row is at index zero, the second at index one, and so on. The next row begins at the index matching the next element.

The results make a pretty good grid.

There is a hidden problem, though. Add another element to the array by changing the preview to the following:

```
GridView(columns: 2, items: [11, 3, 7, 17, 5, 2, 1])
```

You'll now get a rather unhelpful error in the preview, so you'll need to run the view in debug mode for more useful information. Hold down **Ctrl** and click the **Play** button, and select **Debug Preview** from the menu.

You'll now get a much more useful error: **Fatal error: Index out of range**. The last time through the loop row will be 3, and column will be 1. The loop then attempts to access index 7. As the array only has seven elements — zero through six — you're trying to access an element that doesn't exist in the array. You can add a function to perform this calculation and determine if the element doesn't exist.

Add the following function below the numberRows property:

```
func elementFor(row: Int, column: Int) -> Int? {
    let index = row * self.columns + column
    return index < items.count ? index : nil
}
```

This function takes the current row and column and performs the same calculation as before. It then checks that the index is a valid position in the array. If not, it returns nil to indicate this fact. Otherwise, it returns a valid index.

If you're experienced in Swift, you might think you can now change the code at comment //3 to the following:

```
if let index = elementFor(row: row, column: column) {
    Text("\(items[index])")
}
```

Go ahead; make the change and see what happens. You'll get an error message: `Closure containing control flow statement cannot be used with function builder 'ViewBuilder'`. Unfortunately, the current implementation of SwiftUI doesn't deal with optionals in a simple manner. You can use a conditional, just not one to unwrap an optional. Change the code to:

```
if elementFor(row: row, column: column) != nil {
    Text("\(items[elementFor(row: row, column: column)!])")
}
```

It's a more tedious way to write the same code, but this works in SwiftUI. You first check if the result of the function is not `nil` and if so, then you display the element at that index by calling the function and forcing the unwrap.

This looks closer to what you want, but the last row doesn't look quite right, and it doesn't line up with the rest of the grid. When you reach the end of that last row, the code needs to add some spacing to fill in the otherwise empty space.

You'll need to add an `else` after the `if` statement to display an empty text field. Change the code to match the following:

```
if elementFor(row: row, column: column) != nil {
  Text("\(items[elementFor(row: row, column: column)!])")
} else {
  Text("")
}
```

[Screenshot: iPhone showing "Mountain Airport" back button and a centered column of numbers: 11 3 / 7 17 / 5 2 / 1]

You've built a nice adaptable grid of integers, and you've already seen that it will adapt to the list changing underneath. Change the number of columns by changing the preview to:

```
GridView(columns: 3, items: [11, 3, 7, 17, 5, 2, 1])
```

You'll see the grid change to three columns. Now that you have the underlying grid in place, you'll let the caller specify the view inside the grid.

Using a ViewBuilder

The grid in the current form always shows a Text view. You could create a series of grids for each needed view: **GridTextView**, **GridImageView** and so on. However, it would be much more useful to let the caller specify what to display in each cell of the grid. That's where the SwiftUI **ViewBuilder** comes in.

Recall the initial code for this list below:

```
ForEach(0..<items.count) { index in
  Text("\(self.items[index])")
}
```

This provides a view inside the `ForEach` loop that you passed in. `ForEach` uses a ViewBuilder to create a parameter for the view-producing enclosure. You'll now update the `GridView` so it can take such an enclosure to define the contents of each cell in the grid.

Change the definition of the GridView to the following:

```
struct GridView<Content>: View where Content: View {
```

Now add a parameter after `items` to store the `Content` you just defined:

```
let content: (Int) -> Content
```

You also need to create a custom initializer for the View. Add the following initializer below the `content` parameter:

```
init(columns: Int, items: [Int],
     @ViewBuilder content: @escaping (Int) -> Content) {
  self.columns = columns
  self.items = items
  self.content = content
}
```

This new initializer accepts an enclosure named `Content` along with the previous number of columns and and array of integers. It also defines that the enclosure will receive a single `Int` parameter.

With these changes, you can now specify an enclosure for the `GridView`. Your loop can then display the enclosure for each element in the grid. You can use the parameter to pass the current element of the array into the enclosure.

Now change the `ForEach` loop to use the `content` parameter:

```
ForEach(0...self.numberRows, id: \.self) { row in
  HStack {
    ForEach(0..<self.columns, id: \.self) { column in
      Group {
        if self.elementFor(row: row, column: column) != nil {
          self.content(
            self.items[self.elementFor(row: row, column: column)!])
```

```
        } else {
            Spacer()
        }
      }
    }
  }
}
```

Instead of including views within the loop, you call the `content` view which contains the enclosure, and you pass the current element of the integer array as a parameter to the enclosure. Note that you need to wrap the conditional inside a `Group` so the two cases act as a single element.

Change the preview to see the new grid in action:

```
GridView(columns: 3, items: [11, 3, 7, 17, 5, 2, 1]) { item in
    Text("\(item)")
}
```

You'll notice that the layout for the page looks a little off, as the last element doesn't line up with the rest of the grid. To correct that, you'll fix the grid's spacing.

Spacing the grid

For this grid, you'll divide the size of the view among the columns, and you can use a `GeometryReader` to get the view's size. Wrap the `ScrollView` of your `GridView` with a geometry reader by adding this code around the `ScrollView`:

```
GeometryReader { geometry in
  ScrollView {
    // Omitted code
  }
}
```

Now change the `self.content()` enclosure to the following:

```
self.content(self.items[self.elementFor(row: row, column: column)!])
    .frame(width: geometry.size.width / CGFloat(self.columns),
           height: geometry.size.width / CGFloat(self.columns))
```

Here, you divide the width of the view given by the GeometryReader object by the number of columns for the grid. This evenly distributes the width among the columns. You then apply a frame to the view with the height and width set to that value. When using the grid, you'll need to make sure that the number of columns for the grid provides enough space for the contents.

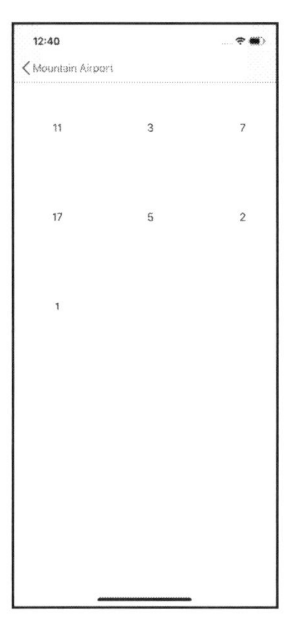

You have a pretty capable grid, but it still only works with an array of integers. The solution for this problem comes in a feature of Swift for just the case when you need to write code independent of specific data types — generics.

Making the grid generic

Generics allow you to write code without being specific about the type of data you're using. You can write a function once, and use it on any data type.

First change the declaration of the view to:

```swift
struct GridView<Content, T>: View where Content: View {
```

You're saying here that you want to use a generic type in the struct. Instead of specifying Int, String or another type, you can now specify T. You can now change the instances of the Int array into an array of type T instead. Change the declaration of the items property to:

```swift
var items: [T]
```

You also need to change the type for the parameter passed into the enclosure. Change the definition of the Content property to:

```swift
let content: (T) -> Content
```

You'll also need to make the change to the custom initializer. Change it to:

```swift
init(columns: Int, items: [T],
    @ViewBuilder content: @escaping (T) -> Content) {
```

And you're done. Seriously! Generics let you pivot from a specific reference of an Int to the generic represented by T. Swift handles the rest. You'll see that your grid still works.

Using the grid

Now that you've written the grid view, you can update the award view to use it. Open **AirportAwards.swift** and change the view to:

```swift
VStack {
  Text("Your Awards (\(activeAwards.count))")
    .font(.title)
  GridView(columns: 2, items: activeAwards) { item in
    VStack {
```

```
      item.awardView
      Text(item.title)
    }.padding(5)
  }
}
```

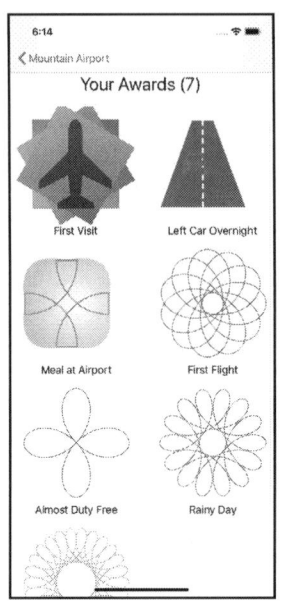

The same grid you used to show integers in the preview shows the awards here. That's the power of SwiftUI, Swift and generics. In this section, you've taken a plain list and encapsulated the views on that page into an array. You then built a view that can display any `Array` as a grid where you can specify how to display the grid. Great work!

Key points

- You build views using `Representable`-derived protocols to integrate SwiftUI with other Apple frameworks.

- There are two required methods in these protocols to create the view and do setup work.

- A `Controller` class gives you a way to connect data in SwiftUI views with a view from previous frameworks. You can use this to manage delegates and related patterns.

- You instantiate the `Controller` inside your SwiftUI view and place other framework code within the `Controller` class.
- Combining `VStack`, `HStack` and `ZStack` will let you create more complex layouts.
- You can use a `ViewBuilder` to pass views into another view when doing iterations.
- Generics let your views work without hard-coding specific types.

Challenge

As written, the `GridView` calculates an even split for each column and sets each element to a square of that size.

You could, instead, pass the calculated size of the grid cell to the enclosure and let it determine the layout. Change the `GridView` to do this and update the Awards View to use the updated grid.

Solution

You can add more parameters to pass into the enclosure. You add the calculated width — a `CGFloat` — as a new parameter. Change the definition of `content` to:

```
let content: (CGFloat, T) -> Content
```

Then update the initializer to include the new parameter:

```
init(columns: Int, items: [T],
     @ViewBuilder content: @escaping (CGFloat, T) -> Content) {
  self.columns = columns
  self.items = items
  self.content = content
}
```

You change the call to `self.content` inside the loop to pass the calculated width to the enclosure instead of applying it to the enclosure.

```
self.content(geometry.size.width / CGFloat(self.columns),
      self.items[self.elementFor(row: row, column: column)!])
```

You then can use the width inside your enclosure. For the preview, you would change the enclosure to:

```
GridView(columns: 3, items: [11, 3, 7, 17, 5, 2, 1])
{ gridWidth, item in
  Text("\(item)")
    .frame(width: gridWidth, height: gridWidth)
}
```

and change the call to the `GridView` in **AirportAwards** to:

```
GridView(columns: 2, items: activeAwards) { gridWidth, item in
  VStack {
    item.awardView
    Text(item.title)
  }.frame(width: gridWidth, height: gridWidth)
}
```

Conclusion

We hope you're as excited about SwiftUI as we are! This new approach to building user interfaces might seem a bit strange at the start. But we're sure that if you've worked through the chapters in this book, you now have a much better understanding of declarative programming and the infinite possibilities of SwiftUI. Remember, SwiftUI is still very much a baby, learning her first steps; it still has a lot to learn and a lot of growing ahead. And you've also just made your own first steps in working with this wonderful new framework.

The possibility of using SwiftUI for all Apple devices opens up the playing field for a greater number of developers on all Apple platforms, which will hopefully turn into many more amazing apps adapted for the iPhone, Mac, iPad, Apple Watch, Apple TV… and even new devices to come!

We encourage you to try to put the book concepts in practice. Combine SwiftUI with UIKit & AppKit and see how well they get along together. Try Stacks, navigation, testing, and all the cool concepts explained throughout the book. Keep learning, and share your projects with us!

If you have any questions or comments as you work through this book, please stop by our forums at http://forums.raywenderlich.com and look for the particular forum category for this book.

Thank you again for purchasing this book. Your continued support is what makes the books, tutorials, videos and other things we do at raywenderlich.com possible. We truly appreciate it!

– The *SwiftUI by Tutorials* team

```
struct ThankYouView: View {
    var body: some View {
        Text("Thank you very much")
    }
}
```

Printed in Great Britain
by Amazon